The County Archaeologies

General Editor : T. D. KENDRICK, M.A.

YORKSHIRE

THE ARCHAEOLOGY OF YORKSHIRE

BY

FRANK AND HARRIET WRAGG ELGEE

WITH 2 MAPS AND 60 ILLUSTRATIONS

METHUEN & CO. LTD.
36 ESSEX STREET W.C.
LONDON

First Published in 1933

PRINTED IN GREAT BRITAIN

PREFACE

WHEN the Editor of this series of County Archaeologies invited us to prepare the Yorkshire volume, we felt no little hesitation in undertaking what we realized to be a formidable task. We cannot claim an intimate knowledge of every region in so extensive and varied a shire. Its broad acres teem with barrows, megaliths, camps, forts, earthworks, and other less conspicuous antiquities. Its museums overflow with thousands of prehistoric, Roman, and Anglian objects. Its ancient churches enshrine innumerable Anglian and Viking sculptures. Its archaeological literature is vast, scattered, uncatalogued. Nevertheless we have essayed to fill a mere pint pot with a gallon of Tadcaster ale.

In this book we have tried to give a concise account of the succession of peoples and cultures from Palaeolithic to Anglo-Viking times. The necessity for compression has made generalization imperative, but as far as possible we have described type objects of each period. We have subordinated museum specimens to field antiquities, but our account of these has had to be cut down to the barest minimum consistent with clarity. Much that is interesting and important has been omitted. We have not burdened the text with names of authorities or footnote references, feeling that the brief bibliography at the end of each chapter, together with the gazetteer, is adequate enough, especially as we have stated the location of most museum specimens mentioned in the text.

Lack of space has prevented us from enlarging upon many alluring aspects of Yorkshire's past, such as the use of Whitby jet, the relation of prehistoric to Roman, Anglian and later settlement sites, the origin of peoples and cultures, comparisons with neighbouring counties, and so forth. Here and there, however, we have ventured to indicate how the past begets the present, and how amidst Yorkshire's wild uplands prehistoric beliefs and practices have lingered down to modern times.

This work is the first attempt to outline Yorkshire's prehistoric, Roman, and Anglo-Viking archaeology as a whole. This arduous task would have been rendered still more difficult without the late W. G. Collingwood's illustrated papers on Anglo-Viking sculpture in the *Yorkshire Archaeological Journal*; Mr. R. A. Smith's account of the Anglo-Viking period, and the late Mrs. Armitage and Mr. D. H. Montgomerie's survey of the earthworks, both published in the *Victoria County History* in 1907 and 1912.

We wish specially to thank Miss M. Kitson Clark, Leeds; Mr. A. L. Armstrong, Warrington; Mr. F. G. Simpson, Newcastle; Dr. A. Raistrick, Shipley; Mr. R. A. Smith, Keeper of British and Mediaeval Antiquities in the British Museum; Dr. W. E. Collinge, Keeper of the Yorkshire Museum; Miss Waller, Principal of the Mount School, York, for important information; and Mr. W. Hornsby, Saltburn, for allowing us to use his unpublished paper on the Roman coastguard fort at Goldsbrough.

Permission to reproduce or to make use of illustrations has been kindly granted by the Prehistoric Society of East Anglia (Fig. 1); Dr. T. W. Woodhead, Director of the Tolson Memorial Museum, Huddersfield (Figs. 5, 24, 27, 36); Mr. T. Sheppard, Director of the Hull Municipal Museums (Figs. 8, 21, 30, plate 10 [i]); Lady Lawson-Tancred, Aldborough Manor (Fig. 28); Sir George Macdonald, Edinburgh (Figs. 23, 29); the late Mr. W. G. Collingwood and the Yorkshire Archaeological Society (Figs. 39, 40, 41); the Yorkshire Archaeological Society (Plate V [i]); Dr. A. Raistrick (Fig. 13); British Museum (Figs. 6, 11, 18, 19, 26, 33); Royal Archaeological Institute (Figs. 17, 15e, 35); Mr. S. B. Gaythorpe, Barrow-in-Furness (Fig. 34, from Atkinson's *History of Cleveland*, 1877); Messrs. Methuen and Mr. R. G. Collingwood (Fig. 22);

Dr. W. E. Collinge (Plates IV, V [ii]), VI, VIII, IX) ; Royal Anthropological Institute (Fig. 20).

We are also indebted to Mr. T. F. Newnam, Redcar, for drawing Fig. 7, and for redrawing Figs. 10, 12, 13, 20, 28 ; Mr. A. L. Armstrong for drawing Fig. 4 ; and Miss Metcalfe, Saltburn, for drawing Fig. 37.

The publication of this work has been delayed by the serious illness of Frank Elgee during the past twelve months, and we owe the warmest thanks both to our Editor and Publishers for their kind help, criticism, and patience.

F. E.
H. W. E.

GUISBOROUGH,
    November, 1932

LIST OF ABBREVIATIONS

A.J.	*Antiquaries' Journal.*
Ant.	*Antiquity.*
Arch.	*Archaeologia.*
Arch. J. . . .	*Archaeological Journal.*
A.B.I. . . .	*Ancient Bronze Implements of the British Isles,* J. Evans, London, 1881.
A.S.I. . . .	*Ancient Stone Implements of the British Isles,* J. Evans, London, 1897. Second Edition.
B.A.P. . . .	*Bronze Age Pottery of Great Britain and Ireland,* J. Abercromby, Oxford, 1912.
Bateman . . .	*Ten Years' Diggings,* T. Bateman, London, 1861.
B.B.	*British Barrows,* W. Greenwell, London, 1877.
B.M.	British Museum.
B.R.A.C. . . .	*Bulletin of Roman Antiquities Committee,* Yorkshire Archaeological Society.
C.I.L. . . .	*Corpus Inscriptionum Latinarum,* VII, Hübner, Berlin, 1873.
E.M.	*Early Man in North-east Yorkshire,* F. Elgee, Gloucester, 1930.
E.R.	East Riding.
G.M.	*Gentleman's Magazine.*
H.M.	Hull Museums.
H.M.P. . . .	Hull Museum Publications.
J.B.A.A. . .	*Journal of the British Archaeological Association.*
J.R.A.I. . .	*Journal of the Royal Anthropological Institute.*
J.R.S. . . .	*Journal of Roman Studies.*
M.	Museum.
Mortimer . .	*Forty Years' Researches in East Yorkshire,* J. R. Mortimer, London, 1905.
N.R.	North Riding.
Nat.	*The Naturalist.*
P.P.S.E.A. . .	*Proceedings of the Prehistoric Society of East Anglia.*
P.S.A. . . .	*Proceedings of the Society of Antiquaries, London.*
P.Y.G.S. . .	*Proceedings of the Yorkshire Geological Society.*
R.B.A. . . .	*Report of the British Association.*
R.Y.P.S. . .	*Report of the Yorkshire Philosophical Society.*
S.M.	Sheffield Museum.

T.E.R.A.S. . . .	*Transactions of the East Riding Archaeological Society.*
T.H.S. . . .	*Transactions of the Hull Scientific and Field Naturalists' Club.*
V.C.H. . . .	*Victoria County History of Yorkshire*, vol. i (1907), ii (1912).
W.R. . . .	West Riding.
Y.A.J. . . .	*Yorkshire Archaeological Journal.*
Y.M. . . .	Yorkshire Museum.

CONTENTS

LIST OF ILLUSTRATIONS
IN THE TEXT

LIST OF PLATES

YORKSHIRE

THE ARCHAEOLOGY OF YORKSHIRE

CHAPTER I

YORKSHIRE

AS everyone knows, Yorkshire, old Michael Drayton's "most renown'd of shires", is the largest English county. With an area of 6,066 square miles it is almost as large as Wales, more than twice the size of Lincolnshire, the next largest county, and forty times the size of Rutlandshire, the smallest. Its coast-line, between the estuaries of the Tees and Humber, measures 120 miles in length. The same distance separates its highest mountain, Mickle Fell, in the extreme north-west from Spurn, a mere spit of sand and shingle at sea-level in the extreme south-east.

To many Yorkshiremen their broad acres appear as an inevitable rule of right, in accordance with the eternal fitness of things. In a sense this is true, because ages before man set foot in the county rivers, sea and mountains had already sketched its outline. On the north there raced the lively Tees ; on the east the North Sea beat against a more or less rock-bound coast ; on the south the broad Humber and its tributary, the Don, sought that sea through dreary marshes and fens ; on the west there towered the rugged Pennines.

Yet the region thus defined by nature does not seem to have been always a tribal or administrative unit in pre-historic or Roman times. For unlike some counties, such as Kent which coincides with the territory of an ancient British tribe, the Cantii, Yorkshire was divided in the La

3

Tène period of Early Iron Age between two tribes, the Brigantes who occupied West Yorkshire and who overflowed into Durham and Lancashire, and the Parisi who occupied the Wolds of East Yorkshire. On the other hand, under the Romans an apparent unity was restored, and it was then that an ancient settlement, situated approximately at the centre of our region, rose from obscurity and became the legionary fortress of Eboracum, the military capital of Britain. This is now known as York, the second city of England.

In Anglian times the kingdom of Deira was probably in the beginning confined to the Wold area, for that region, surrounded as it is by rivers and the sea, may have borne this Celtic name, which means ' waters '. Ultimately Deira embraced the land northwards to the Tees, and westwards the British territories of Loidis (Leeds) and Elmet (Sherburn district), and thus became the southern province of the kingdom of Northumbria, and identical with what is now Yorkshire. In 867 the Vikings conquered Deira, and subsequently divided it for administrative purposes into the East, North, and West Ridings. Naturally their boundaries met at York, but this city remained an independent unit.

Though their boundaries often run along rivers and watersheds, the Ridings themselves do not correspond to natural regions. There are at least twelve of these, the physical characteristics and original conditions of which vitally affected their human settlement. A brief description of Yorkshire's natural regions is therefore an essential preliminary to a survey of its archaeology from the remotest past down to the Viking conquest of a thousand years ago.

A wide, low-lying, central plain, the Vale of York, separating the hill country of West from that of East Yorkshire, is the key to the county. The three belts thus formed traverse the whole length of the shire from south to north, and, though there are certain areas that must be excepted, it may be said that in general they are all drained by the Humber river-system.

The Vale of York forms the northern section of the

Midland plain, and like the rest of that plain it has been excavated out of the soft red marls and sandstones of the Trias formation. Sixty miles long, the Vale varies from thirty miles in width in the south to ten miles at Northallerton, beyond which it again expands in a north-easterly direction to Tees-mouth. It rarely rises higher than 200 feet above sea-level.

In ancient times the forest of Galtres spread northwards from York to and beyond Northallerton, interspersed with heaths on sandier ground, and with bogs and marshes in hollows and along rivers. South of York marshes prevailed, for into this area there streamed the Ouse, the Aire, the Don, the Derwent, and the Trent. Their overflowing waters, swollen by the Humber tides, flooded hundreds of square miles. Patches of these primeval swamps still survive at Marshland near Adlingfleet, Goole Moor, Thorne Waste, Strensall and Askham Bogs, and there are still heaths at Riccal, Skipwith, and Bubwith.

In its natural state the Vale was a barrier against communication between East and West Yorkshire, for early man shunned the forest and dreaded the swamp. He had neither the means nor the inclination to clear the one or to drain the other. He could, however, cross the Vale in three or four places with comparative ease. At Escrick, seven miles south of York, and at York itself, two crescentic ridges, the terminal moraines of a large glacier that flowed down the Vale during the last Ice Age, rose like natural embankments amidst the swamps, to link the eastern with the western hill country. There are traces of similar morainic ridges near Easingwold and Northallerton, but they were less used than the York ridges. That on which York stands was more emphatic, higher, with narrower river-crossings than the Escrick moraine. It therefore became the chief in importance, and is largely responsible for the origin and growth of the city itself.

Though so extensive, the Vale of York is not the only lowland region. The next in size and consequence is Holderness in south-east Yorkshire, nowhere more than 160 feet above sea-level. From Spurn to Bridlington it presents a long dull line of boulder-clay cliffs to the sea, which incessantly wears them away, in some places at the average rate of seven feet per annum. Inland the region extends to the foot of the Wolds and along the Humber shore to the neighbourhood of Hessle. It is drained by a little river, the Hull. Geologically Holderness is the youngest part of Yorkshire. Before the Ice Age a coastline of chalk cliffs swept in a bold curve from Hessle and Beverley northwards to Driffield and Bridlington. Against these cliffs glaciers discharged their cargoes of clay and boulders, sand and gravel, and thus built up a new land of morainic mounds and ridges enclosing lakes and meres in their hollows, only one of which, Hornsea Mere, Yorkshire's largest lake, survives. The prehistory of Holderness in many respects differs from that of the Wolds, including as it does the Maglemose harpoons from Skipsea and Hornsea, the remarkable lake-dwellings, and a special culture of the late Bronze Age.

Holderness is overlooked on the west by the undulating chalk uplands of the Wolds. They may be compared with the Downs of southern England, though they differ from them in their steeper slopes, due to the greater hardness of the Yorkshire chalk. On the whole they are shaped like a boomerang. One point rests on the Humber at Hessle ; the other juts out into the North Sea at Flamborough Head, whose white cliffs average 400 feet in height. The inner curve of the boomerang corresponds to the Holderness boundary. The outer and higher curve is represented by the steep chalk escarpment commanding the Vale of York as far north as Acklam, whence it bends round to the east along the south side of the Vale of Pickering. At Wilton Beacon, a few miles south of Acklam, the Wolds attain their highest elevation of 808 feet.

The Wolds are intersected by a complex series of dry, steep-sloped dales, many of which deeply recess their western escarpment. The largest of these, the Great Wold Valley, splits the northern Wolds into two main ridges and runs eastwards from Winteringham to Burton Fleming and thence via Rudston to Bridlington. Only a paltry stream, the Gypsy Race, now trickles along its broad floor. But in ages long ago, before it was captured by the Ouse, it was the Yore that flowed down the Great Wold Valley eastwards to the sea. Until their enclosure, grass and furze carpeted the Wolds, and on them sheep grazed happily and the stone curlew and bustard found a congenial home. In prehistoric times man also found them congenial ; for they stood up invitingly between the swamps and forests of Holderness and the Vale of York. Despite the fact that many of their antiquities have been collected or destroyed, they are one of England's most important fields for pre-historic research, and without doubt they are still the richest and most varied in Yorkshire.

Another lowland region, the Vale of Pickering, lies between the northern foot of the Wolds and the hill country of North-east Yorkshire. It takes the form of an oval basin twenty miles long and from five to ten miles wide. In the west the narrow Coxwold-Gilling gap links it to the Vale of York. In the east it terminates in the boulder-clay cliffs of Filey Bay. The Vale receives all the rivers from the hill country on the north, which unite within it to form the Derwent. This river does not, however, enter the sea at Filey Bay. On the contrary, it turns inland and flows down a wide gorge through the hills on the south side of the Vale between Malton and Kirkham Abbey. Thence it emerges into the Vale of York to journey southwards to the Humber. This deflection of the Derwent originated during the Ice Age when, owing to its obstruction at both ends, the Vale became the site of a glacier-lake. Its waters rose until they overflowed the surrounding hills at Kirkham Abbey, where they excavated a gorge to such a depth that the drainage of the Vale has followed the same course ever since.

For long after the Ice Age, until comparatively recent times in fact, the Vale, subject to periodical floodings from its numerous rivers, remained a waste of mere and marsh with a few low island-like hills in its midst. Nearly all the Vale has now been reclaimed, and is under cultivation.

Despite its water-logged condition early man frequented the Vale where fish and wild-fowl were plentiful; and his stone axes, lake-dwellings and bronze implements have been found there.

The hills through which the Derwent breaks at Kirkham Abbey constitute another small natural region about fifteen miles long by five wide. Phillips, the pioneer Yorkshire geologist, called them the Howardian Hills, after Castle Howard, the palatial seat of the Earls of Carlisle, designed by the poet-architect Vanbrugh, at the beginning of the eighteenth century. They separate the Vale of York from the Vale of Pickering. The heights overlooking the latter consist chiefly of corallian limestones; those overlooking the former Vale, of grits, sandstones and shales belonging to the Inferior Oolite and Lias formations. The general aspect of these hills is that of pleasant, wooded country, interspersed with mansions, parks, farmlands, and occasional patches of heath, formerly more extensive. Such an aspect it wore even in Roman times.

Both geologically and geographically, the affinities of the Howardian Hills lie with the tableland of North-east Yorkshire, of which they are a south-eastern prolongation connecting it with the Wolds. The tableland itself covers an area of nearly one thousand square miles. Like the Howardian Hills it is divisible into two main regions, the Limestone Hills, built of corallian limestones and their associated rocks—the Middle Oolite formation—and the Eastern Moorlands, based on the shales, grits, and sandstones of the Inferior Oolite or Bajocian formation.

The Limestone Hills, which extend for 34 miles from Scarborough (which is almost encircled by them) to the Vale of York, include the following areas: a lower zone, once scrub and grassland, now usually cultivated, bordering the Vale of Pickering; a higher, more barren tract merging into moor on its northern margin, the Tabular Hills of Phillips; and the Hambleton Hills which soar out of the Vale of York to an edge scarred with precipices, attaining their greatest elevation of 1,234 feet on Black Hambleton. Rivers from the Moorlands cut through the Limestone

Hills in deep wooded ravines. Their southern aspect, dry surface, and proximity to the Vale of Pickering attracted early settlers, and they vie with the Wolds in archaeological interest.

The Tabular Hills roughly correspond to the southern boundary of the Eastern Moorlands, ancient Blackamore, which with its dales occupies an area of about 500 square miles. In the north the moorlands terminate in the high, picturesque Cleveland Hills, amongst which may be mentioned Roseberry Topping (1,057 feet), and Eston Nab (800 feet) commanding the estuary of the Tees. On the east the moors formerly extended more or less to the verge of the long wall of sea-cliffs between Scarborough and Saltburn, but now they do so only at Peak or Ravenscar, the southern headland of Robin Hood's Bay, for thanks to the glacial drift, this area has been largely reclaimed.

The average altitude of the moorland plateau is about 1,000 feet. It is lower on the east than on the west where it attains a maximum elevation of 1,489 feet on Urra Moor on the Cleveland escarpment above Stokesley. From this point eastwards to the sea at Peak, and westwards along the summit of the Cleveland Hills to the edge of the Vale of York, there runs a high watershed, the backbone of the moorland region. Numerous small rivers have their source on this watershed, some falling southwards to the Vale of Pickering, and others northwards to the valley of the Esk which, with Kildale, forms a trough parallel to the central watershed.

These rivers and their affluents dissect the plateau into ridges and spurs of heather-clad moor, between which lie the dales. With their stone-walled fields enclosed in the dark frame of the moor on the surrounding craggy heights, their clear streams murmuring over rocky beds, their red-tiled farms scattered along the slopes, the dales are unique. In ancient times they were more or less forested, as testified by the presence of large pines and oaks in what is known locally as " black land ", the site of former bogs.

We have no evidence that the moorland plateau was ever

forested, though there can be no doubt that scattered trees and scrub once grew at higher levels. From time immemorial the plateau has been heather-clad, with deep peat mosses on the central watershed, in hollow places, and in shallow valleys or slacks of glacial origin.

Owing to their elevation and the sterility of their siliceous soils no attempt has been made to reclaim the moors. Consequently they still retain the same untutored aspect that they wore in prehistoric times. Thousands of round barrows and cairns, numerous stone monuments and many settlement sites make the Eastern Moorlands another of England's great prehistoric regions.

We must now turn to the entirely different hill country of West Yorkshire. Here everything is on a more ancient and a grander scale. Its rocks, unlike those of East Yorkshire which are Secondary or Mesozoic, all date from the Primary or Palaeozoic Age. Its dales, the typical Yorkshire dales, completely dwarf those of the Eastern Moorlands. Its hills, climbing to greater heights, often attain the majesty of mountains.

The western hill country rises unobtrusively out of the Vale of York along the outcrop, averaging ten miles in width, of the Magnesian Limestone. This rock enters the county on the Nottinghamshire border as a prominent escarpment facing west. But as it travels northwards by Conisborough, Wentbridge, Pontefract, Sherburn and Tadcaster, the escarpment gradually becomes less conspicuous. North of Wetherby it fades out altogether, though the outcrop of the limestone can be followed northwards to the Tees by its red soils, good agricultural lands, fine woods, and other features. Early man settled on this belt of country, more particularly where it is breached by the rivers from the Pennines.

West of the Magnesian Limestone foothills the country gradually increases in altitude to the Lancashire and Westmorland border. Generally speaking, the county boundary hugs the watershed of the Pennines which range from 1,000 to over 2,500 feet in height. From this watershed spring the rivers which in their journey east or south-

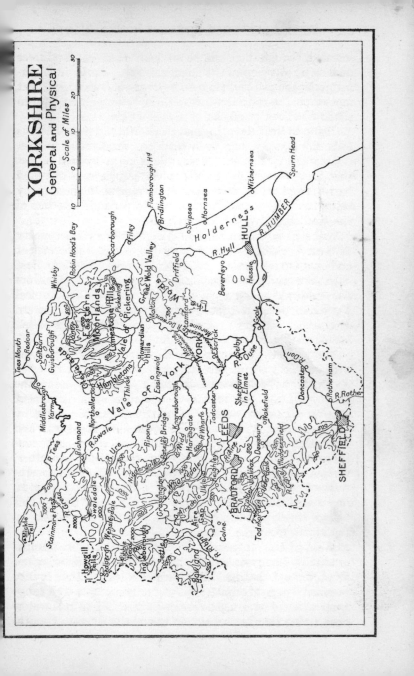

eastwards to the Vale of York have carved out Teesdale, Swaledale, Wensleydale, Nidderdale, Wharfedale, Airedale, Calder Dale and the Don Valley. A few shorter rivers rise on the steeper and often precipitous western slopes of the watershed, and fall into the Westmorland Eden or the Lancashire Lune.

West Yorkshire is cleft by Airedale which, a little west of Skipton, forms that singular depression known as the Aire Gap, about 500 feet above sea-level, the lowest and most accessible of all the passes through the Pennines, and which has been in continuous use since prehistoric times. The country south of Airedale includes two contrasted natural regions, the Yorkshire coal-field and the moors of the southern Pennines.

The coal-field lies between the Magnesian Limestone scarp on the east and the Nottinghamshire and Derbyshire Border on the south, merging gradually into the Pennine slopes on the west. Its altitude varies from 200 to 400 feet, and it consists of a plateau of Carboniferous sandstones, shales, and associated coal-seams, declining east and south-east. It has been much cut up into ridges and spurs by the Don, Calder, Aire and their tributaries. No other part of Yorkshire has been so thoroughly industrialised. Middlesbrough and its neighbouring towns merely fringe the Tees, and Hull alone stands on the Humber shore. Here an entire region has been devastated by mills and factories, collieries and iron-works, enveloped in a pall of smoke that befouls and blights everything it touches. An enormous population is packed into this area, barely equal in extent to the lonely Eastern Moorlands, the most congested centres being the towns of Barnsley, Dewsbury, Wakefield (the administrative capital of the West Riding), Halifax, Huddersfield, Bradford, Rotherham, Leeds and Sheffield. This Tophet now embraces that " pleasant district of merry England " immortalised by Scott, who staged the opening scene of Ivanhoe in that " large forest covering the greater part of the beautiful hills which lie between Sheffield and the pleasant town of Doncaster ". Indeed, the original aspect of the coal-field was largely that of forest broken by heath. Remnants of it can still be seen at the " noble seats of Wentworth and Wharncliffe Park ". Prehistoric relics have often been found in this region, which also contains some well-preserved hill-top camps of a type unknown or at any rate rare in other parts of Yorkshire. Nor is it deficient in Roman roads, camps and forts.

From the coal-field we pass westwards on to the Millstone Grit formation. This consists chiefly of grits and sand-stones, often as coarse as conglomerate. They average half a mile in thickness, cover a wider area than any other rocks in West Yorkshire, and crown its highest mountains. South of Airedale the Millstone Grit region varies from 8 to 12 miles wide. On the Derbyshire and Lancashire border it faces westwards in a series of high rocky escarp-ments such as Stanage Edge (1,368 feet), Derwent Edge (1,765 feet), and Blackstone Edge (1,553 feet), up which climbs the Roman road from Manchester to Ilkley. Near Haworth, where the passionate spirits of the Brontë sisters haunt moorlands grimmer than the witches' heath in Macbeth, the outcrop sweeps round to the north-east. Between Skipton and Keighley it is severed by Airedale, north of which it forms the heights of Rumbles Moor (1,321 feet) on the divide between Airedale and Wharfedale. Thence northwards in a zone from sixteen to twenty miles wide, the formation assumes a more truly mountainous character, soaring to more than 2,300 feet on Great Whern-side and Buckden Pike, at the heads of Wharfedale and Nidderdale. It is traversed by the Yore from Thornton Watless to Thornton Steward, disappearing just south of Richmond-on-Swale.

Nearly the whole of the Millstone Grit region is moor-land. On the higher peaks and plateaux this takes the form of deep peat bogs or mosses, composed almost entirely of the remains of cotton-sedges. These plants grow pro-fusely over hundreds of square miles on the bleak heights, and in summer their white seed-plumes resemble a snow-fall. On the lower slopes, where the rainfall is less heavy and the surface drainage better, heather moor flourishes, though it does not cover so wide an area as the mosses or as on the Eastern Moorlands.

Towards its lower eastern border where glacial deposits mask the sterile siliceous soils formed by the Grit, the land has been reclaimed. And of course Nidderdale, Wharfedale, and to a less extent, owing to the cancer of industrialism, Airedale, are famous for their pastoral and sylvan beauties.

Were it not for the moor which clothes its nakedness, the region would be more savage and forbidding. As it is the Grit protrudes through its clothing at the Cow and Calf Rocks, Ilkley ; the so-called Druid's Altar at Bingley ; Brimham Rocks near Pateley Bridge ; Plumpton Rocks near Knaresborough ; and in other localities. Their weird, awe-inspiring shapes attract thousands of visitors, and the fascination they exercise to-day probably echoes the deeper and more mysterious spell that they wove round the mind of prehistoric man.

Though the Millstone Grit moors do not seem to be so prolific as the Eastern Moorlands, nevertheless they have yielded many prehistoric antiquities which further research is increasing. At the base of the peat mosses we find large numbers of pygmy flints, the earliest evidences of post-glacial man in Yorkshire. On the heather moors round barrows, stone circles and earthworks occur, especially on Rumbles Moor, near Ilkley, celebrated for its cup and ring stones.

If we take the route westwards from Skipton through the Aire Gap we enter Ribblesdale. From Settle, where it emerges from the Craven highlands, to Sawley Abbey on the Lancashire border, the Ribble, one of the few Yorkshire rivers not falling into the Humber, flows through a fairly wide and comparatively low-lying region which is largely pastoral and which contains much of archaeological interest. Its rocks belong to the Mountain Limestone series, though owing to the extensive coating of glacial drift they rarely show at the surface. We are now in the region of the Pennine glaciers, one of the largest of which, cradled in the Craven mountains to the north, streamed down Ribblesdale. Near the Aire Gap west of the Ribble, between Hellifield and Gisburn, the landscape presents an amazing confusion of small and large rounded green hills. Composed of boulder-clay, sand, gravel, or even of solid rock, these hills or drumlins are by no means the least striking of the many physical features fashioned by the glaciers of the Ice Age in Yorkshire.

Below Sawley Abbey the Ribble valley contracts between the heights of Harrop Fell (1,300 feet) and the tabular mass of Pendle Hill (1,831 feet) in Lancashire. Here for more than twelve miles the river forms the county boundary. At Great Mitton the Hodder comes in from the north-west, and for a considerable distance this cheerful and picturesque river also separates Lancashire from York-shire.

The Hodder and its tributary the Dunnop have their source in the wild uplands of the Forest of Bowland or Bolland. Its high fells and knotts consist of the Millstone Grit, clad as usual in moorland, and reaching elevations of more than 1,700 feet on the county boundary. We may note in passing that fell is a common West Yorkshire word for a high hill or mountain. Knott, a much rarer name, is that of an elevated central mass like the Bowland Knotts (1,589 feet), whence fells diverge in various directions. Bowland is traversed by a fine stretch of the main Roman road from Chester to Carlisle.

The fells and knotts of Bowland lie within that ancient division of Yorkshire known as Craven, the Cravenshire of Domesday. It does not, however, correspond to a natural region. For north of Bowland, beyond the valley of the Wenning which falls westwards to the Lune, Craven becomes a limestone country of deep dales and high terraced mountains sweeping northwards in apparent confusion to Mickle and Cronkley Fells in Upper Teesdale, a distance of more than 40 miles. On the west this mountainous tract ranges to the county boundary on the heights above the valleys of the Lune and the Eden. On the east it coalesces with the Millstone Grit region. Apart from two or three small areas of older rocks,

the most conspicuous foundation of this sublime scenery
is the Carboniferous or Mountain Limestone formation
naturally divisible into a lower series, the Great Scar
Limestones, and a higher, the Yoredale grits, shales and
limestones.

The Great Scar Limestone attains its most astonishing
development in north Craven. Everywhere in this region
it appears as grey or white cliffs and scars, with organ-like
columns and flutings. From Ingleton in the west by
Clapham, Austwick, Giggleswick, Settle, Attermire, to
Malham and Kinsey in the east, a succession of high scars
and precipices combine to produce a rocky panorama un-
paralleled elsewhere in Yorkshire. Vertical scars alternate
with slopes or flat terraces often carpeted with bright green
pasture. On the terraces bare limestone pavements or
clints have been eroded into an intricate network of clefts,
channels, or even chasms from a few inches to many feet
in width. Streamless valleys gouge the limestone plateau.
Their waters now travel underground through "cavern
measureless to man", the roofs, floors and sides of which
are encrusted sometimes with beautiful, at others with
monstrous fungus-like stalactites and stalagmites. Should
the roofs of these caverns collapse deep ravines open to
the sky. The grandest example is Gordale near Malham.
More usually fallen roofs produce "pots", irregular funnel-
shaped abysses which plunge down into the heart of the
limestone. To descend and explore these caverns now
ranks with mountaineering as a thrilling recreation.
Archaeologically they are disappointing. Without ropes
and tackle they are inaccessible, so their occupation by
prehistoric man was out of the question, though he did
inhabit many of the drier smaller caves in the scars at
Giggleswick, Settle, Dowkerbottom and Elbolton in
Wharfedale.

Out of the river-trenched platform of the Great Scar
Limestone there spring Yorkshire's noblest mountains.
Spaced over a distance of sixteen miles we have five giants.
Gragarth (2,058 feet), along the narrow edge of which run
the Lancashire boundary; Whernside (2,419 feet), with

four tarns at its northern end; Ingleborough (2,373 feet), whose grassy summit is the site of a prehistoric fortified village; Pen-y-Ghent (2,273 feet), which bears a Celtic name; and Fountains Fell (2,151 feet), formerly the property of the monks of Fountains Abbey near Ripon. Alternating beds of shale, grit and limestone—the Yoredale rocks—form their sharp slopes; weather-defying scarred masses of Millstone Grit their summits. None of them is an isolated peak, not even Ingleborough and Pen-y-ghent, which are simply the highest extremities of long ridges parallel to the valleys between them.

The northern limits of Craven approximately coincide with the disappearance of the Great Scar Limestone beneath the Yoredale rocks, so extensively developed on the uplands dividing the basins of the Ribble, the Wharfe and the Yore. From the area round Blea Moor (1,753 feet), three miles north of the lower end of the Ingleborough massif, rivers radiate in many directions. In some instances their valley heads unite in distinct passes through the mountains. The nodal point of these passes lies about Ribble Head. From the east two high passes come in from Upper Wharfedale; from the west the pass between Ribblesdale and Dent Dale; north-east of Ribble Head a col at 1,474 feet leads over the watershed into Widdale, and thence to Hawes in Wensleydale. Indeed, from Ingleton to Hawes a continuous valley intersects the mountains. The Romans, if not prehistoric man, realised the value of these passes; for at Ribble Head the Roman road from Ingleton to Bainbridge in Wensleydale crossed another from Settle into Dent Dale.

Dent Dale, one of the most beautiful of all the Yorkshire dales, has its headwaters in the noble mountains of Whernside, Blea Moor, and Great Knoutberry Hill (2,205 feet) on Widdale Fell. Its river, the Dee, flows north-west to Sedbergh, near which old-fashioned town it falls into the Rawthey from the north-east. The united river enters the Lune which, for a few miles north of the junction, separates Yorkshire from Westmorland.

In the triangular region outlined by the Lune, the

3

Rawthey, and the county boundary on the north, we find a complex of steep, smooth, grassy hills, the Howgill Fells in marked contrast to the rough, terraced mountains amongst which we have been wandering. They attain their greatest elevation at the Calf (2,220 feet), above the Crag and Spout (waterfall) of Cautley, where we at once see that these fells consist of grey slates belonging to the Silurian and Ordovician systems. More ancient than the Mountain Limestone formation, they can be seen underlying it in the valley of the Greta, upper Ribblesdale and near Malham. In truth the Howgill Fells are geographically alien to our county. Their affinities lie with Westmorland and the Lake District. Henry I assigned them to Yorkshire in 1131. Little seems to be known of their archaeology.

From Sedbergh, Garsdale, the narrow valley of the Clough winds between the mountains of Rise Hill (1,825 feet) on the south, and Baugh Fell (2,214 feet) on the north, both formed of the Yoredale rocks with Millstone Grit summits. A pass at a maximum altitude of 1,059 feet unites the heads of Garsdale and the valley of the Yore. This river has its source near that of Hell Gill Beck, the headwaters of the Westmorland Eden. The twin streams flow parallel to one another for a mile or so and then part company, Hell Gill bending northwards and the Yore southeast along the same valley, which serves as a pass between the Vale of the Eden and Wensleydale.

From the passes at its head Wensleydale extends with widening vistas for more than twenty-five miles eastwards to Masham, where it declines into the Vale of York. No other Yorkshire dale, except perhaps Wharfedale, equals this magnificent valley, famous throughout the land for its vivid green pastures, quaint old-world villages, ruined castles, and superb waterfalls. Sculptured out of the Yoredale rocks, the terraced heights on the south side of the dale, such as Pen Hill (1,685 feet), and Addleborough (1,564 feet), interpose their bulk between charming tributary valleys, each a gem of beauty set within sombre mountains. The upper part of the Bain valley enshrines Yorkshire's most delightful lake, Semmerwater. Local tradition relates that its limpid waters hide a drowned village. Geologists tell us that it is the last of the lakes held up in the lateral valleys by the great Wensleydale glacier. Throughout the dale perched blocks, moraines, roches moutonnées, and green drumlins bear witness to that time

> " When the ice was here, the ice was there,
> The ice was all around ".

Though it has been less investigated than East Yorkshire Wensleydale contains much of archaeological interest : inhabited caves, prehistoric settlement-sites, camps, and Roman remains.

Towards its head the northern slopes of Wensleydale ascend to 2,213 feet at Lovely Seat and 2,346 feet at Great Shunnor Fell. Between these mountains lies the Butter-tubs pass which derives its name from a series of pot-holes in the Yoredale limestone. The pass is in alignment with that between Ingleton and Hawes, and is followed by the road from Hawes to Muker in Swaledale.

Swaledale, though somewhat shorter and narrower than Wensleydale, surpasses its neighbour in wildness. Hemmed in by mountain ridges, the Swale courses amidst green, stone-walled pastures and by stone-built villages to emerge from the dale at the castled crag of Richmond, below which it flows more gently down the Vale of York. Swaledale is rich in glacial remains.

Its rocks, like those of Teesdale, Wensleydale, Nidderdale and Wharfedale, are penetrated by veins of lead. The Romans and earlier peoples mined these veins, and their old workings still survive. Otherwise as yet we know little of the archaeology of Swaledale, once the most isolated of the western dales.

The mountains north of Swaledale, such as Great Pin Seat (1,914 feet), Water Crag (2,176 feet), and Rogan's Seat (2,204 feet), constitute an irregular and in places extremely narrow watershed between the Swale (and its affluents, the Arkle and Marske Becks) and the Greta which flows east-wards to the Tees. The Greta rises on the county boundary where its valley breaches the Pennines at an altitude of 1,436 feet in the broad pass of Stainmore, a route through the Pennines almost as important as the Aire Gap. Over it came a great glacier with its load of granite boulders from Shap Fells in Westmorland, boulders which were dumped far and wide over Yorkshire, even as far south as Doncaster. Prehistoric man used the pass, and the Romans fortified and drove a military road through it, a road that now runs parallel to the railway between Kirkby Stephen and Barnard Castle.

The Stainmore pass traverses high, wild moorlands furrowed to the north by the valleys of Deepdale Beck, the Balder, and the Lune, tributaries of the Tees whose beauties Scott describes in " Rokeby ".

The Lune gathers most of its waters from the southern slopes of Mickle Fell, Yorkshire's loftiest mountain, 2,591 feet high, a flat-topped crescent-shaped mass of Yoredale rocks, with two miles of limestone crags on the inner or south side of the crescent. Nearly all Yorkshire's finest hills and mountains can be seen from its summit. Southwards beyond Shunnor Fell and Lovely Seat rise Ingleborough, Pen-y-ghent, and Whernside. Eastwards, beyond the expansive Vale of York, Black Hambleton, Roseberry Topping, and Eston Nab shrink into insignificance. Westwards, beyond the Vale of the Eden, loom the Lake District mountains, whilst 8 miles to the north-west stands Cross Fell (2,799 feet) in Cumberland, the highest of the Pennines, and the source of the Tees.

The north-west boundary of our county follows the Maize Beck down to its junction with the Tees, which river, from this point to the sea, a distance of nearly 80 miles, divides Yorkshire from Durham. Above Middleton, Teesdale is wild and moory, with enchanting river scenery, for here the Tees flows over the hard basaltic rocks of the Great Whin Sill. A little above Maize Beck it foams and boils down the superb cataract of Caldron Snout. Then after winding for a few miles through a deep ravine excavated in the basaltic plateau of Cronkley Fell, it plunges over the vertical Whin Sill cliffs, 70 feet high, at High

Force. Below this waterfall the dale grows more wooded, and the Tees is

> " Condemn'd to mine a channell'd way
> O'er solid sheets of marble grey ".

Teesdale properly so-called ends near Winston whence the river meanders, often in large loops, across the northern end of the Vale of York to the sea. Extensive salt marshes formerly fringed its estuary, and the navigable channel was so shallow that at low tide the river-mouth could be forded. The Tees has yielded many prehistoric remains, and at Piercebridge and Middleton-one-Row it was crossed by the two main Roman roads from York to Hadrian's Wall.

For Reference : J. Phillips, *Geology of Yorkshire* (1829–36) ; *Rivers, Mountains and Sea-coast of Yorkshire* (1855). P. F. Kendall and H. Wroot, *Geology of Yorkshire* (1924). C. Fox-Strangways, *Jurassic Rocks of Yorkshire* (1892). T. Sheppard, *Lost Towns of the Yorkshire Coast* (1912). F. Elgee, *Moorlands of North-east Yorkshire* (1912). C. Reid, *Geology of Holderness* (1885). R. Tate and J. Blake, *Yorkshire Lias* (1876). P. F. Kendall, *Geology of Yorkshire*, V.C.II.Y., vol. i (1907). F. R. Cowper Reed, *Geological History of the Rivers of East Yorkshire* (1901). A. G. Ogilvie (Ed.), *Great Britain, Essays in Regional Geography* (1928), chaps. xvi-xviii.

CHAPTER II

THE OLD STONE AGE

THAT Yorkshire was habitable before the Ice Age is undoubtedly true. Its pre-glacial fauna all points to a warm climate, very suitable for man. In fact, its species either still live in Africa, or they have their nearest relatives there.

At Sewerby, near Bridlington, the rolled and water-worn bones and teeth of the hippopotamus (*H. amphibius major*), the extinct, straight-tusked elephant (*Elephas antiquus*), and the extinct slender-nosed rhinoceros (*R. leptorhinus*) occurred on a beach at the foot of a pre-glacial chalk cliff. Resting on the beach was an ancient land-surface, consisting of a chalky rubble, with land-shells, covered with a mass of yellow dune-sands, on which were the remains of the mammoth (*E. primigenius*), the giant deer (*Cervus megaceros*), the urus (*Bos primigenius*), and the bison or auroch (*Bison bonasus*). Over the dunes lay the basement clay of the earliest glaciation.

A more varied and instructive assemblage of pre-glacial animals was found in the Victoria Cave, which lies at the base of the Mountain Limestone scars of Langcliff, at a height of 1,000 feet above Settle (W.R.), 1,450 feet above sea-level. Inside the cave a thick deposit of laminated clay of glacial origin divided the cave-earth into a lower layer that preceded, and an upper that followed the earliest glaciation. In pre-glacial times the cave had been the home of hyenas (*H. crocuta spelaea*), a large variety of the African spotted hyena. Mingled with their dung and their bones were the teeth and the gnawed and split bones of the hippopotamus, the straight-tusked elephant, and the woolly rhinoceros (*R. tichorhinus*). In the higher parts of the pre-glacial layer were the bones of the brown bear (*Ursus arctos*), the grizzly bear (*U. horribilis*), the fox (*Canis vulpes*), the urus and the red deer (*Cervus elephas*).

Four miles north-east of Skipton a fissure in the Raygill limestone quarries of Lothersdale yielded the bones of the hyena, straight-tusked elephant, slender-nosed rhinoceros, and the molar tooth of a lion. As they lay beneath laminated boulder-clay, they are obviously of pre-glacial age.

At Armley Gaol, Leeds, the complete skeletons of two adult and one young hippopotami were recovered from a dark blue mud-like clay, in which the living animals must have been bogged, for their bones were found in their natural position. The age of this clay and its relation to glacial deposits have not yet been elucidated. It is probably pre-glacial.

The most prolific bone cave in Yorkshire was that at Kirkdale in the Limestone Hills, near Pickering. This, like Victoria Cave, had been a hyena den for many generations. The remains of between two or three hundred hyenas were scattered throughout a thick layer of sandy mud on the floor. Their bones and teeth were mixed with those of the hippopotamus, lion, straight-tusked elephant, and slender-nosed rhinoceros, characteristic of the warmer pre-glacial fauna ; and those of the mammoth, woolly rhinoceros and reindeer, characteristic of the colder glacial fauna.

A claim has been made that eoliths were found on the Wolds, between Market Weighton and Beverley, and if so, they must have been deposited before the Ice Age, under conditions similar to those just described. But they are not made of Yorkshire flint ; they are in every way identical with the eoliths of Kent ; no other examples have ever been found. So for these reasons we are inclined to think that they have been wrongly located.

The on-coming of the Ice Age is revealed to us by the woolly rhinoceros at Victoria Cave, and the mammoth at Sewerby. Their thick, hairy coats enabled them to endure the rigours of the increasingly glacial climate.

The Ice Age lasted for some thousands of years, during which period much of the original surface of Yorkshire was buried under thick deposits of boulder-clay, with their intervening beds of sand and gravel. This boulder-clay is the debris gathered up and pulverised by the glaciers, over 1,000 feet thick, as they pressed towards the sea from the Pennines, Lake District, Cheviots, Scotland and Scandinavia.

Nowhere is the local history of the Ice Age so plainly readable as in the sections of the glacial deposits extending southwards from Flamborough Head along the Holderness coast, where the following generalised succession of deposits occurs in this ascending order :—

1. Pre-glacial beach and cliff of Sewerby.
2. Basement boulder-clay.
3. Laminated clays of Bridlington.
4. Lower purple boulder-clay.
5. Gravels, sands and loams of Holderness.
6. Upper purple boulder-clay.
7. Hessle and Sewerby sands, gravels and loams.
8. Hessle or uppermost boulder-clay.

It must not be supposed that these deposits were laid down without a break. There were interludes of less arctic weather, when the ice receded, and when glacial fauna easily established and maintained itself.

Its characteristic animals were the woolly rhinoceros, the mammoth, the reindeer, the musk ox, the giant deer, bison and walrus. Their bones and teeth have been found in the glacial deposits of Holderness, near York, at Bielsbeck between Market Weighton and North Cliff, and elsewhere.

It is clear from this list that there appears to be no reason why the remains of man should not be found, as they occur in the Creswell Caves in Derbyshire. A pear-shaped flint implement (3¾″ long) found many years ago on the surface at Huntow, near Bridlington, is considered a typical Lower Palaeolithic hand-axe.

Efforts have been made to discover Palaeolithic implements in the glacial drift and other deposits. In 1922, and again in 1931, E. R. Collins described and figured implements of local chert from Upper Nidderdale. He arranged them in four series, according to their probable age. 1. Implements from a deposit probably due to the melting of the ice, and lying below the peat which covers the tops of the moors. They include triangular points made from tabular chert blocks, cores, and flakes ; a massive scraper ; and a flake with a bulb of percussion. As there is nothing in their form or technique comparable to well-known Palaeolithic types, Collins finds it impossible to date them, though he thinks that they are Upper Palae-olithic. 2. Implements from terraces and river gravels (Fig. 1), consisting of material apparently washed out of the lateral moraines of the Nidderdale glacier at the end of the Ice Age. He records four rolled implements from these beds. 3. Implements from lateral moraines at Scar (980–1,100 feet) and at Byer Beck (950–1,050 feet). They are mostly sharp, but a high percentage are slightly rolled. They include lozenge-shaped points and beaks ; a heart-shaped tool with a cutting edge on one side, the other being in its natural state ; a massive triangular implement ($1\frac{3}{4}$ lb.) ; and a steep-sided scraper, with boldly trimmed edge and flat base. 4. Implements from river-bed gravels, between Goyden Pot Hole and Manchester Hole. These are massive, much rolled, and with few exceptions patinated a light chestnut colour. They include types that resemble early Chellean hand-axes. They occur at the very bottom of the dale, where they were deposited by the glaciers which swept them off an old land-surface.

J. P. T. Burchell has recently described a well-developed industry of flint points, scrapers and gravers from Danes' Dyke, Flamborough. They occurred on an old land-surface below a weathered deposit which, on being cut back, proved to possess all the features of a boulder-clay, containing chalk fragments and an abundance of Cheviot and Scottish erratics. At Beacon Hill this deposit was more earthy, though containing the same kind of erratics. At its base, and resting on the surface of the Upper Purple Boulder-clay, or, where that is absent, on sands and gravels, he found a similar industry. He assigns both to the Upper Mousterian culture.

Burchell regards the Danes' Dyke clay as the result of direct glacial action. On the other hand, the Geological Survey regards the Beacon Hill bed as a landwash comparable to the Coomb deposits of southern England, and not as a true boulder-clay. If Burchell's views are right, then the industries antedate the last glaciation of East Yorkshire ; if the Geological Survey is right, then they must be post-glacial.

A deposit similar to that at Beacon Hill caps the well-known glacial sections at Kelsey Hill and Burstwick, 10 miles east of Hull. It contains similar erratics, and in it Burchell found scattered flakes and cores, and at its base signs of an occupation level.

Below this bed is a rather stoneless clay which he calls the " Hessle boulder-clay of inland sections ", and which because of its colour he equates with the Upper Purple clay of Danes' Dyke and Flamborough. If this correlation is correct, then the deposit cannot be the Hessle clay, a term reserved for the foxy red clay with Cheviot and Scottish erratics, the Upper Purple clay of the coast being rich in western erratics. However this may be, the clay overlies sands and gravels usually considered to be the moraine of the western ice. They have yielded bones and teeth of mammoth, rhinoceros, reindeer, bison and walrus. In them Burchell found several flint implements of which he figures a Levallois flake (Fig. 1), and an ovate hand-axe, and which he refers to the Early Mousterian culture. These appear to be the first Yorkshire implements from a deposit containing Palaeolithic fauna.

Another flint implement ($1\frac{3}{4}''$ long) found at a depth of 4 feet in the uppermost boulder-clay, between Grosmont and Sleights in Lower Eskdale, has been compared with a Mousterian point.

As we have not yet been able to examine the sections and implements described by Collins and Burchell, we are not in a position to criticise their conclusions which, it must be admitted, have not met with general acceptance.

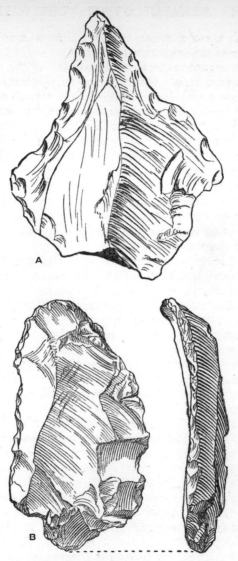

FIG. I.—PALAEOLITHIC IMPLEMENTS

A, Nidderdale (chert) ; B, Burstwick (flint)

Natural size

That their researches are serious attempts to throw light on Palaeolithic Yorkshire cannot, however, be gainsaid, whatever the ultimate verdict may be.

With regard to the Upper Palaeolithic remains in Yorkshire, there is likewise little to be said, though the representative Upper Aurignac, proto-Solutré, and Creswellian (Aurignac under La Madeleine influence) cultures are found near at hand in the Creswell Caves of Derbyshire. Nevertheless, at Windy Hill (1,000 feet) on the Pennines, two miles south of Blackstone Edge, and twelve west of Huddersfield, eighty flakes and twenty chert tools of the developed Aurignacian Series occurred in the lowest layer of a site occupied before any of the deep peat which clothes the hill had begun to form. These tools included two large carinated planes, a large parrot-beak graver, and two hammer stones or choppers. Their occurrence shows that Upper Palaeolithic man reached Yorkshire in early post-glacial times.

The evidence adduced in this chapter makes it perfectly clear that only before and after the Ice Age, or during its milder intervals, was it at all possible for Palaeolithic man and his contemporaries, the great mammals, to enter Yorkshire. For this reason alone his remains cannot be so numerous as in those parts of southern England which escaped glaciation, or which were only glaciated once or twice. It is not altogether vain to hope that patient research will reveal further evidence as to the relationship between Palaeolithic man and the glacial and inter-glacial periods in Yorkshire.

For Reference : W. Boyd-Dawkins, *Cave Hunting* (1874). R. A. Smith, *Flint Implements of Special Interest, Arch.*, lxxii, 1922. E. R. Collins, *Early Palaeolithic Implement in Yorkshire*, P.P.S.E.A., ii, 1922 ; *Palaeolithic Implements of Nidderdale*, op. cit., vi, 156–73, 1930. J. P. T. Burchell, *Upper and Lower Palaeolithic Man in Yorkshire*, op. cit., vi, 226–33. T. Sheppard, *Palaeolithic Man in Yorkshire, Nat.*, 1930, 287–92.

CHAPTER III

THE MESOLITHIC AGE

IN the last chapter we learned that Upper Palaeolithic man lived on the Southern Pennines in early post-glacial times. This phase, from about 10,000 to 7000 B.C., is known as the Arctic Period. It was succeeded by the Boreal Period, during which the climate was warm and dry. Birch-heath forest, with oak, alder and hazel, became widespread, even on the Pennines. From 5000 to 3000 B.C. a warm moist climate prevailed in what is termed the Atlantic Period.

Archaeologically the Boreal and Atlantic Periods cover the Epi-palaeolithic or Mesolithic Age. These terms have been devised for a series of cultures following the Upper Palaeolithic. They carried on the Palaeolithic tradition, which, after flourishing for tens of thousands of years, was finally passing away. Viewed in this light the Mesolithic Age becomes invested with the melancholy peculiar to dying institutions and civilisations. Hunting, fishing, and food-gathering had been man's only method of living since he sprang from the ape. During the Mesolithic Age they were still primary but soon destined to become subsidiary to the cultivation of the ground and the domestication of animals. In other words, the gates of Eden were closing against Adam ; he was soon to earn his bread by the sweat of his face.

Yorkshire has yielded remains of three more or less contemporaneous Mesolithic cultures, the Azilian, the Maglemosian, and the Tardenoisian. The Azilian and Tardenoisian are often bracketed together as one culture, though there seems little reason to doubt that the Azilian began earlier, while the Tardenoisian persisted later.

In Yorkshire the Azilian culture, which takes its name
from the Mas d'Azil cave in the Pyrenees where its time
position was first determined, is represented by a flat
barbed harpoon of reindeer antler from the Victoria Cave,
Settle (Fig. 2). It is of early Azilian type, being without
the basal perforation characteristic of later harpoons.
Associated with it were three rude flint flakes, charcoal,
broken bones of the brown bear, red deer or stag, horse
and short-horn ox.

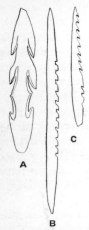

FIG. 2. — ANTLER
HARPOONS

A, Victoria Cave, W.R.
(3½″), *Giggleswick School
Museum*; B, Hornsea
(10″), C, Skipsea, E.R.
(5″), *British Museum*

The antiquity of these remains can
be gauged from the circumstance that
they lay directly upon glacial clay,
covered by 10 feet of debris. The
uppermost 2 feet had accumulated since
Roman times, which in their turn were
represented by a deposit 2 feet thick,
rich in Romano-British relics. Between
this and the Azilian level the deposit
was 6 feet thick. Assuming that the
pre-Roman debris had accumulated at
the same rate as the post-Roman, 2 feet
in 1,500 years, we get the date 4500 B.C.
for the Azilian occupation. Though
this date, owing to inevitable variations
in the rate of accumulation, cannot be
regarded as absolute, it nevertheless
carries us a long way towards the 6000
B.C. which on other grounds has been
assigned to the Azilian Age.

No other Azilian objects seem to have been found in
Yorkshire. In Holderness, however, the relics of a contemporaneous culture have occurred. Known as the Maglemosian, this is considered by many archaeologists to be
the North-European equivalent of the Azilian, which is
essentially of French and Spanish origin. It derives its
name from Maglemose (great moss), formerly a freshwater
lake, situated near Mullerup on the west coast of the
Danish island of Zealand. Here in 1900 the Danish
archaeologist, Dr. Sarauw, first discovered the remains of

a primitive fishing folk who lived upon raft-like structures in shallow water. Their implements were chiefly made of bone and antler, and include harpoons, chisels, axes, perforated hammers, sockets for stone tools, fish-hooks, awls, needles, spear-heads and knives. They also used flint scrapers, knives, borers, axes, and other tools known as pygmy flints. Ignorant of agriculture and pottery, they had one domestic animal, the dog. The associated animals and plants all indicate that this folk lived during the warm Boreal Period, about 6000 B.C.

The Maglemose culture has been detected in North Germany from Hanover to East Prussia, as far south as Boulogne in France, and as far west as Yorkshire, where it obtained a foothold in and around the ancient meres of Holderness, for the North Sea was then a land-surface.[1] At Skipsea Whitow a typical antler harpoon (Fig. 2) was found in 1903 by the late Mr. Beaumont Morfitt, lying in silt at a depth of 5 feet beneath lake-peat, and immediately under the skeleton of an Irish elk or giant-deer. Other associated animals were the red deer, reindeer, and ancient ox. A. L. Armstrong, who first described these remains, states that it resembles one from Mullerup.

The harpoon occurred below high-water mark on the beach at Skipsea where coast erosion exposes silt deposited on the bed of an ancient mere. From this silt and the overlying peat Armstrong recovered a dozen flint implements, scrapers, ridged flakes, piercers, etc. Two flint implements from Skipsea in the Morfitt collection are like others from Sværdborg, a Maglemosian station in Zealand. Armstrong also records two flint Maglemosian hand-axes (5″ long) found in peat at Skipsea. Their most distinctive feature is a cutting edge formed by the removal of bold flakes uniting at the medial ridge which with the side edges is much battered and bruised. They are the oldest known axes in Yorkshire.

In 1905 another harpoon was found under lake-peat, 12 feet below the present surface, near Hornsea Mere. The

[1] A Maglemose harpoon has recently been dredged up 50 miles N.E. of Cromer, *Ant.*, June 1932.

type is essentially Maglemosian, occurring frequently at Mullerup and Sværdborg (Fig. 2).

In 1889 a rare implement was found in the Calf Hole or Elland Cave at Skyrethorns on the edge of Malham Moor, W.R. The original is lost, but casts were made of it at Owens College Museum, Manchester. The implement was made of reindeer antler, into which was fixed the canine tooth of a boar, and it was used as an adze (Fig. 3). Such tools are typical of the Maglemosian culture, and, as might be expected, the tool was associated with the bones of the bison and the reindeer. Further research is bound to reveal more evidence of the Maglemosian culture.

The most abundant and widespread implements of the

FIG. 3.—BOAR TUSK IMPLEMENT IN ANTLER HAFT
Calf Hole Cave, Skyrethorns, W.R. (7″)

Mesolithic Age are ' pygmy ' or microlithic flints (Fig. 4), which, though belonging to each of its three cultures, more particularly characterise that named after Tardenois in France. Thousands have occurred in Yorkshire : they are most abundant on the moors of the Southern Pennines, where they must be looked for at altitudes of over 1,000 feet, beneath the peat which now covers the softer sandstones. In Mesolithic days these open spaces were sufficiently well-drained to form the best possible camping-grounds for the microlithic hunting-folk. The flints occur always within a small area ; sometimes one site only can be traced, sometimes several on the same hill, just as if the ground had been occupied one year after another. Nowhere is their age more instructively revealed than in sections excavated by Mr. F. Buckley on Warcock Hill, Marsden, near Huddersfield (Fig. 5). He cut through three feet of peat, and reached a layer of grey sand, 6″

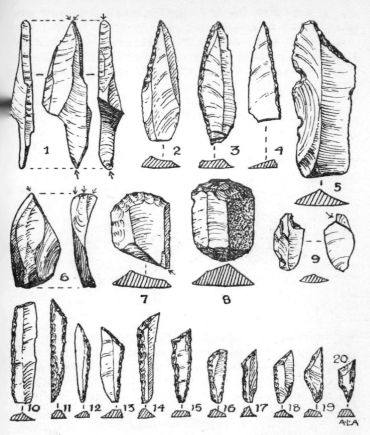

FIG. 4.—MICROLITHIC FLINT IMPLEMENTS

Developed Aurignacian type (latest phase of Upper Palaeolithic and pre-Tardenois) : 1. Double-ended angle-graver, Siss Cross, Danby, N.R. 2. Backed blade, S. Yorks. moors. 3. Point of Châtelperron type, Cock Heads, Glaisdale, N.R. 4. Gravette point, S. Yorks. moors. 5. Notched and shouldered blade with scraper end, Pickering Moor, N.R. 6. Graver, Salt Cliff, Bridlington.

Tardenoisian tools : 7. Combined end scraper and graver. 8. Double-ended keeled scraper, S. Yorks. moors. 9. Micro-graver, Cupwith Hill, W.R. 10–20. Pygmy tools, Eastern Moorlands, Pennines, and S. Yorks. moors.

Natural size

thick, resting on the original rock. At the base of this sand he found unpatinated microlithic implements and waste flints with birch and oak charcoal. Above them another floor in the grey sand contained white-patinated 'pygmies' and waste flint, associated with birch charcoal.

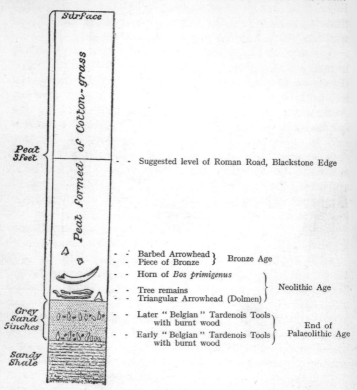

FIG. 5.—SECTION OF PEAT WITH REMAINS, WARCOCK HILL, MARSDEN, W.R.

At the base of the peat a flint arrow-head of late Neolithic type was found amongst the remains of birch and oak trees. In the lower peat layers there occurred the horns of the ancient ox, and at a higher level a piece of bronze and a barbed Bronze Age flint arrow-head.

These sections show that the men who made microliths were wandering over the Southern Pennines not only before the Neolithic Age, but also before any peat, which in some places is 10 feet deep, had begun to form, and when these hills were clothed with heather moor and oak-birch scrub. From this circumstance we may infer that the ' pygmy ' flints date back into the Boreal Period, when the climate was too warm and dry for peat to accumulate.

A study of the pygmy flints discloses a broad-blade industry which has been compared with the Early Tardenois of Belgium, and a narrow-blade industry more or less peculiar to the Pennines, probably developed from the Aurignacian culture of Upper Palaeolithic times. These can be subdivided into an earlier series which is unpatinated and is characterised by the angle and the true graver (Fig. 4) and a later often patinated series, distinguished by the micro-graver, indisputably the key tool of the Tardenois culture—a graver being a tool used either for the ornamental carving of bone, ivory or wood, or for such useful purposes as the making of bone pins, or as gouges and chisels.

In the Huddersfield area, which has been systematically investigated, the most important sites are the following :—

1. Windy Hill. Above the Aurignacian flints (p. 28) there was a densely packed Early Tardenois workshop, containing over 5,300 flints, including 100 broad-blade microliths.

2. White Hill. 15 sq. yards yielded 1,200 flints, including 100 broad-blade pygmy tools. One of the latest sites in the district. Near it Mr. Buckley found a row of 35 flints, arranged like the teeth of a saw, 1½" to 2" apart.

3. Lominot. Several workshops of varying size. One consisting of two round emplacements has produced an industry similar to that of the Early Belgian series found in the cave of Remouchamps.

4. March Hill (1,340 ft.). One of the most famous flint sites of the Pennines. More than 6,000 pieces of flint and nearly 500 tools from 4 sites. Narrow-blade industry. Angle-graver the commonest tool. Related to the Azilian of France.

5. Cupwith Hill. Several thousand pieces of flint; many small tools, including 100 micro-gravers. Main workshop represents transitional period when the angle-graver was replaced by the micro-graver.

6. Dean Clough. Prolific area with a number of small workshops and thousands of pieces of flint. The angle-graver is rare and poorly made. The most characteristic tool a small pear-shaped point rarely found elsewhere.

It must be understood that these small tools were presumably mounted in bone or wood to serve as harpoons, arrow-heads, saws, fish-hooks, cutting-tools, borers, and the like. Associated with them in most cases were found pieces of chert, or chert implements, indicating an acquaintance with more northern districts. Red ruddle and brown hæmatite are general, and graphite (from Cumberland) occurs. These were probably used, not only for personal adornment, but for colouring the tools themselves as was the custom among the aborigines of Australia : red being symbolic of the life force, and therefore potent. Round shale objects were also found.

South of the Huddersfield area Tardenois implements are plentiful on the moors west of Penistone and Sheffield. They range from 1,000 to 1,700 feet ; but a station has been located at 400 feet on Wincobank Hill between Sheffield and Rotherham. Sites are most numerous on Derwent Edge, Cut Gate and Langsett Moors, Moscar Edge, Stanedge, and Higgar Tor.

Typical implements include long narrow knives, saws, borers, end-scrapers, round scrapers often no larger than a threepenny-piece, micro-gravers, blades with battered backs, small notched tools and triangles, usually of flint, but sometimes of chert and Derbyshire lydian stone. Hearths and fire-cracked cooking stones occur on the sites. Scattered over the moors are many flat neatly shaped sand-stone discs (2 to 4 inches), most probably used for throwing at small game. Similar discs have also been found in Bronze Age camps (p. 84) and on Roman sites.

Though these microlithic implements resemble the older Huddersfield series in general character, they suggest a

PLATE I

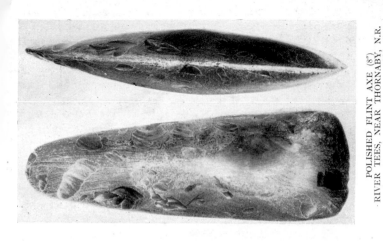

POLISHED FLINT AXE (8")
RIVER TEES, NEAR THORNABY, N.R.

Middlesbrough Museum

MESOLITHIC FLINT HAND AXE (5¾")
COCK HEADS, GLAISDALE, N.R.

northward movement of their makers rather than one southward from the Huddersfield district. They seem to represent the final development of those characteristic of the Upper Palaeolithic Age in the cave known as Mother Grundy's Parlour at Creswell, Derbyshire, especially in the occurrence of Châtelper—on and Gravette points, typical implements of that age (Fig. 4).

In North-east Yorkshire pygmy flints are again found on sandy knolls at altitudes from 825 to 1,300 feet. At Cock Heads, Glaisdale (1,300′), a Châtelperron point occurred, and a finely flaked flint axe which, as it is much battered along the side edges, must have been held in the hand when used (Plate I). Sites on the north Cleveland moors are characterised by narrow blades with flaked or battered backs, occasional angle-gravers, borers, scrapers, etc. True micro-gravers are rare.

The makers of the microlithic flint implements always chose to camp on sandy ground, the usual explanation being that such ground was naturally drained and more or less treeless. But this explanation is superficial, since their camps are unknown on chalk or limestone which offer the same inducements. Possibly, in the mind of micro-lithic man sand was endowed with magical properties, and a religious significance. The special attributes of sand were probably noted first in Egypt where it acts as a preserver of the dead, and where also countless creatures apparently hatch out of the sand, as if it were a veritable giver of life as well as a preventer of corruption. Thus sand became a holy thing, a thing to be sought after and associated with. This belief has held throughout the ages. Sand was often used in the burial rites of the Bronze Age, and even in our own times sand has been strewn in the streets at weddings, emblems drawn in it, and old verses reveal that the custom is associated with the notion of fertility. Records of these practices come from Knutsford in Cheshire, Newcastle-on-Tyne, and Sunderland.

For Reference : A. L. Armstrong, *Maglemose Remains of Holderness*, P.P.S.E.A., vol. 4, 1923 ; *Flint and Stone Implements of the Sheffield District*, Proc. Sorby Scient. Soc., i, 1929. T. Sheppard,

The Maglemose Harpoons, Nat., 1923, 169–79 ; 1930, 193–4.   F. Buckley, *Microlithic Industry of the Pennine Chain*, 1924.   F. Elgee, *Early Man in N.E. Yorkshire*, chap. 5.   J. A. Petch, *Early Man in the Huddersfield District*, Tolson Memorial Museum Publication, No. 3, 1924.   M. A. Canney, *Sand in Magical and other Ceremonies*, Discovery, 1926.   W. Boyd-Dawkins, *Cave Hunting*, 1874.   T. W. Woodhead, *History of the Vegetation of the Southern Pennines*, Tolson Mus. Publications, No. 5, 1929 ; Journ. Ecol., xvii, 1929.

CHAPTER IV

THE AGE OF LONG-BARROWS AND STONE AXES

THE interval between the Mesolithic Period and the dawn of the Early Bronze Age is usually termed the Neolithic Age, and is still very obscure. We do not know when microlithic man ceased to hunt our moors and dales, nor what became of him, but we must suppose that new cultural and perhaps racial elements were imposed upon him. By this time the peoples of the Eastern Mediterranean were living in settled communities ; they had domestic animals ; they cultivated the land ; they knew the art of pottery ; they made copper and bronze axes, and imitated them in stone where copper was not to be had. Some were adventurers and traders, and they coasted as far as Britain and Ireland in search of gold, tin, copper, pearls and the like. Such intercourse, naturally enough, left its imprint on the inhabitants, who began to lead a more settled existence, who adopted the use of the ground and polished stone axe in contradistinction to the unpolished hand-axe hitherto employed. They also developed an elaborate ritual of the dead which reached its highest expression in the chambered long-barrows.

Neolithic remains are reported from caves in the West Riding. The evidence is not altogether satisfactory, depending chiefly on flints and animal remains characteristic of the period. The most certain seems to come from the Elbolton Cave, near Thorpe, Wharfedale. The upper cave-earth contained several human skeletons, and numerous hearths, around which were numerous sherds of thick hand-made pottery said to be of Neolithic type. A large number of bone pins, skewers, spoons, and a ' whistle ' accompanied the pottery, together with bones of wild cattle, sheep, ox, goat, poultry, wolf, and fox. A few fragments of flint were found, and many pot-boilers.

An example of a very early settlement site is to be found in the so-called lake-dwelling of West Furze, near Ulrome, in northern Holderness. At a depth of 10 feet there lay a platform, 60 by 90 feet, of tree trunks resting on a thick layer of brushwood, beneath which was a deposit of sand and gravel merging horizontally into peat not more than 2 feet thick. Originally this deposit formed the bed of a shallow mere above the surface of which the log platform had been raised by means of the brushwood, and secured by poles fixed to the logs and driven into the lake bed. From either end of the platform a narrow causeway led to the shore.

Amongst the logs were many hammer-stones or pounders with abraded edges, a few stone rubbers including an oval stone more than a foot wide with a flat, smooth surface, many flint scrapers, knives, saws, deer-horn picks, seventeen circularly perforated ox bones and horns used as adzes, and a piece of burnt ironstone coated with ruddle. Under and around the platform lay a great accumulation of bones and teeth of the red deer, ancient ox, wolves, boars, beavers, foxes, otters, and domestic animals,—the horse, pig, goat, sheep, dog and short-horned ox.

The great age of this dwelling may be inferred from the fact that above it there lay a second floor of the late Bronze or Iron Age (p. 102) which as far as we know had no cultural connection with the older structure, which recalls the raft-like abodes of the Maglemose folk of Denmark, just as the perforated ox bones resemble Maglemose tools. As the dwelling rested on two feet of peat it must be later than the Maglemose harpoons (p. 31) which came from under lake peat. It may have been the home of a folk descended from Maglemose fishers and hunters.

Another type of evidence of a settled community is to be seen in the long-barrows. These are burial mounds or howes, more or less oblong in shape, with one end higher and often wider than the other They have not yet been detected in the Vale of York, and only one has been found in West Yorkshire,[1] but in East Yorkshire about twenty-five, including a few that have been destroyed, are known. One stands at an altitude of 1,200 feet on Kepwick Moor on the Hambleton Hills, and another at 800 feet on Sleights Moor in lower Eskdale. These are the only known long-barrows on the Eastern Moorlands, so rich in round-barrows, and they are situated at a higher altitude than the other long-barrows of East Yorkshire. On the Lime-stone Hills eight are distributed from Scarborough to Wass at altitudes between 275 and 675 feet. Two on the Howardian Hills at Yearsley and Westow stand at 550 and 150 feet respectively. About twelve occur on the Wolds at altitudes of about 500 feet. The most con-spicuous and accessible is that on the brink of the chalk escarpment on Flotmanby Wold, and close to the high road from Folkton to Hunmanby.

Three formerly stood near the Scamridge Dikes between Scarborough and Pickering; but only one, the Howe Hill, survives. At Rudston near Bridlington two long-barrows formed a V, their lower, narrower ends being in contact. One of them measured 255 feet long by 45 feet wide and 3½ feet high at the west end, and 35 feet wide and 1 foot high at the east end, probably the largest in the county, though that on Flotmanby Wold is very nearly its equal in size. Its twin was slightly smaller. Others vary from 170 feet in length (Kilham) to 60 feet (Wass), with their higher ends from 9 to 3 feet. The shorter barrows are wide in proportion to their length.

Thirteen barrows have their longer axes running east and west; seven, north and south; four, south-east and north-west; and two, south-west and north-east. The east or northern end is usually the higher.

Seventeen long-barrows have been excavated, three destroyed; the rest offer themselves for investigation, and, which is more important, for preservation as the oldest known human monuments in the county.

In eleven barrows the interments were restricted to a narrow space along the longer axis, rarely extending beyond

[1] See p. 64.

the middle, and usually at the higher end. On Kepwick Moor the fragmentary bones of five or six people were spread over a distance of 8½ feet on the original surface beneath a barrow more than 100 feet long. In another near Cropton on the Limestone Hills many imperfect human bones and skeletons lay in hollows 2 to 3 feet deep at the east and west ends ; beneath them were three graves each enclosing a skeleton, one without the skull, associated with leaf-shaped flint arrow-heads.

These are the only two Yorkshire long-barrows known to contain unburnt human bones ; in most the interments had been subjected to the action of fire, not before, but *after* they had been deposited in the barrows. At Rudston there were the fragmentary remains of at least four people ; at Westow, seven ; at Scamridge, fourteen or fifteen ; and at Market Weighton as many as twenty-six.

It is thought that many of the bodies had originally been deposited in some other place such as an ossuary, before being finally buried and burnt in the long-barrow. This view also seems to account for the disjointed and imperfect condition of the skeletons. The bones were laid in a line on the ground, or in holes or trenches, or on a layer of flagstones. They were then surrounded with wood or other fuel, and the barrow was built over them in such a way that when the fuel was ignited the fire spread along the deposited remains to flicker out in the heart of the mound. The consequence was that bones nearer the end of the barrow where the fire was started were often so thoroughly burnt as to be cremated ; others further inside were often merely scorched or escaped the fire altogether.

Wherever measurable the skulls proved to be long or dolichocephalic, that is having a breadth not more than 75 per cent of the length. This proportion is termed the cephalic index, and when associated with other skeletal features, such as stature, affords a clue to the racial affinities of early man. From the Scamridge long-barrow a woman's skull, index 56, is so long as to suggest distortion after birth ; and a young man's skull, index 67, had been violently cleft at death. Two other skulls from the same barrow had indexes of 71. At Rudston two male skulls measured 68 and 72.

Long-barrow man was not in the habit of providing his dead with articles for use in the spirit world. But in a long-barrow on the Limestone Hills at East Ayton near Scarborough, several objects were found beneath a large cairn on the top of which lay burnt limestone rubble, mixed

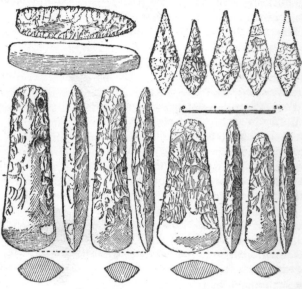

FIG. 6.—FLINT AXES AND ARROWHEADS
From long-barrow, East Ayton, N.R.
British Museum

with potsherds, animal and human bones, thus recalling similar deposits in other long-barrows. In this particular cairn there were two masses of human bone, each with a rude flint arrow-head, and not far away a thin flat stone partly concealed five finely-flaked leaf and lozenge-shaped arrow-heads ; four flint axes with rounded butts, sharp slightly incurved sides, and polished cutting-edges ; two flint knives, two rude flints, boar tusks, and a deer-horn socket for the axes (Fig. 6).

No settlement sites have been identified, but at Hanging Grimston near Acklam at the north-west angle of the Wolds there occurred the remains of a single dwelling beneath the east end of a long-barrow. It consisted of a circular pit 9½ feet wide and 6 feet deep, approached by two sloping and slightly curved passages 24 and 27 feet long. In the pit were the upper and lower jaws of at least twenty pigs with the tusk points broken off and arranged in four heaps; antlers and bones of the red and roe deer; the thigh-bone of a medium-sized person; and a plain dark earthenware vessel with rounded base and wide shallow neck. A similar bowl came from one of the passages, and two others from under an oblong grave situated to the east of the middle of the barrow, but the interments had decayed away. These vessels measured from 12 to 13 inches in diameter, and from 3¾ to 6 inches deep. These are distinctively local examples of what is known generally as ' Windmill Hill ' pottery, a neolithic ware, of frequent occurrence in Yorkshire, that takes its name from a Wiltshire hill-fort, and is found in southern England, the Cotswolds, Yorkshire, and Scotland. Mr. Stuart Piggott, in a recent study of this pottery,[1] remarks that it probably reached Yorkshire either about the same time as, or after, the Beakers (see next chapter), so that although it is of *neolithic* form it probably flourished in Yorkshire at a time when the Bronze Age had already been established in southern England. We may remark in passing that the other variety of neolithic pottery (Peterborough ware) is only poorly represented in Yorkshire, which is surprising in view of its predominantly eastern distribution and of the fact that the Peterborough type bowl is the ancestor of the food-vessel (see p. 66).

The hut-pit appears to have been horizontally roofed with logs covered with soil and chalk grit, and thatched with heather or rushes. Layers of black matter on the floor suggest that both it and its occupants were destroyed by fire. The pit then seems to have been used as a grave, and a barrow heaped over it by digging earth out of two

[1] *Arch. Journ.*, lxxxviii (1931), p. 67.

broad trenches flanking the sides. Prehistoric man often turned his dwellings into graves.

The Yorkshire long-barrows agree with those of south-west England in form, in the disjointed and fragmentary character of their multiple interments, in the type of skull, and in the presence of leaf-shaped flint arrow-heads. They differ in not enclosing burial chambers constructed of large upright stones supporting a large cover or capstone, and sometimes approached by roofed stone passages. When free-standing such chambers are known as dolmens. These do not occur in Yorkshire. It may be noted that in the long-barrows at Yearsley, Wass and Scamridge loose or drystone walling stood in the same position as corresponding stone-work in the chambered barrows. Everything indicates that the Yorkshire long-barrow culture is a later and degenerate form of that of the south-west of England.

Long-barrow man probably entered Yorkshire from Lincolnshire, where his remains are fairly numerous, by crossing the Humber where it breaches the chalk between Brough and Hessle. Thence he wandered northwards and initiated a route along the western margin of the Wolds by Market Weighton and Hanging Grimston to Westow. There he forded the Derwent and moved over the Howardian Hills by Yearsley, and on to the Hambleton plateau as far north as Kepwick. He also initiated routes along the heights north and south of the Great Wold Valley eastwards to the coast at Filey and Bridlington Bays. Old trackways and modern roads still follow in the footsteps of long-barrow man.

Unlike the hunter of the Mesolithic Age long-barrow man in Yorkshire chose to live on the chalk and limestone. Not only were these rocks naturally dry, but they were free from forest, and offered rich pasturage for his domestic animals.

Flint arrow-heads like those from the East Ayton long-barrow have occasionally been found on the surface, as at Keld Slack, Newton near Pickering.[1] But it does not follow that they must all be of long-barrow age, for they

[1] Mortimer, fig. 301A (p. xliii).

have also occurred in the round-barrows of the succeeding
Early and Middle Bronze Age. A similar survival is
probable in the case of some of the polished stone axes,
hundreds of which have been found in Yorkshire. It is
customary to assign all these objects to the Pre-metal Age,
but we have little or no direct evidence that they date
from a time anterior to the use of bronze. Many no doubt
do so; but others may have been made and used long
after bronze was known. Yet for convenience's sake we
shall conform to custom and describe the chief Yorkshire
axes in this chapter.

We have seen that Mesolithic man was provided with
flint hand-axes bearing no trace of the grinding or polishing
characteristic of most later axes, which were also mounted.
Here and there, however, unpolished flint axes have been
found, which, since they differ from the Mesolithic type,
are probably of later date. Two or three with rounded
butts and sharp sides from Scamridge and the Wolds are
only from 2 to 2½ inches long. Another (5¾″) from
Bempton, though narrower, resembles the ovate implements of the Old Stone Age.

An axe from Nova near Pickering, with its cutting edge
formed by the removal of a large flake, is very like the
Thames " pick ", frequent in or near that river, and usually
assigned to the Pre-metal Age. The Nova tool, like the
pick, is a roughly-flaked flint bar which no doubt served
many purposes. The pick seems to be much rarer in
Yorkshire than in the south. A related implement from
Charleston near Bridlington is more or less chisel-like.
Smaller flint chisels are reported from Dalton and Helperthorpe on the Wolds.

Flint axes with a ground or polished cutting-edge have
occurred more frequently, and a good example comes from
Sawdon on the Limestone Hills near Scarborough. It is
5″ long, triangular in shape, with sharp sides, and a narrow
butt, near which are a few polished patches caused by the
axe moving in its horn or wood socket. Other localities
for this type are Ruston, Allerston, Skelton near York,
and Seamer Carrs. Small specimens 2 to 2¾″ long have

been picked up on the Wolds. More rarely this type of axe was made of greenstone or felstone. One (3″) from Grindale near Bridlington is curved in the direction of its length. Another rather like it found in a cremated burial in a round-barrow on Seamer Moor near Scarborough shows that the type was known in the Bronze Age.

A large greenstone adze with a markedly curved blade was found in 1868 at a depth of 6 to 10 feet when digging the foundations of the Railway Gas Works at York. It formed one of a hoard of flint implements confined within a space about one foot square, and comprising numerous flakes, scrapers, knives, three arrow-heads (one of long-barrow type), and fourteen flint axes, one of the same type as those from the East Ayton long-barrow. This type has also been found in other parts of the county, one (4¾″ long) comes from an altitude of 1,000 feet on Booth Moor near Huddersfield ; two from near Bridlington and one (4¾″) from Garton are in the Mortimer Museum at Hull.

Closely related to the East Ayton type is a longer and narrower flint-axe with a polished or ground cutting edge and pointed butt. It has been found at Arram, Kilham (9¼″) and Cranswick Carr (9″) in East Yorkshire. An example in blue flint from Armthorpe near Doncaster is supposed to have served as a dagger as well as an axe. A boldly flaked axe (7″) from Ampleforth, N.R., with sharp sides and pointed butt, is most probably an example of the long narrow type which never reached the polishing stage. This and the East Ayton type were no doubt contempor-aneous, for they have been found together in a Derbyshire round-barrow of the Early Bronze Age.

Completely polished axes of flint are numerous. A magnificent specimen 8″ long, with thin rounded butt and sharp sides, comes from the Tees between Yarm and Thornaby (Plate I) ; another (7½″) from Holme-on-Spald-ing Moor in the Vale of York west of Market Weighton ; other examples are recorded from Thorn Marsh, Norton near Malton, Knaresborough, and Fimber.

Even more numerous are polished axes of stone other than flint. A favourite material was greenstone, the volcanic ash of Borrowdale in Cumberland. A trade with this region has been invoked to account for the fact that more than half the stone axes in East Yorkshire are made of this rock. But it must not be overlooked that the glacial drift also contains greenstone boulders, and these may have sufficed to meet all requirements. Garton in Holderness has yielded a completely polished greenstone axe (6½″) with thin sides and round butt ; at Cottingham near Beverley three of broader type were found together.

Another rock was clay-ironstone which occurs as nodules in the Lias and other shales of East Yorkshire. Evans figures a fine example (7½″) from Oulston in the How-ardian Hills. It is rather thin and flat, with sharp sides and a rounded butt. The Middlesbrough Museum exhibits one from Guisbrough in Cleveland. Another associated with a cremated interment in a barrow on Seamer Moor demonstrates that this type was used in the Bronze Age.

There is another type of axe in which the sides have been flattened by grinding and polishing. Flat-sided flint axes have occurred at Upsal in Cleveland, Scamridge and Allerston on the Limestone Hills. Other materials seem to have been more frequently used. Good examples come from Barugh (6½″) in the Vale of Pickering ; Carnaby near Bridlington (3½″, clay-slate) ; Nunnington (7″, calcareous nodule) ; and Holme-on-Spalding Moor (7″, limestone). Another example (5″) from Harome near Helmsley is double-bladed, with the sides slightly incurved.

A few axes have been found in which the sides have been flattened, so that the implement has an almost rectangular section. One (8½″) found at Ness at the west end of the Vale of Pickering, made of dark slaty rock, has a round butt nearly as thin as the blade. Further examples come from Gilling, Heslerton Carr and Airedale. This rare type is practically identical with the rectangular flint axes of the Scandinavian dolmens and passage-graves. A narrow chisel-like axe (6″) of oblong section and made of slate or limestone from Swinton near Malton has been compared with similarly shaped but longer Danish flint axes.

We have one or two implements which closely resemble

the so-called " shoe-last " celts or axes of an early culture
centred on the Danube.   These tools, which come from
Whitwell on the Howardian Hills and Osgodby near Thirsk,
have broad flat sides, one face flat and the other rounded
and sloping down to an adze-like blade.   The butt forms
a rounded point.   They are about 5″ long by 1½″ wide, and
like their Danubian originals they could have been used
as hoes.   The type was most probably introduced into

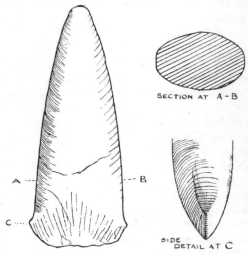

SECTION AT A-B

SIDE
DETAIL AT C

FIG. 7.—STONE AXE, BRIDLINGTON TYPE (5″), STAINTON,
CLEVELAND, N.R.

Middlesbrough Museum

Yorkshire from Germany, where identical specimens have
been found near Worms.

The last axes we shall describe have a circular, or oval
section, owing to the rounding of their sides.   In the
Boynton collection in the Yorkshire Museum there are
two of flint, one polished all over, the other at the cutting
edge only.   They were found at Peak, the southern headland of Robin Hood's Bay.   The type is more numerous
in stone, especially at or near Bridlington where they
formerly abounded.   These Bridlington axes (Fig. 7) range

5

from 5 to 8 inches in length, and taper from the curved blade to the more or less conical butt. Made of basalt or greenstone they are often much weatherworn, a condition suggestive of considerable antiquity. At Bridlington plenty of raw material amongst the glacial boulders was available, and an extensive axe-manufacturing industry was carried on. Unfortunately we have no exact details of their provenance, and so we are unable to identify the site of the industry. They were exported to other parts of the country, and have occurred at Willerby (E.R.), Crambe (N.R.), West Melton near Mexborough, near Aldborough, Sherburn in Durham, and in the Cambridge region. That they are a fairly early type may be inferred from the occurrence of similar axes in the upper level of the Danish shell-mounds. This similarity, together with their prevalence near the coast, points to intercourse between Yorkshire and Denmark; but in which country the type first occurred has not yet been determined.

Variants of this type are not infrequent. A short, broad form found at Easton near Bridlington has the thick truncated butt roughened so as to fix it more firmly in its socket. A clay-slate axe (10″) from Pilmoor in the Vale of York has the blade rather narrower than the butt, which is thick and pointed. Somewhat similar examples come from North Holme in the Vale of Pickering (10″) and Barmston in Holderness (10½″). Then we also find narrow chisel-like axes of oval section, made of grit at Sherburn, E.R. (5½″) and schist (4½″) at Thixendale.

Shorter and triangular oval axes in greenstone (4″, 4½″) have occurred at Seamer near Scarborough, and in quartzite at Scampston (4″) and Birdsall near Malton (5″). Their likeness to axes from the Eastern Mediterranean, and Spain, Brittany, and Ireland indicate their Atlantic (and ultimately Mediterranean) origin. A polished basalt axe (3½″) of oval section, found in an Early Bronze Age barrow seven miles east of Pickering, shows that this type survived into the Metal Age. Occasionally the oval type has a narrow butt and expanding blade, as in a greenstone example from near

Malton. A flint axe from Ebberston is of similar shape, the narrower butt-end being unpolished.

Shouldered axes from Ryedale and Menethorpe no doubt owe their peculiar form to that of the pebbles from which they were made. A few examples have a circular or oval hollow on each face, by means of which they were more easily grasped.

No census has been made of the Yorkshire stone axes. The total cannot be fewer than a thousand. The reason for their popularity was their usefulness. With them men could fell trees, fashion wooden utensils, hollow out canoes, and split the heads of their enemies. Moreover, stone axes could be made wherever suitable stone was available. So in Yorkshire we find the axe people relying chiefly on local rock for their implements. Most of their flint axes were made out of boulders of black, pink, grey or brown flint scattered throughout the glacial drift, exposed on the coast and more rarely inland. The Yorkshire chalk, it is true, contains flint nodules ; but its flaking quality is so poor that it seems to have been rarely used. Flint boulders and pebbles, if not implements, must have been imported into West Yorkshire, where flint does not exist, by way of the ridges across the Vale of York (p. 5), which even at this early date had become recognised traffic routes. Other flint may have been derived from the Grimes' Graves mines in Norfolk, for an axe of the Bridlington type was found there ; or even from Sussex, for our long flat axes (p. 47) appear to have affinities with types from the famous Cissbury mines.

Stone axes are more numerous in East than in West Yorkshire. Generally absent from the higher moorlands, they are most abundant on the Limestone Hills and the Wolds. They are frequent on the coast, by rivers, and even in low-lying regions such as Holderness, and the Vales of Pickering and York. In the Vales they have usually been discovered on hills which in prehistoric times were encircled by marsh, such as the gravel-capped hill at Holme-on-Spalding Moor. As axes are essentially household tools the majority of places where they have occurred

must mark the site of settlements of which all other traces
have vanished. Scarborough, Sheffield, Doncaster, Leeds
and York all had their beginnings in the humble huts or
villages of the axe people.

Those who wish to investigate ancient Yorkshire could
not do better than compile a catalogue of its stone axes
in which their size, form, material, locality and associations
should be set down   This would illuminate and extend our
knowledge of relationships which have been no more than
hinted at in this chapter.

For Reference : R. A. Smith, *Lake Dwellings in Holderness*, Arch.,
vol. xlii, 1911.   W. Greenwell, *British Barrows*, 1877.   J. R. Mortimer, *Forty Years' Researches*, 1905.   F. Elgee, *Early Man in N.E.
Yorkshire*, chap. 6.   J. Evans, *Ancient Stone Implements of Great
Britain*, 1897.   R. A. Smith, *Hoards of Neolithic Celts*, Arch., vol.
lxxi, 1921.   T. D. Kendrick, *The Axe Age*, 1925.   T. Sheppard,
Materials used in the Manufacture of Stone Weapons, T.E.R.A.S.,
vol. xxiii.

CHAPTER V

THE EARLY BRONZE AGE

OUR account of the Yorkshire long-barrows should dispel the misconceptions that prevail concerning them, such as that they consist of two or more round-barrows joined together, or that they are a local peculiarity of the round-barrow culture of the Bronze Age.

These notions owe their origin to the fact that two or three long-barrows, in addition to their own characteristic features, disclosed others typical of the Early Bronze Age. Below the Helperthorpe long-barrow, for example, there were two small graves (one containing a cremated burial) at the east end ; and three larger, deeper graves at the west end, the interments in which had decayed away, and in one of which there were two flat rectangular jet beads, both beads and graves being of Early Bronze Age type. The body of the barrow enclosed typical Yorkshire long-barrow interments.

These long-barrows clearly reflect the mingling of long-barrow man and the people who buried their dead in graves under round-barrows, the men of the Early Bronze Age. During this age we have the earliest known indications of the use of bronze implements in Yorkshire. Roughly dating from 2000 to 1500 B.C., it may most conveniently be divided into two phases more or less contemporaneous, and distinguished by two kinds of pottery—the beaker and the food-vessel, both having been found associated with bronze awls, knives, daggers, and axes.

At Kellythorpe Farm near Driffield the railway from Market Weighton passes over the site of an instructive Early Bronze Age barrow. About 4 feet high, it covered a cist or stone box made of oolitic grit slabs about 4 and

3 feet long. They were 2½ feet wide, and sunk to that depth in the ground below the barrow, and covered by a lid or capstone (6 feet by 4 feet and 7 inches thick). On the bottom, paved with small irregular pieces of grit, there lay a man's skeleton on its left side, with the head to the east, the knees drawn up, and the arms bent towards the face,—the so-called sitting, flexed or contracted position. His skull was of the round or brachycephalic type, i.e. with an index exceeding 80; and as his thigh-bone was 19 inches long, his stature cannot have been less than 5 feet 10 inches. The body had originally been swathed in a linen shroud, fragments of which remained. Behind the waist was a small bronze knife or dagger (3½″), thin and flat, with the point broken off, a bevelled edge, a broad one-riveted tang, and fragments of its wooden handle and sheath. At his neck lay three large conical amber beads with V-shaped basal perforations. On his right forearm there rested a fine-grained greenstone oblong plate, an appliance worn by bowmen to protect the wrist from the recoil of the bowstring. Four gold-headed bronze pins had secured it to a leather arm-band, which, except for the bronze buckle, had decayed away. As the guard was on the right wrist it looks as if the man had been left-handed. Above his knees lay the head of a hawk, symbol of sun-worship. Behind the feet stood a beaker (7″) [1] which originally held a food-offering.

Such a burial could only have been that of a ruler, who was to enjoy in the spirit world the weapons and implements he had treasured in this. No trouble had been spared in honouring his remains. Even the stones of his cist had been brought from afar, Filey Brigg, 18 miles distant, being the nearest place whence they could have been obtained.

This is a typical Early Bronze Age burial. Not only is it quite different from those of long-barrow man, but it is that of a different people who, because of their pottery, have been christened the 'beaker people'. They played an important part in the prehistory of Yorkshire and of

[1] Formerly known as drinking-cups.

England, and their descendants are still living amongst us.

In Yorkshire at least 151 whole or fragmentary beakers have been found. Of these 133 come from the Wolds, the greatest settlement region of the beaker people in the country, since this figure is more than one-third of the total number of beakers from England and Wales. Yet, despite the abundance of their pottery, no actual village of the beaker folk has been discovered on the Wolds. In Yorkshire our knowledge is entirely derived from their burial mounds.

Canon Greenwell of Durham and J. R. Mortimer of Driffield excavated most of the beaker barrows in East Yorkshire. Their discoveries can be studied in their standard works, and in the British and Hull Museums. To the late Lord Abercromby we are further indebted for a comparative study of beakers, their classification, their chronology and their origins. Indeed, he was the first to assign to the beaker folk their rightful position in the ancient history of our island. For details on these matters the reader is referred to his monumental work on Bronze Age pottery. Here we can only glance at the beakers and their provenance, their associated objects, the physical character and origin of their makers, their distribution and their relation to the early bronze trade in Yorkshire.

Beakers are all hand-made, and in Yorkshire they range from $4\frac{1}{4}$ to $9\frac{1}{4}$ inches in height, though an exceptionally small beaker only $2\frac{1}{2}$ inches high was found at Aldro (E.R.). The ware is thin, and made of clay mixed with sand or powdered stone. They are yellowish, drab or light brown, more rarely red, and are occasionally burnished. The neck is sometimes encircled by raised ribs or mouldings, and six Yorkshire examples have handles. Decorated horizontal bands alternate with plain bands, usually covering the whole vessel (Fig. 8).

The general custom was to deposit a single beaker with a single burial in a grave, 3 to 4 feet deep, under a round-barrow. Cist-burial like that at Kelleythorpe was exceptional, though one is also recorded from Egton in lower

Eskdale, and included the remains of a bronze knife-dagger. Furthermore, two cists were found side by side at the bottom of a grave 10½ feet deep, below a round-barrow on the Wolds above Rudston. In one there lay the flexed skeleton of an aged man on his left side, the normal position of these burials. A beaker stood behind his head, and the bones of two very young children behind his feet. In the second cist a beaker had been deposited with a cremated burial, a most exceptional occurrence.

The large primary graves under barrows in Garton

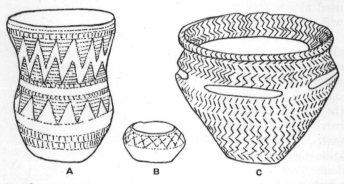

FIG. 8.—BRONZE AGE BEAKER, PYGMY VESSEL, AND FOOD VESSEL
A, Painsthorpe (6″); B, Calais Wold (1″); C, Hanging Grimston (6″), E.R.
Mortimer Museum, Hull

Slack near Driffield were regarded by Mortimer as pit-dwellings. He was led to this conclusion by the discovery of two such dwellings near barrows which had yielded eight beakers. One dwelling was 9 feet long by 5½ feet wide at the bottom, and 4¾ feet deep, the sides sloping outwards all round. Near the centre the site of a hearth was strewn with numerous splinters of animal bone. The dwelling must have been provided with a thatched roof sloping all round to the ground.

Beaker barrows range from 27 to 120 feet in diameter, and from nothing (in instances where they have been ploughed down) to 9 feet in height. One on Folkton Wold was surrounded by a trench; another at Willerby was trenched round the inside, while a third at Hanging Grim-ston enclosed a broken circle of stones, each about 2½ by 2 feet and 15 inches thick. Within this ring were burials. Perhaps such trenches and circles were thought to have the magical property of imprisoning the ghosts of the dead.

Besides being provided with bronze knives or daggers, the beaker folk also possessed small slender awls or prickers of bronze, about 1¼ inches long, square in the middle, and tapering to a point at each end. They were probably used to sew skins together, and have usually been found with the skeletons of women.

Another of their implements was the flat bronze axe, although no direct association with a beaker has been recorded. In a barrow on Wold Farm, Willerby, there were four flat axes, three ornamented, and all with glassy surfaces. They seem to have been a votive offering, for they accompanied no burial. In another part of the barrow there was a secondary interment of a skeleton with a beaker. As similar axes have been found with knife-daggers of beaker age, there seems little reason to doubt that the beaker folk used the flat axe, many of which have been found on the Wolds (Fig. 15).

The beaker folk also used flint implements ; amongst them, the barbed and tanged arrow-head, three small examples of which were found in a beaker grave at Thwing. As is to be expected, they are frequent as surface finds. Other flint tools include knives, worked flakes, and round scrapers. In a barrow at Garton Slack a flat polished axe of black flint (2⅞ inches) with flattened sides demonstrates that many Wold axes of this type can be attributed to the beaker folk.

Their most characteristic flint implement was the dagger. A fine example (6¾ inches) from a barrow in Garton Slack was actually leaning against a beaker. A finer example (6¼ inches), broader, and deeply notched near the butt end so that it could be better bound to the handle, was associated with an inhumation in the same locality. Another dagger is recorded from Cottingham

on the Wolds north of Hull. They rank among the most
superb examples of flint craftsmanship in this country.

Associated with the Garton Slack dagger was a perforated
stone battle-axe. Another of the same kind occurred with
a cremated burial and beaker fragments in a grave near
Towthorpe. They may be termed the beaker type, and
are copies of perforated square-butted copper axes found

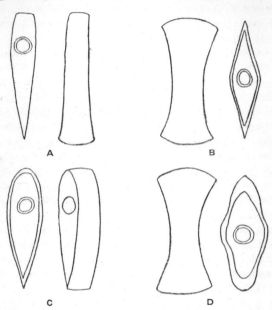

FIG. 9.—STONE AXES AND THEIR METAL PROTOTYPES

A, Copper axe (8″), Denmark ; B, Copper axe, Cretan type (5¼″), Whitby (*Skipton Museum*) ; C, Stone axe (5½″), Beaker type, East Yorks. ; D, Stone axe (3¾″), Huggate, E.R. (*British Museum*)

in Scandinavia, Hanover and Silesia (Fig. 9). The round-
butted examples recall the pierced copper axes of Thermia
in the Grecian Archipelago.[1]

Though an oval jet bead [2] of long-barrow type occurred
in a barrow at Maiden's Grave Farm, Burton Fleming, the
beaker folk were the first to use Yorkshire jet to any

[1] *B.M. Bronze Age Guide*, 1920, fig. 174*b*.   [2] In B.M.

extent. On the Wolds conical buttons with V-shaped basal perforations were frequent. "Pulley" rings were also made, about an inch in diameter, and pierced like the buttons. At Middleton-on-Wolds a necklace of seven large flat rectangular beads ornamented with diamond-shaped patterns minutely punctured, together with many smaller cylindrical beads, was found with a beaker burial. Jet was worn not only as an ornament, but as a charm to avert evil. Such a belief was held in Roman times, as Pliny testifies in his *Natural History*.

The beaker folk were essentially round-headed, or brachycephalic. They had prominent brow ridges, large strong teeth and square, massive jaws, giving them a ferocious appearance. They were of somewhat stocky build, their stature varying from 5 feet 3 inches to 5 feet 10 inches. They included a few tall long-headed folk, skeletons of this type having been unearthed at Aldro (index 70, stature 5 feet 11·3 inches), and Garton (index 72, stature 5 feet 10·3 inches).[1] It is clear then that beaker man differed both culturally and physically from long-barrow man who, though long-headed, rarely exceeded 5 feet in height.

Such marked differences point to new-comers, and it is generally agreed that the beaker folk invaded eastern England directly from the Rhinelands, in which region a similar culture was widespread. The beaker has a much wider range than this. Whether it originated in Spain whence it penetrated into Central Europe, or vice versa, is still an open question. A few of the Yorkshire beaker folk undoubtedly came from Denmark, for two beakers from the Whitby-Pickering area have the ornamentation restricted to the neck, as in beakers found in the single graves of the Danish stone battle-axe people. In many respects the Yorkshire beaker barrows resemble those of the same people in Central Germany, who like the Danish were tall long-heads. The Aldro and Garton skeletons

[1] Three male skeletons nearly 6 feet high, and with dolichocephalic skulls (one 70·51) were found without pottery in a barrow at Borrow Nook on the Mid-Wolds. *Y.A.J.*, xx, 491–2.

unquestionably belong to this race, which appears to be ancestral to the modern Nordic race, the tall fair-heads so famous in the stormy annals of the north.

On the Wolds the beaker folk met and mingled with long-barrow man, as revealed by the Helperthorpe and Cropton long-barrows (pp. 42, 53). This mingling is further displayed in a few round-barrows, of which the most striking example is the Howe Hill, at the foot of the southern slope of the Great Wold Valley near Duggleby. With a basal diameter of 125 feet, it has a flat top 47 feet across, and it is 22 feet high; though originally it must have been 8 or 10 feet higher, and the top rounded. Its size alone bespeaks the monument of no mean chieftain.

The Howe had been raised over a circular central grave, 11 feet wide and $8\frac{1}{2}$ feet deep, dug out of the solid chalk with stag-horn picks, two of which were found in the barrow. In the grave there lay four crouched-up skeletons accompanied by a fine leaf-shaped arrow-head, a superb partially polished flint axe ($9\frac{1}{2}$ inches), a round-bottomed bowl, and a perforated stag-horn hammer reminiscent of those from the West Furze pile-dwelling. Close by was a second, shallower grave enclosing a flexed skeleton, and many flints, a long bone pin, ten boar and two beaver tusks, and ox vertebræ. At the western edge of this grave, with its head lying over the brink of the large grave as if contemplating the occupants, was the skeleton of a man about seventy years of age, markedly long-headed (68·8) and 6 feet 3 inches in stature. In front of his face lay a rare flint implement of oblong shape with rounded corners, $2\frac{3}{8}$ by $1\frac{3}{16}$ inches, somewhat curved, and only $\frac{1}{16}$ inch thick,—a supposed knife.

Above in a clayey mound were four further skeletons, one of a very young child, another of a boy from 6 to 10 years old, and five cremated burials. Over this inner mound a bed of chalk grit $4\frac{1}{2}$ feet thick enclosed more than forty cremations. The interments had all been made on one occasion, for they were sealed under an unbroken band of blue Kimmeridge clay 1 foot thick. A mass of roughly quarried chalk $9\frac{1}{2}$ feet thick covered the clay.

Now, whilst the bowl, the arrow-head and the axe are identical with those of long-barrow man, the shape of the barrow and its graves coincides with those of the Early Bronze Age invaders. We have no more instructive example of the mingling of the two peoples than this. Dr. Garson stated that the skeletons agree entirely with those of long-barrow man. Many no doubt do, especially those with statures averaging 5 feet and with indexes as low as $65\frac{1}{2}$. One, however, with an index of $79\frac{1}{2}$, verges on brachycephaly, and therefore approximates to the beaker type, whilst two with indexes of 74·7 and 75·3 suggest a cross between the long- and the round-heads. The old man, nine inches taller than the next tallest skeleton, must surely have been of the same stock as the long-headed stone battle-axe people. Though no battle-axe was interred with him, nevertheless the boar and beaver tusks from the same grave may well have formed one of those animal tooth necklaces so characteristic of the continental battle-axe folk.

A Nordic giant he probably was, a pioneer adventurer from across the North Sea, who, with the masterfulness of his race, had made himself ruler over the gentler and slighter long-barrow folk of the Wolds. At his death, men, women and children were sacrificed, some burnt, and all buried in the Howe, so that they might accompany their lord into the spirit world. Only in this way can we reasonably interpret the features of Duggleby Howe.

The Howe probably preceded the full beaker culture, nor is it the only one of its kind. Mortimer remarks on its resemblance to Willy Howe (125 feet in diameter) near Wold Newton in the Great Wold Valley ; and to Mickle Howe (250 feet in diameter, 50 feet high) at the foot of Garrowby Hill. To these we may add another, 200 feet in diameter, near Oulston on the Howardian Hills.

It was the Wolds that attracted the invaders, because they combined favourable physical conditions with accessibility. The distribution of beakers shows that their makers overspread the whole region, the chief inhabited centres being Garton Slack (altitude 50 to 100 feet),

Rudston, and especially the north-west angle between Garrowby and Aldro, whence more than fifty beakers are recorded. Small settlements were established on the Limestone Hills near Pickering, on the Hambletons near Boltby (altitude 1,000 feet), and in the Whitby area. As not a single beaker has been discovered on the Eastern Moorlands it is clear that the beaker folk avoided this uninviting region.

From the Wolds they pushed into West Yorkshire via the morainic ridges across the Vale of York. Two beakers come from York itself. Beaker fragments have been found on Baildon Moor near Shipley in Airedale, Entwhistle Moor near Widdop and Lea Green near Grassington in Wharfedale. The beaker folk also settled near Ferry Fryston, where the Aire breaches the Magnesian Limestone. Stone battle-axes of beaker or derivative type have occurred at Holme-on-Spalding Moor, Burstwick in Holderness, Pickhill, Jervaulx, and elsewhere; flint daggers at Ragstone near Huddersfield and Topcliffe-on-Swale. These objects suggest a wider distribution of the beaker folk than that indicated by their pottery. But on the whole in West Yorkshire their remains are very scarce.

Soon after the beaker folk had settled down they began to deposit food-vessels instead of beakers with their dead. This change of custom led to the extinction of the beaker and to the development of the cinerary urn, characteristic of the Mid-Bronze Age culture of England.

Food-vessels are about the same height as beakers, but they are broader and heavier, being more stoutly made, of a reddish, brownish or yellowish fire-baked clay (Fig. 8). Their ornamentation, usually simpler than that of the beakers, is more varied; their form less rigid. Some have handles, others feet; one or two have lids, and many have perforated lugs or ears, by means of which they could be suspended. They rarely possess features in common with the beakers, although the two types were partly contemporaneous. But they performed the same office, holding offerings to the dead.

Food-vessels are most abundant on the Wolds where 254 have been discovered ; 66 come from North-east Yorkshire, where they are most abundant on the Limestone Hills between Scarborough and Pickering ; 10 have occurred on the Howardian Hills, and they have been found on the coast at Huntcliff, Boulby, Hinderwell, Lythe, Peak, Scarborough and Flamborough. They do not appear on the Moorlands, in Holderness or the Vale of York. In West Yorkshire they are more frequent than beakers, occurring at West Tanfield where the Ure breaches the Magnesian Limestone, at Ferry Fryston (2), Baildon Moor near Shipley, Grassington in Wharfedale, Pule Hill near Huddersfield (4) and near Halifax.

Food-vessels are not only more than twice as numerous as beakers, but are more widely distributed, and so indicate a growing population.

Like the beakers, food-vessels are usually found singly in barrows ; sometimes they are found in the same barrow with the beaker. Again, two food-vessels were sometimes associated with one interment as at Huntcliff ; more rarely one vessel did duty for several interments. Thirty-four barrows have yielded three vessels each, while four vessels were found in each of three barrows, and five in each of two barrows.

Where stone was available, food-vessel man buried his dead in cists, often surrounded by one or two stone circles, fourteen instances being recorded from the Howardian and Limestone Hills. Twenty-seven other cist burials in the same locality, although containing no food-vessels, belong to the same age. The cists divide themselves into two types : a larger, from $9\frac{1}{2}$ to 5 feet long by 5 to 3 feet wide and 5 to 3 feet deep ; and a smaller, from 5 to $2\frac{1}{2}$ feet long by 3 to 2 feet wide, and from 3 to 1 foot deep. They are made of stone slabs set on edge ; usually four in the smaller variety. The floor was oftener paved with small stones than with single slabs ; but single slabs were nearly always used for the cover-stone, which sometimes weighed more than a ton. The slabs were usually made rigid in the ground ; sometimes they were completely sunk beneath the surface,

thus forming what is termed a cist-grave.   Near Pickering a
rock cleft 15 feet long by 4½ feet wide and 4 feet deep had
been roofed by a block of stone weighing two tons, over
which a barrow 78 yards in circumference and 8 feet high
had been piled.   Embedded in stiff red clay, associated
with a small polished axe and six other flint implements,
lay a man's skeleton.

Sometimes more than one cist occurs in a barrow.   In
Hedon Howe, near Langton south of Malton, five were
arranged in cross-wise fashion.   The centre cist held the
skeletons of an old man, a woman of 60, and the arm-bone
of a person 25 years old ; the second cist a leaf-shaped
flint arrow-head and the bones of a middle-aged adult ;
two others were practically empty owing to decay ; in
the fifth lay the flexed skeleton of a person of 30.   A
beaker and a food-vessel were also discovered in association
with cremated remains.

At Brow Quarry on the Cleveland coast near Staithes
as many as seven cists were found together.   Cists have
also been found as secondary interments in long-barrows
at Wass (1), Yearsley (with food-vessel) and Westow (3),
and even as a primary burial in a long-barrow on Bradley
Moor (W.R.).[1]   On the Wolds where suitable stone was
absent the cists were constructed of wood, and have consequently usually perished.

To this period belong the heavy oak tree-trunk coffins,
6 to 7½ feet long and 2 to 4 feet wide.   The trunks were
split lengthwise, one half forming the lid, resting on the
other half, hollowed out to receive the corpse.   In the
coffin from a barrow near West Tanfield there was a food-
vessel ; in another at Sunderlandwick near Driffield were
the remains of three skeletons ; a third in the Howe Hill
near Brotton held the fragmentary bones of a brachycephalic man ; in a fourth at Rylston in Craven the body
had been wrapped in a woollen shroud ; the fifth and best-
known example can be seen in the Scarborough Museum.
The coffin, square at one end, rounded at the other, lay
at the bottom of a pit-grave 10 feet deep, below a barrow

[1] *Y.A.J.*, xxx, 252.

3 feet high, on Gristhorpe Cliff. It enclosed the skeleton of a tall brachycephalic man whose shroud had been made of animal skins, fastened with a bone breast-pin. He was provided with flint implements, a two-riveted bronze knife with a whalebone pommel, and a bark food-vessel.

These tree-trunk burials prove intercourse with Jutland and Schleswig where such were frequent towards the end of the Early Bronze Age, about 1600–1400 B.C. The coffins represent the dug-out canoes in which their makers voyaged across the North Sea and up our rivers. Such canoes have been found in the Calder near Stanley Ferry ($17\frac{3}{4}$ feet long, with pointed bow and square stern) ; in the Tees near Thornaby (12 feet long, with pointed bow and stern) ; in Giggleswick Tarn (8 feet long) ; at Owthorne in Holderness (12 feet long, square stern) ; at Marton near Boroughbridge ; and at Hull.[1] To this day the Australians and Polynesians lay their dead in canoes or hollowed-out logs suggesting a canoe, so that they may return to the home of their fathers across the sea.

In material possessions food-vessel man differed little from the beaker-makers. In a food-vessel barrow on Riggs Farm near Thixendale there was a stone battle-axe, rather more hollowed out than the beaker type. No flint daggers or wrist-guards have been found with food-vessels ; but flint knives, scrapers, spear- and arrow-heads, leaf-shaped and barbed, are numerous. In a Rudston barrow where both beakers and food-vessels occurred there were 3 leaf-shaped arrow-heads, 2 borers, 17 scrapers, and 79 flint saws, many very finely serrated, some along both edges and glazed by use. Many of these saws when mounted in the underside of the shorter arm of a bent stick would form a sickle. Sickles of such a nature were necessary, as the grains of wheat in a food-vessel at Hanging Grimston testify,—these particular specimens being the earliest positive evidence of agriculture in Yorkshire.

Bronze awls, knives, daggers and ear-rings were also used by food-vessel man. In a barrow on the Wolds near Butterwick the skeleton of a young man was accompanied

[1] These dug-out canoes are not necessarily of the same age.

6

by a three-riveted bronze knife-dagger, furnished with an ox-horn handle and a wooden sheath. On it lay a flint knife, and below it a bronze awl. In front of his chest were five conical jet buttons, and one of sandstone engraved to form a cross, at the hips was a flat bronze axe (4″) made of 87·97% copper and 10·74% tin. A bronze dagger from Towthorpe (6″) has a well-developed midrib, three engraved lines parallel to the cutting edge, six rivets, and a rudimentary tang. Two bronze ear-rings ($1\frac{1}{2}$″) were found near the skull of a boy 8 to 12 years old at Garton Slack.

It is clear from the above account that food-vessel man had more bronze goods than beaker man, that he more frequently interred his dead in cists and practised cremation. Often, too, he surrounded his graves with stone circles before building up the barrow. He was more varied physically, for round, long, and intermediate types of skull have been found with food-vessels. The round skulls are similar to those associated with beakers. A long skull (index 72) of a man 6 feet in height from Garton Slack probably belongs to one of the stone battle-axe race. The intermediate skulls point to intermarriage with the short-statured long-headed folk of the long-barrows. Thus the mingling of the Bronze Age invaders with long-barrow man had become even more intimate amongst the food-vessel folk, and a new culture and race were evolving.

As in most primitive tribes it is the women who are the potters, it appears likely that the intermarriage of the beaker folk with women of the long-barrow race caused the food-vessel to triumph over the beaker which became extinct. For the food-vessel was derived from the round-bottomed bowls used by long-barrow man and his contemporaries, especially the type that is known as Peterborough ware. It has a round base, and a deep moulding or neck between the overhanging brim and the shoulder. It was often decorated by pressing twisted cord into the wet clay to form zigzag or herring-bone patterns. By flattening the base of such bowls the food-vessel was invented.

Ireland has been suggested as the original home of the food-vessel, for there early types are numerous. Some types may, however, have originated in Yorkshire where the food-vessel is more abundant than elsewhere in the British Isles. In any case Ireland exerted a strong cultural influence on East Yorkshire, for many food-vessels are closely related to Irish types ; Irish jet beads have been found near Bridlington ; jet necklaces have the same shape and ornamentation as the gold lunettes of Ireland ; and many features of Yorkshire cist-burials, notably that in the Hedon Howe, are Irish.

How did this come about ? It was due partly to the stimulus given to the bronze trade by the invasion of the beaker folk, and partly to the fact that Yorkshire was traversed by a trade route between Ireland and Scandinavia and North Germany (Fig. 10).

We do not know whether the Yorkshire copper was ever used by Bronze Age man. That in the Lake District may have been worked by him. He would reach it by way of the Stainmore Pass. The occurrence of a large beaker period battle-axe and a flat bronze axe at Bowes shows that a route already existed whereby the Cumberland copper could be transported to East Yorkshire. Abercromby pointed out certain similarities between Yorkshire and Cumberland beakers. The route appears to have gone by Dalton (between Bowes and Richmond) where another flat axe was found, and also barrows containing cists, pottery, and skeletons.

Ireland, where gold, copper, and to a less extent tin abounded, was undoubtedly the chief source of supply. It had become an important and prosperous trading centre, and ideas, as well as trade, flowed into Ireland from the Continent. A knowledge of copper and bronze had come to it from the Mediterranean through the medium of traders and prospectors, who may have introduced the idea of the megalithic tomb. Irish gold lunulæ were exported to France, Hanover and Denmark. Many Irish and some Yorkshire food-vessels are ornamented with triangles and lozenges imitating wood-carving, a style found in South and Central Germany, Alsace, and the Rhineland.

The map (Fig. 10) shows how metal traders, by traversing Yorkshire, could follow an almost direct route between Ireland and Denmark. It was before the days of paved roads, so every advantage the physical configuration of the country offered would be eagerly seized. Sailing from Ireland across the Irish Sea, the traders pushed up the Ribble and its affluent the Calder as far inland as Read where, four miles from the Yorkshire border, three flat bronze axes have been found. Thence they would strike in a north-easterly direction to the Aire Gap, the lowest Pennine Pass, or over Ickornshaw Moor to Steeton in Airedale, both localities for flat axes. Then they journeyed not actually down Airedale itself but most probably along the broad plateau clothed with heath and scrub dividing it from Wharfedale. On the plateau the route ran eastwards by Adel, and Bramham Park to the Wharfe, which was crossed either by canoe or ford near Tadcaster. The route then probably divided, one branch running along the Escrick moraine, and another following that at York. These ridgeways more or less converged at Stamford Bridge on the Derwent, east of which the route climbed Garrowby Hill on to the Wolds. Here it split into three, one line running along the southern slope of the Wolds to Bridlington Bay, a second through Sledmere and along the heights south of the Wold Valley, and the third along the heights commanding the Vale of Pickering, both the latter terminating at Filey Bay. The coast thus reached, the traders set sail for the continent.

Traffic up the Don and Rother valleys is also indicated by flat axes at Goole, at Conklow near Rotherham, and a beaker battle-axe near Sheffield.

The more minutely our cross-country route through the Aire Gap is studied, the more clearly do we realize its important influence on the ancient culture of the Yorkshire folk. The occupation of Airedale by beaker and food-vessel man certainly confirms the route. Flat axes found there mark the position of small settlements. A tree-trunk coffin at Rylston proves that traders came thither from Denmark. By this route the many Irish

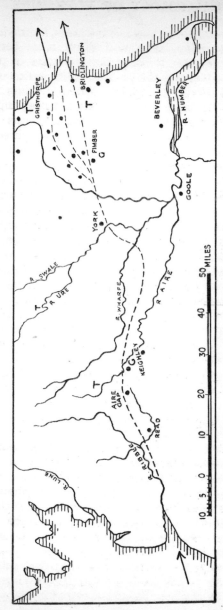

FIG. 10.—SKETCH MAP SHOWING LANCASHIRE AND YORKSHIRE SECTION OF THE EARLY BRONZE AGE

TRADE ROUTE BETWEEN IRELAND AND SCANDINAVIA

- - - Route   T Tree-trunk Coffins—Danish type
● Flat Bronze Axes   G Grooved Stone Hammers—Mediterranean type

influences reached the Wolds. And so we find gold-headed rivets at Kelleythorpe, and many flat axes in the neighbourhood. It was in this seemingly roundabout way, too, that Mediterranean objects and ideas drifted into Yorkshire. For example, two grooved stone hammers from near the route at Keighley in Airedale and at Fimber on the Wolds are identical with Spanish axes and Egyptian axes of the XI and XII dynasties (2200 to 1800 B.C.).

A bronze dagger found with a beaker at Brough-on-Humber has Spanish affinities. A unique double-bladed copper or bronze axe with a large oval shaft hole said to have been found in Whitby is very similar to a well-known Cretan and Ægean copper axe of about 2000 B.C.

Stone copies of this type of axe have occasionally occurred in East Yorkshire. One was found with a skeleton in a barrow on Huggate Pasture. A superb example, $6\frac{1}{2}''$ long and made of whinstone, comes from Tees-mouth. Others are recorded from Pickering and Cowlam (Fig. 9).

These axes were undoubtedly ritualistic, for in the Cretan world the double-axe, along with other objects, was a symbol of a divine being, the Great Mother, a belief in whom seems to have existed in East Yorkshire.

This is first clearly shown in the three so-called " drums " made of local chalk, from a beaker barrow on Folkton Wold (Fig. 11). They lay behind the skeleton of a child, about 5 years old, the smallest touching the head, the others the hips. Whilst part of their ornamentation is similar to that on Yorkshire beakers, the rest is of Mediterranean origin. The curious owl-like face occurs on vases from Hissarlik, the ancient Troy ; on clay vessels of the early metal age in Spain ; and on standing-stones in the Gard and Marne valleys in France. As the four-rayed star is found on the base of Irish food-vessels, and concentric circles within horseshoe-like markings on megalithic tombs in Brittany and at New Grange in Ireland, we may therefore be sure that the drum ornamentation and the ideas it symbolised reached East Yorkshire from the Mediterranean by way of Ireland and our trade route.

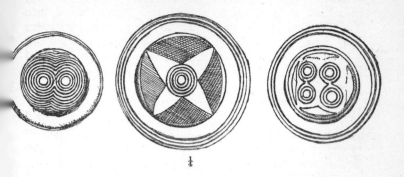

FIG. 11.—CHALK CARVING, FOLKTON, E.R., WITH DETAIL OF TOP
ABOVE (LEFT), AND TOPS OF TWO SIMILAR CARVINGS

British Museum

The owl-face even occurs on bowls of the passage-grave period in Denmark.[1]

Abercromby regarded the " drums " as domestic idols or baetyls, the symbols of a goddess or earth-mother ; and that they were placed with the child so that it should carry them as offerings to the great Mother-goddess of the underworld under whose protection it would pass at death. This interpretation is based on the researches of the late M. Déchelette who had shown that the owl-face belonged to a female divinity, a primitive personification of maternity, a warden of burial-places, and a mother-goddess whose worship was widespread in the Ægean, Gaul, and Britain in the Early Bronze Age.

Sometimes she was represented by figurines, like one with the owl-face from Pamphylia in Asia Minor, and again by standing stones of special shape as often in France. She may also have been regarded as triune, in which case the three " drums " become even more significant.   As we shall see in the next chapter, the worship of a mother-goddess or goddesses may possibly supply an explanation of stone triangles and other Bronze Age remains of the Eastern Moorlands, often associated in local folklore with witches, and a mysterious being known as the Old Wife.

Early Bronze Age man also believed in a sky or sun-god. It was usual to inter the dead with their faces toward the sun.   The hawk's head in the Kelleythorpe cist points to sun-worship, for in Egypt this bird was a sun-symbol, and the sun-god Ra was sometimes depicted with a hawk's head. In the Ægean a four-spoked wheel often represented the sun.   From this symbol was derived the four-rayed " star " on one of the chalk " drums ", and cruciform designs on jet buttons, food-vessels and other objects, with which we may also associate the cross-wise cists in Hedon Howe.

Concentric circles may also have been sun-symbols. They are inscribed at the centre of the star on the " drum." They were engraved on the stones of cists at Cloughton and Peak, the latter with a star at the centre.   They are particularly numerous on Rumbles Moor near Ilkley,

[1] Ekholm, *Reallexikon der Vorgeschichte,* 1927, plate 84, fig. C.

though in this region they may be rather later than the Early Bronze Age. A few can still be seen *in situ* ; others are preserved opposite the church at Ilkley, and there is a series of casts in Leeds Museum. Often there is a hollow in the centre, which, when enclosed by a single circle, forms the well-known "cup and ring." A stone with several such symbols was associated with the tree-trunk coffin at Brotton, and many cup-stones without rings. These cup-stones may have held offerings to the dead, and are, we find, of Mediterranean origin.

At the close of the Early Bronze Age, about 1500 B.C., Yorkshire had risen to an important position in the life of ancient Britain. Lines of communication and centres of population then founded have, in many instances, never been forsaken. Their situation was almost entirely governed by natural conditions, and population was densest on the Wolds and eastern Limestone Hills, all of easy altitude, and clothed with pasturage on which the beaker and food-vessel folk grazed their sheep, goats and cattle, grew wheat, and hunted an abundance of wild game. On the coast small communities foreshadowed Yorkshire's picturesque fishing villages. The Eastern Moorlands, even now the most thinly-peopled region in the county, were then practically uninhabited. In West Yorkshire, more inaccessible and mountainous, population was sparsely distributed in riverside settlements on the Magnesian Limestone, and on or near traffic routes crossing the Pennines. Men, bronze goods, and ideas entered the county along the Rother valley, over the Stainmore Pass, and above all through the Aire Gap, which largely if not wholly contributed to the establishment of a direct trade and culture route linking Ireland with Scandinavia.

For Reference : W. Greenwell, *British Barrows*, London, 1877 ; *Researches in Barrows in Yorkshire*, etc., Arch., lii, 1890. J. R. Mortimer, *Forty Years' Researches*, 1905. J. Abercromby, *Bronze Age Pottery of Great Britain and Ireland.* O. G. S. Crawford, *The Early Bronze Age Settlements of England*, Geog. Jour., 1912. F. Elgee, *Early Man in N.E. Yorkshire.* T. Bateman, *Ten Years' Diggings*, 1861. *B.M. Bronze Age Guide*, 1920.

CHAPTER VI

THE MID-BRONZE AGE

THE Mid-Bronze Age was the final outcome of that mingling of cultures and races revealed in the barrows of food-vessel man. Its distinguishing burial custom was the enclosure of the cremated dead in hand-made urns. In a barrow on the coast at Hinderwell Beacon, in one of the Three Tremblers on Wykeham Low Moor near Scarborough, and in others on the Wolds, there have been found urns, which, except in being larger, are identical with food-vessels. Urn-burial spread until it became general over a large part of the country, the urn undergoing development until it culminated in vessels two or more feet high, with massive overhanging rims ornamented with impressions of twisted cord similar to those on the Neolithic bowl and the food-vessel.

Small pots from one to three inches high have often been found singly in large urns or in association with cremated bones. Many resemble food-vessels and serve the same purpose, though, in course of time, they deviated considerably from their prototype. They are often pierced with circular holes or slits, a feature that occurs in pottery of this age found in the Channel Islands and western France.

More than 450 urns have been found in Yorkshire, and scores must have perished.[1] They are at least three times as numerous as beakers, and half as numerous again as food-vessels. The contemporary pygmy-vessels or 'incense-cups' total 170 (Fig. 8).

---

[1] On being asked what he had done with the urns or 'pankins' in the barrows which he had cleared from his land, a Cleveland farmer replied, "Deean wiv em? Why, Ah've brussen 'em oop wi' mah feeat; and mah lad bunched 'em ti bits."

PLATE II

CINERARY URN (18″)
British Museum

ROUND BARROW

ROBIN HOOD BUTTS, DANBY LOW MOOR, N.R.

These figures indicate an increase of population, which spread over the Wolds, the Howardian and Limestone Hills and the coast north of Scarborough. Not only did the Urn Folk inhabit the same areas as their ancestors, but they were the first to settle within the Eastern Moorlands. They lived in the Vale of York on Hutton Moor, at Howefield between Rainton and Baldersby, on Thornborough Moor near West Tanfield (Fig. 12), and in West Yorkshire, chiefly in Airedale, but also in Ribblesdale and Calderdale, at Sheffield and Doncaster.

The urns were usually placed in round barrows ranging from 18 to 80 feet or more in diameter, and from 2 to 12 feet in height (Plate II). Hundreds still stud the Eastern Moorlands where they are generally strung out alongside ancient trackways running up the ridges between the dales. Sometimes the barrows are arranged in groups of three, as the Three Howes or Kid's Huts near the Falcon Inn on the Scarborough and Whitby high road ; more rarely after the seven stars of the Plough, a grouping formerly to be seen near Cloughton, Ugthorpe, and on Huggate Wold.

Most of the moorland barrows are built of grit and sandstones gathered from the surface. Their base is often encircled by massive blocks within which there occasionally lies a second concentric circle. Earth, clay and turf were also used, usually mixed with sand, which in many instances is the sole constituent, having, as the reader will remember, a magical significance (p. 37).

The urns in the barrows were usually deposited just below, on or above the original surface of the soil, sometimes inverted, often upright and covered with a flat slab. Urns in cists are rare, only six instances being known.

Many urns are found as secondary interments. At Ferry Fryston on the Aire urns had been buried just below the summit of a barrow that had been erected over Early Bronze Age burials (p. 62). They have been found on the Wolds in food-vessel barrows. On the moors there are often primary and secondary urn burials, suggesting a sort of family mausoleum. For instance, in the Herd Howe on Girrick Moor there were 14 urns, 3 pygmy vessels, two cremations with no pottery, and a primary deposit of burnt bones and potsherds. Most of the large moorland barrows, nearly all of which have been mutilated and plundered, no doubt enshrined several successive interments.

The objects associated with urns are neither so varied nor so numerous as those of the Early Bronze Age. Flint implements are most frequent—tanged and barbed arrowheads, leaf-shaped arrow-heads (rare), scrapers, worked flakes, knives. Flint daggers have never been found. The only flint axe recorded is a broken one from Raven Hill barrow at Peak. Stone battle-axes have occasionally been found resting on cremated bones in urns, so perfect as to suggest a ceremonial usage. Bone pins and needles, jet beads and amulets have been found in or near urns. Associated with a large urn at Garton Slack, Mortimer found an antler-tool identical with those at the Neolithic Camp, Windmill Hill, near Avebury. A stone found over an urn on the Eston Hills was carved with symbols which hark back to Upper Palaeolithic, Mesolithic and Neolithic times.

Bronze implements have rarely been found, though tanged knives are recorded from Calais Wold, Baildon Moor, and Crookes near Sheffield ; awls from Peak, Wykeham Moor, and Sherburn Wold ; knives from Hanging Grimston and Broughton-in-Craven ; bronze fragments from Kilburn and Midhope, W.R.

In the Vale of York southwards from Northallerton to Sessay and Boroughbridge, and thence up the Ure to West Tanfield we have a region in which there appears to be a definite association between its occupation by the urn folk and flanged bronze axes. These are a later development of the flat axe, the sides of which were at first hammered up into narrow flanges. At a later stage they were cast with wide flanges, thus enabling them to be more firmly fixed to the haft. Six examples of this wide-flanged type come from this region. Still later, a ridge between the flanges prevented the axe from being driven too far into and splitting the haft. Stop-ridge axes, or palstaves, as they are usually termed, have been found at Rainton and Cundall Manor. As these tools succeeded the flat axes of beaker and food-vessel man, it follows that they must have been used by the urn people (Fig. 15).

Flanged axes have also occurred along the southern edge

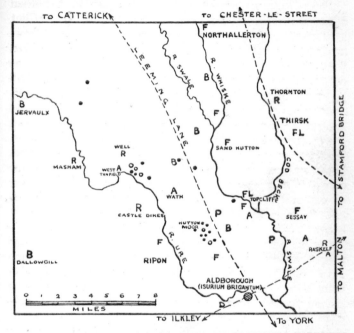

FIG. 12.—PREHISTORIC AND ROMAN REMAINS IN CENTRAL YORKSHIRE

- - -	Roman road	B	Large Stone Axe, perforated
R	Roman site	F	Flanged Bronze Axe
O	Circle	FL	Flint Dagger, Arrow-head
•	Barrow	P	Bronze Palstave
A	Stone Axe	D	Devil's Arrows, Megaliths

of the Vale of Pickering; along the eastern margin of the Wolds, on the Wolds at Cowlam, Middleton and Pockthorpe, round Barmston in northern Holderness, at Holme-on-Spalding Moor, Sutton-on-Derwent, and York; in Airedale, Upper Wharfedale, Ribblesdale, at Ingleton, Leyburn in Wensleydale, Reeth in Swaledale, at Sandal

Magna and Stanley Ferry on the Calder ; and in North Cleveland. None have as yet been found on the Eastern Moorlands.

It is now clear that the flanged axe is more numerous and more widely distributed than the flat axe. The copper and tin of which they are made most probably reached Yorkshire from Ireland by the Aire Gap route.

Palstaves, which had a similar range, ultimately displaced the flanged axe, and varieties with a loop handle survived into the late Bronze Age (p. 91).

The urn folk sometimes interred their dead within circles of earth and stone. At Higher Stone Cross Farm above Todmorden in the Calder Gap, at least 8 urns and 3 pygmy vessels had been placed within a circular bank of earth 3 feet wide and 30 yards in diameter. The central urn contained a pygmy vessel which held several human teeth, a cylindrical bone pin, twelve jet and stone beads, a triangular bronze knife and a bronze pin. Similar circles are found adjoining urn-barrows on the Eastern Moorlands. Circles found by Dr. Raistrick near Grassington in Wharfedale and near Askrigg in Wensleydale are surrounded by an outer trench and closely resemble the so-called disc barrows of Southern England.

Three most impressive circles 550 to 600 feet in diameter occur on Thornborough Moor. They consist of high banks of earth and stone, with a wide inner ditch enclosing a flat central area. Two of these circles are surrounded by an outer ditch ; the third has probably been filled in by the plough. There is evidence that the banks were crowned with standing stones. Each circle has an exit and an entrance cutting through the bank, and not only do the three circles, though 660 and 1,100 yards apart respectively, lie in an almost straight line running N.W. and S.E., but the six breaks in the banks are in similar alignment. Two other circles of a like nature stand not five miles away on Hutton Moor, near Ripon ; and in each instance barrows with cremations and urns adjoin them. These circles were clearly ceremonial meeting-places of a plentiful population ; and the rites practised there are echoed in some measure in many of our folk-dances and round games, so beloved by children throughout the generations. Some legends, and stories too, go back to this cultural epoch.

The best-dated example of a stone circle occurs on Danby Rigg in Eskdale. Originally it consisted of a bank of earth and stones 6 feet wide and $3\frac{1}{2}$ to 4 feet high, and 42 feet in diameter. On the inner side, at the cardinal points, there stood four large upright stones, only one of

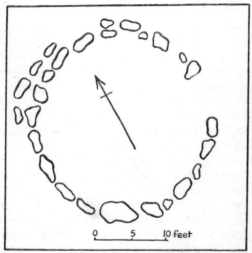

FIG. 13.—STONE CIRCLE AT YOCKENTHWAITE, WHARFEDALE

which survives. It is about 6 feet high, and $4\frac{1}{2}$ feet wide, and deeply weather-worn. Buried at the centre were two urns inverted over cremated bones.

There are a number of stone circles, 22 to 25 feet in diameter, in West Yorkshire ; and judging from the scarcity of earlier remains in this area, they may date from the Mid-Bronze Age. At Horncliffe, Yockenthwaite (Fig. 13), and Grubstones on Burley Moor, the stones form an unbroken fence ; at Carperby, Bradup and the " Twelve Apostles " between Bingley and Ilkley they are regularly spaced. In some instances, as on Malham Moor, they stand on an earthen bank, enclosing a low central mound.

It is clear that we have now tracked down many settlement areas. Hutton and Thornborough Moors invited settlers because they constituted open country on sand and gravel at low elevations, watered by the Swale and Ure. The region seems to have received both its people and its bronze goods from East Yorkshire by way of the Howardian Hills or the Ouse. River-traffic in dug-out canoes and other primitive craft must always have played a great part in the ancient life of Yorkshire, for in many respects this was the easiest way of penetrating into the interior.

On the Eastern Moorlands we can still see the remains of villages and small inhabited sites, a favourite position being the lower end of a spur or ridge between two valleys. Such spurs were easily defended on their most accessible side by constructing earthworks or dikes across them ; the surface was comparatively dry and usually sandy ; the sheltered slopes cultivable ; and springs and streams yielded an unfailing water-supply.

One of the best preserved settlements of these folk lies two miles west of Castleton in Upper Eskdale. It occupies the extremity of a spur known as Crown End, rising steeply for 300 feet between the junction of Hob Hole Beck in Baysdale and the Esk in Westerdale. The spur is about two-thirds of a mile wide, and reaches a maximum elevation of 775 feet.

Below the crest of the ridge stands a broad circular dry-stone wall 4 feet high in which standing stones are embedded. It has an entrance and an exit on the east and west, and though much smaller, recalls the Thornborough circles.

Enclosures north of the circle are undoubtedly prehistoric fields. Against three lengths of irregular walling running east and west the earth is banked up, forming distinct terraces on the hill-side known as lynchets, an infallible proof of cultivation where the ground is sloping. Field lynchets of to-day are often a yard or more high.

In preparing the ground the primitive farmer removed

the smaller stones, piling them up to form enclosures. The heavier stones still remain, a fact which shows that the ground was turned over with mattocks or digging sticks. The crops were reaped with flint sickles and the grain ground with stone pounders in hollowed-out stones known as saddle-back querns. One is recorded from High Castleton, opposite Crown End.

There are about 40 shallow pits on this settlement site. Occasionally two are in contact, an arrangement often to be found elsewhere. But further excavation is necessary before we can form a definite opinion about them. In the six we have excavated we have found nothing but burnt stones and charcoal, and large quantities of charcoal in their vicinity. We believe them to be merely fire-pits ; fires being necessary to keep the wolf and the herds of deer, the wild boar, the wild ox and the bear at bay.

South of the circle are three large barrows of the urn-period type, and many smaller cairns, 8 to 12 feet in diameter. Similar cairns are sprinkled over the moor to the west, forming a cemetery. Wherever excavated these cairns have disclosed no grave goods or human remains. They were evidently heaped over unburnt bodies which have entirely perished. Their abundance signifies that they are the burials of the humbler villagers, the large mounds containing cremated burials being reserved for chiefs.

About half a mile west of the settlement a dike straggles across the spur. This comprises a rampart 2 feet high and 6 feet wide, a ditch $2\frac{1}{2}$ feet deep and 7 feet wide, and a low outer bank set with a continuous wall of stone slabs. Twelve of these are *in situ*, the largest about 3 feet high and 5 feet wide. Originally the dike may have traversed the ridge as a complete defence work 400 yards long ; it has been sadly plundered.

Though no objects of the urn culture have been found on Crown End the settlement must belong to that epoch. On Danby Rigg, three miles to the east, the stone circle from which came two urns stands in a cemetery containing a thousand cairns and belonging to a settlement similar to that on Crown End. It is situated between 700 and

7

1,000 feet high, on and around the ridge dividing Danby Dale from Little Fryup.   There are lengths of irregular dry-stone walling, seemingly indicating field boundaries.   Pits are less frequent than on Crown End, but this settlement has been more disturbed.   On the south the cemetery is bounded by a dry-stone wall about 400 yards long.   The ridge is further traversed 700 yards to the south-west by the Double Dikes, two ramparts separated by a deep fosse at the east end ;   three ramparts with two intervening fosses at the west end.   At one time the outer rampart was set with upright stones like those on Crown End.

In the area between the two cross-ridge works there is a burial circle 70 feet in diameter, enclosing a central grave. Cairns occur near the Double Dikes, but rarely elsewhere. This spur must have been a long-inhabited site, but it is so devastated that it does not afford much more illuminating evidence of the first order (Fig. 14).

In Little Fryup Dale there are three squarish prehistoric fields, one above the other, and about 100 feet above the stream.   As they are more regular in shape than those on Crown End they may represent clearings made by the Rigg dwellers at a later period when the Celtic field system had been generally adopted.

Defensive works like the Double Dikes are frequent on the Eastern Moorlands, and are invariably associated with cairn groups, urn-barrows and the like.   They consist of a stone-parapetted rampart and ditch, as on Girrick Moor, Guisborough Moor, and Horn End in Farndale.   On Castleton and Glaisdale Riggs there are two ramparts half a mile and 400 yards apart respectively.   On John Cross Rigg, three miles west of Robin Hood's Bay, four ramparts and three intervening trenches 100 feet wide in all and half a mile long defend an area bounded on three sides by boggy valleys.   At a spur settlement at the foot of the Tabular Hills near Blakey Topping the cross-ridge work consists of a wall of upright slabs only, apparently more of a boundary than a defence.   All the more powerful works stand across ancient ridge-ways defined by round-barrows, and some of them are still used.   Trackways, still

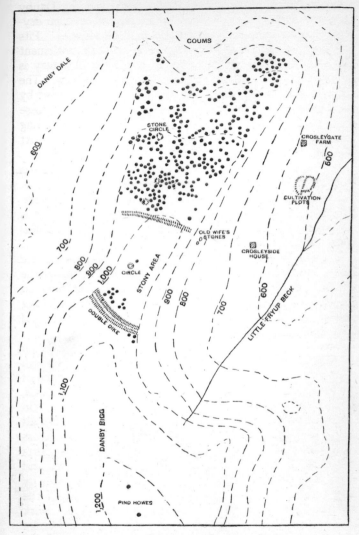

FIG. 14.—BRONZE AGE SETTLEMENT SITE, DANBY RIGG, N.R.

The black dots represent barrows. The plan is 1¼ miles wide

visible as hollow-roads, radiate from every settlement site.

The Urn Folk also lived on the Eston Hills where the moors reach their most northerly limit. Urn barrows, cairns, and flint implements occur freely, but the most striking antiquity is a large semicircular camp, perched on the edge of a sandstone cliff at Eston Nab, the highest point. It consists of a rampart, 9 to 14 feet high, and an outer fosse 5 to 8 feet deep, measuring about 350 yards in circumference. Two well-defined causeways bridge the fosse.

Excavation has shown that the camp dates from the Mid or Late Bronze Age. The fosse was originally about 7 feet deeper than to-day. The outer slope of the rampart is of earth, and originally banked up a high dry-stone wall, the collapsed ruins of which litter both the fosse and the inside of the rampart. Within the camp were unearthed two lines of stones about 100 feet long and a yard apart, which defined the site of hearths, for both they and the rubble infilling were well-fired. Fragments of a coarse, reddish-brown pottery (like that found with late Bronze Age implements in Heathery Burn Cave, Co. Durham) were scattered amongst the stones, together with flint chips and implements (including a tanged and barbed arrow-head), stone rubbers, quartzite pounders, three small stone discs resembling those of Mesolithic Age (p. 36), and numerous small pieces of calcined human bone, probably the remains of cannibal feasts.

Elsewhere in the camp scrapers and other small flint tools were unearthed. On the cliff-edge, about half-way between the rampart ends, cremated interments amongst stones were associated with a food-vessel, burnt and unburnt leaf-shaped flint arrow-heads, scrapers and flakes. These interments point to an occupation of the site anterior to the building of the camp.

Similar semicircular camps situated on the edge of cliffs occur at Boltby, N.R. (1,075 feet), and at Castleberg, Nesfield on the Wharfe (400 feet).

Shallow pits, barrow-groups, circles and entrenchments

survive on Rumbles Moor near Ilkley, on the Sheffield Moors and elsewhere in West Yorkshire.

On the sandstone terraces of Addleborough mountain near Bainbridge in Wensleydale there are numerous well-preserved hut-circles within and without massive dry-stone walled enclosures of irregular outline. Those near the Devil's Stone on the south-west terrace can be seen in plan from the summit. A second series occurs on the south terrace, and a third on the other side of the valley to the south. Many enclosures have been cultivated. Near the third series a large cairn, the Stone Raise, covered a skeleton in a cist,[1] suggestive of a Bronze Age date for the sites (p. 63).

Lowland settlement was also widespread during the Mid-Bronze Age, as on Hutton and Thornborough Moors, Skipwith Common, and at Hutton Rudby, where urns have in each case been found. Stone hearths associated with tanged arrow-heads and scrapers and a fragment of bronze have been found on the Esk bank at Sleights. Occasionally barrows and often flints occur low down in our eastern dales, affording the last relics of the small settlements of the urn folk, who, with their digging sticks, actually initiated the farms of to-day.

We must now examine the stone monuments of this culture in greater detail. They consist of unhewn large or small upright stones arranged in circles, rows or triangles. Whilst most circles guard burials as on Danby Rigg, some seem to have been places where religious rites only were performed, for as yet no burials have been found within them. In Sleddale-in-Cleveland a circle of this kind stands on a natural ledge two-thirds of the way up the eastern slope, and it consists of 16 stone pillars, not more than 3 feet high, evenly spaced in a circle 30 yards in diameter. There are no signs of a bank or ditch. There are many barrows and other stones in the vicinity.

Adjoining the settlement site at Blakey Topping there stand three pillars about 6 feet high, the remains of a circle 18 yards in diameter.

---

[1] Whaley, *History of Askrigg*, 79–80.

More impressive are the High Bride Stones at an elevation of 900 feet on Sleights Moor above Grosmont in Lower Eskdale. Though only six stones remain erect, the original arrangement can be reconstructed from those that have fallen. There are two circles, one about 12 yards in diameter is represented by three stones averaging 7 feet in height and another stone 4 feet high ; the other circle of about the same dimensions consists of three upright stones 2 to 3 feet high, with at least 8 lying in the heather. Monoliths stand outside the circles on the north and south, extending for about 150 yards.

To the west of the High Bride Stones and on a hill-side terrace stand the Low Bride Stones. One group contains at least 86 pillars not more than 5 feet high, enclosing an area about 170 feet square. A second group, south of the former, makes an irregular line of 26 uprights, extending for 70 yards. The stones are deeply weather-worn, and many have fallen over. Unlike the High Bride Stones, which certainly were sacred, the Low Bride Stones, of similar potency, are the remains of field-walls.

On Moorsholm Moor there are four small stone pillars arranged equidistantly in a straight line running east and west. To the north-west of these stands a fifth, rather taller. On Dunsley Moor near Whitby three oblong slabs have been set up on edge between the Swart Howe and another large barrow.

At least seven stone triangles are known, and with one exception, close to barrows. In most the stones are less than 3 feet high ; in others they are from 5 to 7 feet. At Simon Howe on Goathland Moor they are almost in a straight line, with two nearer together. An impressive example, with stones 3 to 5 feet high by 3 to $4\frac{1}{2}$ feet wide, stands on Ramsdale Hill top south of Robin Hood's Bay near the Scarborough and Whitby highroad.

Single standing stones are very frequent, usually associated with barrows.

In East Yorkshire, owing to the absence of suitable stone, megaliths are rare. Yet it contains the tallest monolith in the county, if not in England. It stands even yet on a sacred site, in Rudston churchyard, five miles west of Bridlington. It is 25½ feet high, 3½ feet higher than the tallest sarsen at Stonehenge, and is 6 feet wide and 2¼ feet thick at the base. It has been shaped out of a block of grit, the nearest outcrop of which occurs in the cliffs and scars of Cayton and Carnelian Bays over ten miles away. It does not appear to have been noticed that on the north-east side of the churchyard there is an upright stone of grit, rudely triangular in shape, and 3 to 4 feet high. Near it is a cist of sandstone slabs, probably unearthed by some sexton. Moreover, the churchyard is circular in shape. Here we have a striking example of the permanence of sacred sites, and of the ingenuity of the early Christians who grafted their religion on to pagan custom (p. 188).

Our most famous megaliths, made of millstone grit from Abbey Plain, Knaresborough, 7 miles away, are the Devil's Arrows or Three Sisters at Roecliffe near Boroughbridge (Frontispiece). They stand in an almost north and south line. The northernmost is 18 feet high and 22 feet round; the central stone, 22½ feet high and 18 feet in perimeter, stands 200 feet to the south; the southern stone, of similar size, stands 370 feet away. According to Leland, who visited them between 1535–1543, a smaller stone stood 6 to 8 feet from the central one, and Camden (t. Elizabeth) also states that there were two middle stones, one of which had been displaced in the hope of finding money!

That most Yorkshire standing stones date from the Bronze Age is indisputable. There is no evidence that they were erected by Neolithic man. As they are most frequent in regions in which Early Bronze Age remains are scarce or absent, but in which those of the Mid-Bronze Age abound, the majority cannot be any earlier than that age. Even the Devil's Arrows, weather-worn as they are, need not be any older, for they adjoin the Mid-Bronze Age settlements of Thornborough and Hutton Moors.

The upright stone cult first reached this country from the Mediterranean, where it attained its sublimest expression in the Egyptian obelisk. Through the agency of the earliest metal-traders and the chambered long-barrow folk it slowly made its way to the north, and was eventually adopted by the Early Bronze Age invaders, reaching its maximum development in the Mid-Bronze Age.

Many upright stones were of phallic significance, promoting life. Belief in these symbols was widespread, and so strong that it survives even to this day in remote places such as the Eastern Moorlands.

Until quite recently Cleveland farmers used to erect in their fields stone pillars, in shape exactly like prehistoric menhirs, and 3 to 4 feet high. They spoke of them as rubbing-stones. When we remember that in Celtic lands contact with upright stones was believed to conduce to human fertility, we may be certain that the initial use of these rubbing stones was to promote the welfare and multiplication of the flocks and herds.

Standing stones are frequent in prehistoric field-walls on the moors as at the Low Bride Stones and at Crown End. They recall the lines of upright stones in the ricefields of Assam where they are erected to ensure bountiful harvests. Many prehistoric monoliths can be seen incorporated in modern field-walls on the moors. Old stone gateposts leading into fields are sometimes phallic in shape, and though their significance is no longer remembered, the gatepost when renewed is usually a slavish copy of the original. The pillars of buildings, the posts of our doorways, the obelisks over our graves, and our various types of bevelled fencing may be all survivals of the lively faith and practices of the Bronze Age folk.

But life was twofold : " male and female created He them." Our stone triangles were probably erected as symbols of the triune mother-goddess, a faith derived from that of the Cretan and Mediterranean region. In the last chapter we saw that her worship was prevalent in Yorkshire during the Early Bronze Age ; that her face was found on the chalk " drums " from Folkton Wold, and that she was thus represented on menhirs in France, these being very broad at the base in contradistinction to most standing stones. We have found stones that represent her in shape, and we hope in time to find her face on some overturned stone which has got thus protected from the weather.

Her cult must have persisted throughout the Bronze Age, and religious ceremonies took place at her stone-monuments. The name Bride which is given to circles on Sleights and Bilsdale Moors, as well as to uncanny natural rock-masses on Pickering Moor, seems to be the same as that of the great Celtic goddess of fire and fertility, Brigit, otherwise known as Brig, Brid or Bride. From inscriptions we know she was the tutelary deity of the Brigantes, the powerful British tribe who dominated Yorkshire in Roman times (p. 122). Many Scottish and Irish customs still testify to her influence.

Equally suggestive is the name Old Wife, which is directly associated with standing-stones and Bronze Age settlement sites on the Eastern Moorlands. We have the Old Wife's Stones on Danby Rigg, the Old Wife's Neck, an upright stone on the John Cross Rigg entrenchments, and the Old Wife's Stone near a settlement site on Bilsdale West Moor. The only feasible explanation of this association is that the Old Wife was none other than the mother-goddess of the Bronze Age urn folk whose cult was practised at monoliths, triangles and circles. Her worship no doubt persisted on the moors until the coming of Christianity, when it fell into contempt, and she was dubbed the Old Wife. In spite of the fact that standing stones were Christianised and called or entirely replaced by crosses, and that the sign of the cross was carved on them, as at Crown End where there is a striking example, in order to dispel once and for all the older associations, worship of the Old Wife was secretly carried on as witchcraft. Our witch-lore is directly associated with Bronze Age settlement sites. We tested this association recently. Half a mile east of Captain Cook's monument (an obelisk) on Easby Moor is the Devil's Court, where, according to tradition, witches congregated under the presidency of their lord and master. We therefore examined the Court, and found what we expected, a typical moorland Bronze Age settlement site, with stone-walled enclosures, shallow pits, flint implements, and many barrows, one of which is named Nanny Howe, after a famous witch, it is said, who also frequented Nanny Nook, a right-angled bend in a stone wall near Wayworth Farm, Commondale, marking another settlement site.

A witch story related by a native 25 years ago attempts to explain two conspicuous natural features two miles apart, on Pickering Moor ; Blakey Topping, an isolated hill, and the Hole of Horcum, a deep basin-shaped valley. The local witch had sold her soul to the devil on the usual terms, but when he claimed it, she refused to give it up, and flew over the moors, with the devil in hot pursuit. Overtake her he could not, so he grabbed up a handful of earth and flung it at her. He missed his aim, and she escaped. The Hole of Horcum remains to prove where he tore up the earth and Blakey Topping where it fell to the ground.

From our point of view the significance of this story lies in the fact that between the Hole and the Topping there is a Bronze Age settlement site at Blakey Farm, with its stone circle. The rough trackway leading from the Hole to the circle is known as the Old Wife's Way, presumably also marking the witch's flight. This, together with other Old Wife's Ways, preserves as it were Bronze Age church tracks.

Space forbids the further discussion of the late survival of Bronze Age beliefs and practices in wild and isolated regions like the Eastern Moorlands, where the descendants of the original urn people no doubt continued to live until they came in contact with the Scandinavian settlers of the ninth and tenth centuries.

For Reference : As in Chapter V. J. C. Atkinson's papers in G.M., 1861–5. W. C. Lukis, *Flint Implements and Tumuli of Wath near Ripon*, Y.A.J., i, 116–26. A. Raistrick, references in Chapter VII. See also Gazetteer.

CHAPTER VII

THE LATE BRONZE AGE

OUR knowledge of the Late Bronze Age, which may be dated from about 1000 to 500 B.C., depends almost entirely on bronze weapons and implements. Few habitation sites have been discovered, and no earthworks or other field antiquities have yet been assigned to it in Yorkshire. This is all the more noteworthy, inasmuch as the bronze trade flourished as never before, and bronze craftsmanship attained its most complex, varied and extensive development. Moreover, the Late Bronze Age culture comes in fully developed. There are few links between it and the culture of the Mid-Bronze Age, and its connection with the Urn Folk is obscure.

Late bronze implements far exceed both in number and bulk those of the Early and Mid-Bronze Ages. Hundreds have been discovered in Yorkshire, and new finds are recorded almost yearly. Faced with this wealth of objects we can only describe the chief types, their distribution and provenance.

We begin with the palstave, one of the few implements of the Mid-Bronze Age which continued in use in the later period. In 1867 many palstaves were ploughed up on Hotham Carrs Farm, at the foot of the Wolds between North Cave and Market Weighton. They proved to be a hoard, and with them was a bronze mould in two halves fitting into each other by means of slots and dowels. Some of the palstaves exactly fitted the mould, showing that they had been cast from it by a process which will be described later. This is the only known palstave-mould from Yorkshire.

In late palstaves the space between the flanges below

the stop-ridge was filled up. In some this space is left plain, as on a looped example from Kirby Moorside ; in others it is ornamented with ridges, as in examples from Hotham, Doncaster, and elsewhere. A palstave from Sandtoft, Doncaster, has the blade set transversely, an exceptional feature.

Eventually, the palstave was displaced by the looped socketed axe or celt, the most characteristic and abundant tool of the Late Bronze Age (Fig. 15). Where and how the socketed axe arose has not been settled. One view maintains that it was a development of the continental winged axe, in which the flanges or wings were bent over to form a socket with a central partition or septum. At least four winged axes have been found in Yorkshire, one at a depth of 40 feet at Alexandra Dock, Hull (Fig. 15) ; a second, amongst a hoard of socketed axes at Westow on the Derwent ; a third, on a scrap-heap at Pickering ; and a fourth in the Hotham Carr hoard. As the winged axe is a French or German tool, these specimens must have been brought into Yorkshire by traders or invaders. By casting the wings as one piece, and leaving out the septum, the winged axe could be transformed into the socketed axe. A socketed axe from Givendale on the Wolds is ornamented with raised crescents reminiscent of wings (Fig. 15). Another view maintains that the socketed axe was independently invented, perhaps outside Europe. But however that may have been, the socketed axe was certainly introduced from the Continent, together with many other bronze novelties.

Though socketed axes have often been unearthed singly, they are most numerous in hoards, twenty-one of which have been found in Yorkshire. The largest comes from Earsley or Yearsley Common, on the Howardian Hills near Easingwold. It contained more than 100 axes which, as they were associated with much rough metal and cinders, evidently marked the site of a workshop.

The next largest hoard, comprising 48 celts, 6 gouges, 3 chisels, a knife, a dagger, and a ring, was found at Westow. At Bilton a hoard of 34 implements was discovered, at

Kirby Malzeard 28, at Scalby 17. Smaller hoards have occurred at Roseberry Topping, Keldholm, Sproatley, Lowthorpe, Skirlaugh, Middleton, Acklam, Leppington,

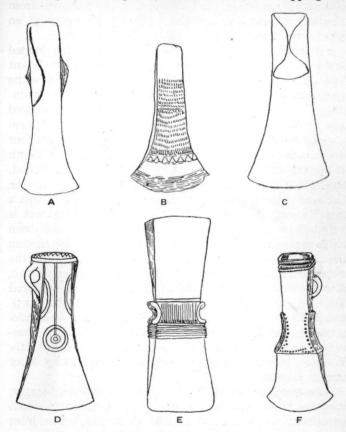

FIG. 15.—BRONZE AXES

A, flanged (5″), Cleveland, *Middlesbrough Museum*. B, flat (6″), Willerby, E.R. ; D, socketed (4″), Givendale, E.R. ; F, socketed, 'waisted' type (5″), Beverley, *British Museum*. C, winged (6″), Hull, *Hull Museum*. E, socketed, Etruscan type (6″)

Hanging Grimston, York, Bramham, Shelf, Stanley Ferry, and Hunslet near Leeds. In 1719 what is described as a bushel of celts was found at Brough-on-Humber. Many of these were founders' hoards, as testified by the presence of lumps of copper.

Sixteen axes and a socketed, collared gouge were found in a gravel-pit where the high road crosses the railway at Everthorpe near South Cave. With them were three broken lenticular copper cakes from a crucible, the raw metal for the manufacture of bronze. An analysis of an axe gave the following result, and an analysis of another Yorkshire axe is added for comparison.

						Everthorpe	*Yorkshire*
Copper	.	.	.	.	.	66·88	81·85
Tin	.	.	.	.	.	10·54	12·30
Lead	.	.	.	.	.	22·36	2·63
Iron	.	.	.	.	.	Nil	Trace
Sulphur	.	.	.	.	.	0·18	Nil
Nickel	.	.	.	.	.	Trace	0·13
Silica	.	.	.	.	.	do.	Silver 0·07
						99·96	96·98

In the second example the contents are more or less normal. In the Everthorpe axe the percentage of lead is unusually high, a feature also shown in bronze axes and swords from the Heathery Burn Cave in Weardale, Durham. The lead was no doubt added in order to save copper which had to be brought from afar, whereas lead was abundant in both West Yorkshire and Weardale. Yorkshire lead-working must therefore date back to the Late Bronze Age. There is, indeed, a lead socketed axe from Seamer Moor near Scarborough, which may have served as a model for making the clay moulds wherein most bronze implements were cast; because bronze moulds, such as that for pal-staves from Hotham, and another for socketed axes from Roseberry, may have been used merely for making wax models.

Fragments of clay moulds for axes, scabbards, daggers, and swords were found by Mortimer near Fimber on the Wolds, though at the time he did not realise their character. They have been described by Sheppard and are exhibited in the Mortimer Museum at Hull. From them the following method of casting bronzes has been demonstrated: A mould in two halves was made, either by modelling or by pressing it round an implement, or a wax or lead model. The halves were tied together with fibrous thong. A clay core for the socket was next inserted and kept in position by coarse clay covering the whole mould. Through a hole in this outer casing molten bronze was poured into the mould which was prevented from bursting by the pressure of the outer covering.[1]

After casting, axes were sharpened on whetstones, examples of which are recorded from the Roseberry Topping and Keldholm hoards. Sometimes the ridges or lines left by the junction of the mould valves on the sides were ground down. Usually these lines are straight, but on an axe from Walling Fen near Everthorpe they are wavy, and therefore indicative of a mould with interlocking valves.

The average length of Yorkshire celts is from 4 to 6 inches; small examples (2 to 2¾") come from Thornton Dale (N.R.), Sproatley and Lowthorpe (E.R.). They are usually ornamented with three ribs on the face; four-ribbed axes are rarer. One from Broughton near Malton has four ribs with a central ring ornament on one face, and four ribs ending in pellets on the other, a French type of ornamentation. Plain axes come from Glaisdale, Bilton and Yearsley.

The presence of moulds proves that many socketed axes were made in Yorkshire; others, however, are unmistakably foreign importations. One with a solid blade, separated from the oblong socket by a waist, resembles Etruscan and Italian celts, and is said to have been found in Yorkshire (Fig. 15). A looped waisted axe with chevron ornamentation, found with a looped palstave and another socketed axe, between Towton and Ulleskelf on the Wharfe below Tadcaster, is identical with those from the south of France.[2] Another from Beverley can be seen in the British Museum (Fig. 15).

---

[1] *Nat.*, Oct. 1930.
[2] Salisbury Museum. This has been confused with the Etruscan axe, see *Arch. J.*, viii, 91, *A.B.I.*, 132, and cp. with *V.C.H.*, i, 414.

Contemporaneous with the socketed axe was the bronze sword, a weapon the like of which had never before been seen in Yorkshire (Fig. 16). At least twelve examples are known, and fragments have often been found in hoards of socketed axes. Three types stand out clearly:

1. A short rather broad-bladed weapon with a well-defined midrib. Two examples have occurred, one in Alnwick Castle Museum still retains its bronze hilt and pommel; the other (18½″) from Brompton (N.R.) shows

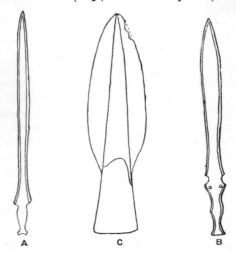

A   C   B

FIG. 16.—BRONZE SWORDS AND SPEAR-HEAD

A, (27¾″) Ebberston, N.R., *Sheffield Museum*
B, (18½″) Brompton, N.R., *Edinburgh Museum*
C, (4½″) West Furze Pile Dwelling, Holderness, *Yorkshire Museum*

how the hilt was fastened to the wings by a pair of rivets and raised flanges on the T-shaped tang.

2. A longer and more slender weapon curving in considerably towards the base of the blade, with the midrib less prominent or absent. Several examples are known. One from the Tees at Middlesbrough is 21¾ inches long, with a long slot in the tang, and a rivet-hole in each wing. Examples from Leven and Lowthorpe (E.R.) have rivet holes in the tang.

3. In this type, known as the Hallstatt, after a celebrated Late Bronze and Early Iron Age site in the Austrian Tyrol, there runs a slight bead parallel to the edge of the blade, ending about three inches from the point. The wings or butt are slightly concave, and the end of the tang more or less hexagonal, and notched. There are two Yorkshire examples ; one without the tang was found at Scarborough, and the second (27¾″), associated with human bones, was found ten miles inland at Ebberston. Along with this was a second sword, and a typical bronze chape, an object which was attached to the top of the scabbard and hooked against the back of the thigh when the sword was being unsheathed. In these types a blunt space at the base of the blade enabled the swordsman to get a firmer grip. The swords were provided with wooden or leather scabbards which, like the hilts, have perished.

An ancient Egyptian sword not unlike ours is inscribed with the cartouche of Seti II who reigned about 1205 B.C. A discovery like this enables us to date the Late Bronze Age culture with some confidence, remembering of course that it entered England much later.

Bronze Age warriors were armed with spears much more commonly than with the sword. The evolution of the bronze spear-head in Britain from the tanged and socketed daggers of the Early and Mid-Bronze Ages was worked out by Greenwell and Brewis. The oldest socketed spear-heads in Yorkshire were fastened to the shaft by a rivet through the socket, as in an example from Bawtry on the Notts. border. At a later stage loops were attached to the socket, through which the thongs binding the spear-head to the shaft were passed. Doncaster supplies a good specimen of this type. Later still, the loops were made in the base of the blade, well shown in examples from Northallerton, Hatfield, Lowthorpe, Stanwick, and Morley. These forms probably antedate the Late Bronze Age, during which a type with lunate or circular openings in the blades was prevalent, as in spear-heads from Kirby Moorside and Middleham (15¼″).

The latest and most abundant type has no loops or blade

openings (Fig. 16), and a bronze pin often fixed the shaft in the socket. A broad, short spear-head and a broad long one from Finningley can be seen in Doncaster Museum ; a barbed example comes from Ferriby (E.R.), and an Irish example from Arnold (E.R.).[1]

Bronze spears are frequent in hoards. Fragments of 8 were found at Bilton together with the upper part of a sword and 7 socketed axes. One spear has a series of shaded chevrons on the outside of each wing of the blade, and a similar series separated by lines round the socket. This ornamentation is typical of the Bronze Age, even occurring on cinerary urns. It seems to have been engraved on the wax model from which the spear was cast.

The Bronze Age warrior also carried a shield or buckler. Thoresby, in his " Ducatis Leodiensis " (1715) figures what appears to be the only Yorkshire example. It was probably found near Leeds, and shows a series of concentric ridges alternating with circles of small studs inscribed round a central hollow boss. Such shields were made by hammering and indenting a bronze disc about 2 feet wide.

Thus armed with sword, spear and shield, and perhaps withal mounted, the Late Bronze Age warrior surpassed any that the country had hitherto beheld. A peculiar bugle-shaped bronze object in the Roseberry Topping hoard is regarded by some as a piece of horse-harness, by others as a sword belt fastener. The bones and teeth of the horse have been found in Yorkshire Bronze Age barrows.

The spear and the sword were the most distinguishing weapons of this age. The only Yorkshire example of a rapier,[2] from Flotmanby near Filey, with a broad central rib notched on each side of the base, probably dates from the Mid-Bronze Age. A small pointed oval object from Scamridge 2″ long, and with a hollow midrib, could have served either as a socketed arrow-head or tip of a light spear. What are described as tanged spear-heads have been found at Cawthorn, Scarborough and Seamer Carr.

[1] H.M.   [2] Scarborough M.

The last instance is, however, identical with a tanged knife found with socketed axes in Reach Fen, Cambridgeshire.

Small tools such as socketed gouges, chisels and hammers are frequent in hoards ; bronze razors, numerous in other parts of the country, do not seem to have been recorded.

That the Late Bronze Age folk were cultivators is proved by a small socketed bronze sickle from the Roseberry hoard, and the bronze point of a ploughshare found in Holderness, a unique implement.

Gold ornaments imparted a touch of splendour to this age. At least 17 have occurred in Yorkshire. Though they were not definitely associated with bronze axes or swords, still, as the association has been noted elsewhere, and as nearly all of them have been found where the Late Bronze Age culture was dominant, their ascription to this age cannot be wide of the mark.

In 1850 six massive penannular gold rings of rude workmanship, ranging from 6 oz. 10 dwts. 17 grs. to 19 dwts. 15 grs., were found a little below the surface at Bowes at the entrance to the Stainmore Pass, where a bronze spear-head with a looped socket also occurred. These rings may have served as money, but no proportionate relation exists between their weights. A penannular ring (14 dwts.) was ploughed up at Cawood on the Ouse between Selby and York.[1]

In the British Museum we can see four penannular gold bracelets with thickened and spiral terminals from Cottingham near Hull, and a fifth from Greta Bridge, N.R.

The peculiar gold ornament shown in Fig. 17 was dug up at Swinton Park near Masham. Two others are recorded from Ripon. They no doubt served as dress fasteners, but it must not be overlooked that iron objects of the same form, known as manillas, were formerly used as money in West Africa.

More striking are two gold girdles. That from Yeadon, six miles north-west of Leeds, was made of two plain,

[1] *P.Y.G.S.*, x, 324.

cylindrical gold rods twisted together and increasing in thickness towards the terminals. It is said to have been found in a barrow.

In 1843 a second torc was ploughed up on the site of a barrow in a field abounding with flint implements at Camboots, Scalby, near Scarborough. It was made of a twisted triangular gold bar, 35 inches in circumference, and terminating in small hooks. Unfortunately it has disappeared.

These gold ornaments came into Yorkshire from Ireland, which in the Bronze Age was the El Dorado of Western Europe. The majority are identical with Irish examples, and their greater frequency in West Yorkshire points to

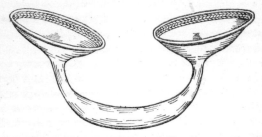

FIG. 17.—BRONZE AGE GOLD ORNAMENT (5″), SWINTON, NEAR MASHAM, N.R.

their introduction by way of the old routes through the Aire Gap and over the Stainmore Pass.

Late Bronze implements are most abundant south-east of a line from Everthorpe through Driffield to Flamborough, and especially in Holderness, east of the River Hull. Another important centre lay along the northern margin of the Vale of Pickering. In West Yorkshire, while more or less absent from Swaledale, Nidderdale and Wharfedale, they have occurred in some numbers between Tadcaster on the Wharfe and Leeds, with an extension up Airedale into Ribblesdale and Calderdale. Another centre extended from Ripon to Masham on the Ure with sporadic examples in Wensleydale and in the Don Valley near Sheffield and Doncaster.

This distribution reveals that the Late Bronze Age culture was essentially that of a lowland or valley folk amongst whom there was an extensive traffic in bronze goods. This traffic must have been chiefly in the hands of traders or tinkers who journeyed from settlement to settlement, bartering their bronzes for food and shelter, repairing and casting implements, and collecting scrap metal for re-melting. They must have drawn their supplies of tin and copper from Ireland, Cornwall, or even the Continent, connections with which are proved by the French and Etruscan axes. These assume a greater significance when we learn that old bronzes from every part of Europe were collected by Italian traders and founders who built up large depots round Bologna, and of whom our travelling bronze traders and tinkers may have been agents or pupils.[1] In any case they constituted a class of craftsmen from whose ranks the uninitiated were excluded, and whose trade secrets were jealously guarded.

In pursuit of their calling, they followed and confirmed the trackways established during the Early Bronze Age. The routes from Brough to Westow along the western edge of the Wolds, that across the York ridges to Tadcaster, Airedale and through the Aire Gap with Ireland as its ultimate objective, and that over the Stainmore Pass were all utilised. What seems to have been a new route ran inland from Scarborough to Helmsley along the base of the Limestone Hills, whilst Yoredale, which was probably sought for its lead, appears to have been reached either from York or from Westow via the Howardian Hills and Easingwold. Where these routes crossed rivers, by ford or by ferry, bronze hoards often occur, as at Brough-on-Humber, York-on-the-Ouse, and Keldholm-on-the-Dove. A hoard found in the Calder near Stanley Ferry may point to a drowning fatality.

The occurrence of a large hoard at Westow, and of three others in the neighbourhood, is due to the fact that here the route from Brough crossed the Derwent to ascend the Howardian Hills, and that near the crossing it was joined

[1] Gordon Childe, *The Bronze Age*, 202.

by roads from York and the coast.   At these river-crossings settlement sites inevitably established themselves ; sometimes floods would hold the traveller up ; in many cases he would have to engage a ferryman to take him across the river.   And so prehistoric inns or hostelries arose at river-crossings, the rude precursors of modern inns still so frequent at these points.   A notable instance is the Morritt Arms at Rokeby, which stands where the Bronze Age trade route to the Stainmore Pass forded the Greta, and near which the Bronze Age gold bracelet was found.

No late bronze implements have been discovered in the Yorkshire round-barrows, or in any recognised burial-place. This, in conjunction with their absence from the settlement sites of the Urn Folk on the Eastern Moorlands, indicates the coming of a new culture, not piecemeal, but suddenly, and fully developed. Our county yields convincing evidence that this culture was that of continental people whose leaders were armed with bronze swords.

The prevalence of the culture in south-east Yorkshire, especially Holderness, where remains of the Urn Folk are unknown, points to its introduction by new-comers with a different mode of life.   This area was the most accessible to settlers from across the North Sea.   Throughout the Bronze Age it was sprinkled with lakes, meres and low wooded hills, and backed by the gentle slopes of the grassy Wolds.   The new-comers, owing to their efficient bronze axes, were in a far better position to make forest clearings than their predecessors of the Early Bronze Age who naturally preferred the Wolds.   Very few habitation sites have been found, as the people built for themselves log cabins which quickly perish, unless preserved by the growth of peat.   Pile-dwellings in Holderness and the Vale of Pickering prove that logs were used, and that the ultimate origins of the new-comers must be sought amongst the Swiss and other continental lake-dwellers.

The most important pile-dwelling discovery was that of West Furze near Ulrome in northern Holderness.   It had been built on the site of a somewhat similar structure of early Neolithic Age (see p. 40).   The later occupation level lay 2 feet above the older, and on it there occurred a bronze socketed spear-head (Fig. 16). Its log piles, sharply pointed, had been driven down into the top of the already decayed logs of the older structure. Bronze axes had undoubtedly been used to sharpen the piles, for in the Yorkshire Museum there is a bronze socketed axe from an adjacent lake-dwelling at Barmston, and others have been found in the neighbourhood.

Its occupants, unlike those of the more ancient level, indubitably used pottery. A hand-made vessel of plain brown ware with incurving lip was undoubtedly designed after continental prototypes of the Hallstatt and La Tène cultures which prevailed on the Continent when iron was first extensively used, but which, in Britain, impinged upon and partly interfused with the Late Bronze Age culture. Other pottery showed that the site was continuously occupied until the Roman period. Three human skulls were found. Further pile-dwellings have been noted round West Furze, and also at Sand-le-mere near Withernsea. Many more must be concealed in the peat-filled hollows of Holderness.

In 1893 a pile-dwelling was discovered on the banks of the Costa Beck in the Vale south of Pickering. Many piles, 4 to 5 feet apart, were observed at a depth of 6 feet, and also sticking up in the stream itself. Nearly 60 different patterns of jars or urns from 6 to 18 inches high ; the bones of 4 people, including those of a young woman not more than $4\frac{1}{2}$ feet tall, and whose skull was missing, and of a child ; and numerous bones of the deer (three species), horse, ox, and sheep, the skulls of the goat, wolf and beaver were recorded. No metal and no stone implements appear to have been found.

In 1925 Col. E. Kitson Clark, Dr. Kirk and Professor Ormerod re-excavated the site.[1] Their trenching revealed heavy clay ($2\frac{1}{2}$ to 4 feet thick) laid down by the Costa, resting on peat containing brushwood, piles, and other signs of habitation. Below these were the remains of aquatic plants resting on sand which in its turn lay on the

Kimmeridge Clay. Some piles had been sharpened by a metal tool, many were untrimmed. The few animal bones included those of the pig and short-horned ox, a small slender-limbed horse and the dog.

Many potsherds were found, but so impregnated with black mud that their true colour was obscured. They have been regarded as later than the Bronze Age, and probably earlier than the Roman. Further research may prove that the settlement was founded in the Late Bronze Age. A Romano-British vessel found on the site proves its occupation in Roman times.

One other occupation site of a folk who used socketed axes is known, on the Castle Hill at Scarborough, an outlier of corallian limestone which rises sheer out of the sea to a height of 280 feet between the North and South Bays. The summit forms a fairly level plateau about one-third of a mile long from north to south, and rather less in width. On it the Romans erected a coastguard fort, below the foundations of which F. G. Simpson discovered more than 40 prehistoric rubbish pits (1½ to 7 feet wide, 2 to 6 feet deep), sunk from a contemporaneous occupation level. Two socketed bronze axes and fragments of two others were found on the floor, and the fragment of a fifth in a pit. A broken bronze chisel, a socketed bronze gouge, three nail-headed pins, part of an awl, three rings and a bronze bracelet also came from the floor level. That bronze smelting was carried on was testified to by the fragments of a rough earthenware crucible, bronze scoriæ, and a " jet " or trimming from a bronze casting.

The occupants wore woven garments, as proved by seven convex pottery spindle-whorls. They ate the flesh of the horse (domestic), ox, sheep and pig, roasted over circular or oblong cobble-stone hearths, or cooked in pots partially sunk in the ground, and made to boil by dropping heated stones or pot-boilers into the water.

Other objects included pieces of jet rings, a crescent-shaped shale pendant supposed to have been associated with moon worship, a shale article shaped like a bottle stopper, and two fragmentary amber and glass beads.

Flints were frequent. There was also a perforated whetstone.

There was much broken hand-made pottery containing numerous limestone particles. It included large bucket- or barrel-shaped vessels ornamented with finger-tip impressions on the rim or shoulder, or oftener on raised bands below the rim. This is a typical Late Bronze Age ware, of continental origin, frequent in the south, but not known in the north until found here. Other vessels, more or less globular, with an S-shaped profile and vertical or everted rims, have close affinities with Dutch and South German pottery of the Hallstatt culture. There can be little doubt that the folk who settled on the Castle Hill came directly from overseas, most probably from the Rhineland. It is not unlikely that they were armed with the bronze swords of Hallstatt type, as found at Scarborough and Ebberston.

It is probable that the other Yorkshire swords were the weapons of an earlier band of invaders who settled in Holderness and along the northern margin of the Vale of Pickering. They must have come into contact with the Urn Folk, with what result can only be surmised. We have suggested elsewhere that this invasion caused the Urn Folk to seek refuge in the Eastern Moorlands, which until then had been more or less uninhabited. The new culture did not penetrate on to the moors, for bronze weapons or tools have never been discovered there. The Urn Folk of the Wolds and Airedale were in a position to acquire bronzes from the traders whose routes traversed those regions. An exchange would be made for food, shelter and right of way. It appears probable that at the end of the Bronze Age the Urn Folk still retained possession of the Moorlands, and the high Wolds ; and that the bronze swordsmen, lovers of the lowlands, dominated Holderness, the Vale of Pickering, and to a less degree Airedale and Yoredale.

For Reference : B.M. *Bronze Age Guide.* Evans, *Ancient Bronze Implements.* V. Gordon Childe, *The Bronze Age,* 1930. F. Elgee, *Early Man.* H. J. Peake, *The Bronze Age and the Celtic World,* 1922. T. Parker Brewis, *The Bronze Sword in Britain,* Arch., lxxiii, 1924.   Brewis and Greenwell, *Evolution of the Bronze Spear Head in Britain*, Arch., lxi, 1909.   O. G. S. Crawford, *A Prehistoric Invasion of England*, Ant. J., ii, 1922.   T. Sheppard, *Papers on Yorkshire Bronzes*, Nat., 1917, 1918, 1921, 1923, 1924, 1926, 1928, 1930.   T. Boynton, *Bronze Implements in the East Riding*, P.Y.G.S., ix, 1887.   E. Evans, *The Sword Bearers*, Ant., iv, 1930.   A. Raistrick, *The Bronze Age in W. Yorkshire*, Y.A.J., xxix ; *Bronze Age Settlement of the North of England*, Arch. Aeliana, 4th Series, viii, 1931.   R. A. Smith, *Lake Dwellings in Holderness*, Arch., xii, 1911 ; *Pre-Roman Remains at Scarborough*, Arch., lxxvii, 1928.   J. Holmes, *Discoveries of Bronze Implements in the W.R.*, P.Y.G.S., vii, 1872 ; ix, 1887.

CHAPTER VIII

THE IRON AGE

WE must always remember that no hard and fast line separates one period from another. This is well illustrated in the transition from bronze to iron displayed in the celebrated cemetery at Hallstatt in the Austrian Tyrol, from which the earlier stage of the Iron Age derives its name, and which has there been dated from 1000 to 500 B.C. This transition was shown at the Scarborough Castle Hill, where, in one of the rubbish pits, there was part of a plain iron pin associated with Hallstatt pottery. We have already seen that this was contemporaneous with Late Bronze Age implements. Apart from the Scarborough finds, definitely Hallstatt remains of a foreign character are rare, though in the Yorkshire Museum there is an early Italian boat-shaped Hallstatt brooch, found near Boroughbridge, and probably dating from about 500 B.C.

It was not until the later phase of the Iron Age that iron displaced bronze in Yorkshire. This phase takes its name from a fortified military post, dating from 250 to 100 B.C., situated in a small bay, known as La Tène or the Shallows, on Lake Neuchâtel in Switzerland. The term covers the centuries from about 400 B.C. to the Roman conquest, subdivided into La Tène I (400–300 B.C.); La Tène II (300–100 B.C.); and La Tène III (first centuries B.C. and A.D.).

Remains of La Tène culture are abundant on the Wolds, where barrow groups are its most conspicuous feature. The best preserved are the so-called Danes' Graves, four miles north of Driffield. Here, on a wooded slope, two hundred crowded barrows can still be seen; formerly there were five hundred or more. They are like inverted shallow bowls, from 10 to 33 feet wide, and from 1¼ to 3½ feet high. Many are encircled by a shallow trench. The body, or more rarely bodies, had usually been buried in oblong graves cut in the chalk, rounded at the corners, and averaging 5 to 3¾ feet long, and 1½ feet deep. The bodies were contracted. Out of 71, 57 were laid on the left, and 14 on the right side, no point of the compass being regarded.

The most frequent objects in the graves were hand-made vessels, poorly-worked and imperfectly fired (Fig. 18). Small pieces of flint were mixed with the clay, which was

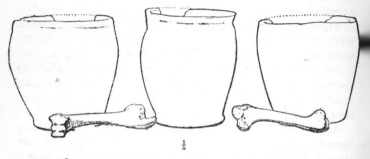

⅕

FIG. 18.—IRON AGE FOOD VESSELS, DANES' GRAVES, E.R.
British Museum

blackish and unornamented. They had served as food-vessels, and four held the humerus bones of young pigs. In one grave the complete skeleton of a pig was observed. Both Bronze Age and Iron Age burials reveal that the pig was held in high esteem both as food and as a cult animal. In the Eastern Moorlands to-day a special cake is eaten after a pig-killing, the last relic of an elaborate ritual. At Christmastide we can still see row upon row of sugar pigs for sale, harbingers of good luck and of plenty, and in many homes the chief dish on Christmas Day is pork.

Many iron brooches occurred in the graves, only one of which, made on the safety-pin principle, was perfect. Two bronze brooches belong to a British type, transitional between La Tène I and II. Instead of being arched, as in other La Tène brooches, the back is concave, and the curved pin works on a pivot, not on a coil or spring. In one the back was elaborately ornamented with raised designs in vitreous paste.

Other ornaments include two plain armlets of thin iron wire; parts of a jet armlet; bronze wire armlets ornamented on the outside with paired, grooved lines, or with 13 equidistant round knobs; a plain blue glass bead, and a few tubular beads of thin bronze; a fine bronze pin, the head consisting of a large ring enclosing a cross with round bosses of what may be coral at the centre and in the middle of each arm, the grooves on the edge of the ring are filled with the coral, and a boss is fixed on the pin.

The most significant discovery was a chariot deposited with two men in a large grave. The iron tires of two wheels were $2\frac{1}{2}$ feet in diameter, at their centre were the thin iron hoops that had bound the hubs. Two iron linch-pins held the wheel to the axle; there were two bronze-coated iron snaffle bits, a hollow bronze ring, four iron rings, two coated with bronze, and other minor metal objects.

At Arras and Hessleskew on the Wolds about half-way between Market Weighton and Beverley there was another Iron Age barrow-group nearly as large as the Danes' Graves. The burials were of the same character, but the grave-goods were more numerous and varied. In the happily named King's barrow there was the skeleton of an old man lying on his back in a large circular grave. Near his head were the skulls of two pigs, and on each side the iron tire of a chariot wheel nearly 3 feet in diameter, and its nave hoop of iron coated with bronze. Under each wheel lay the skeleton of a small horse. There were also two linch-pins, two bits of bronze-coated iron, two larger and two smaller rings of the same material.

Another chariot burial (Plate III) was that of a woman about 35 years of age. She lay on her left side, her left hand in front of her face. Behind her head were the bones of two pigs, and underneath it a circular iron mirror. (A similar mirror was found at Arras.) In addition to the chariot remains, snaffle bits and harness rings, there was a bronze cover for the end of her whip shank. She was probably a British Queen, who, like Boudicca, Queen of the Iceni, and Cartimandua, Queen of the Brigantes, drove her chariot into battle.

A third chariot burial contained also the bronze boss of a shield and two objects of stag-antler, probably the cheek-pieces of a leather bridle.

In another barrow there were nearly 100 round glass beads near the neck of a contracted female skeleton. Blue in colour, some have zigzags and others annulets of white glass upon them. In front of her lay an amber ring, and a brooch ornamented with white shell or coral, and a circular bronze pendant inlaid with coral and vitreous paste. Close to her were a torc-like bronze armlet, a bronze-coated iron armlet, a penannular bronze armlet, two small bronze rings, a bronze pin, an unusual gold finger-ring, and a pair of bronze tweezers.

Other objects from Arras include bronze armlets and rings, a jet ring, a conical chalk spindle whorl, and a bronze looped socketed axe, one inch only in length.

Chariot burials have been found at Westwood near Beverley, and also on the Limestone Hills. In a barrow at Cawthorn the chariot had been placed on the surface, and then covered with sand on which its outline was clearly imprinted, that of the wooden pole being 7 feet long.

At Low Langdale, near Stanwick (N.R.), 4 sets of elaborately ornamented bronze harness-trappings (linch-pins, bits, harness rings, cheek-pieces) two tiny metal bowls, and embossed gold and bronze ornaments were found in a pit 5 feet deep. Iron hoops were found near by, and there was also an iron sword of developed La Tène II type, in a bronze scabbard with a loop for suspension half-way along. Two others have been found at Cotterdale above Hawes and at Flasby between Skipton and Settle. Early and Middle La Tène swords have guards and scabbard mouths in the form of ogee curves, and a good example (Fig. 19), together with the skeleton of a long-headed man, comes from Grimthorpe near Pocklington. It is two-edged, and

PLATE III

TIRES AND NAVES OF CHARIOT WHEELS, IRON MIRROR AND
HORSE BITS, EARLY IRON AGE BARROW, ARRAS, E.R.
British Museum

SWASTIKA ROCK CARVING, ILKLEY, W.R.

the iron tang of the handle is provided with two oval iron plates between which a wooden grip had been fixed. The scabbard is ridged on both sides, one being of bronze and the other of iron. The bronze chape is heavily moulded. Along with this La Tène II sword were the remains of an iron spear-head, several bone arrow-heads, and the bronze fittings of a shield.

A sword from Bugthorpe has a bronze scabbard with finely engraved foliate pattern with basket-work hatching, typical La Tène motifs. It was found with a pair of bronze studs and also a remarkable pair of bronze ornamental discs, bearing red enamelled bosses, the enamel being applied as a thinnish coating on a clay core which was pinned to the metal plate. An iron sword with enamelled bronze handle fittings, of later date (certainly not earlier

$\frac{1}{6}$

FIG. 19.—IRON AGE SWORD, GRIMTHORPE, E.R.
British Museum

than about A.D. 50), comes from Thorpe near Rudston. In this the mount at the scabbard-mouth has been transferred to the base of the grip. The enamelled ornaments are in the form of small circular studs containing cruciform and triangular designs in red, blue, and yellow enamels. The bone plates of the handle can still be seen.

Another typical La Tène II sword was found with an extended male skeleton at North Grimston, together with a sword of entirely different type, the shorter anthropoid sword, in which the handle is of bronze, the pommel being in the shape of a human with uplifted arms, the legs forming the guard, the body the grip. A second less perfect example was found at Clotherholme near Ripon. This type is descended from a Hallstatt sword with branched pommel.

Isolated La Tène objects have sometimes been found, the most noteworthy being a bronze collar, found under a stone transom at Embsay near Skipton ; a bronze bridle-bit from Rise in Holderness, ornamented with red and blue enamel-work, the artistic glory of Britain during the Early Iron Age ; and the Ilkley swastika, a fertility symbol (Plate III). It can be seen, engraved on a rock on Addingham High Moor, west of the town. The design is essentially characteristic of Late Iron Age craftsmanship, as will be realised by comparing it with that of the triskele on a gold torc from Clevedon, Somerset, and figured on the cover of the British Museum Early Iron Age Guide.[1] According to Dr. Raistrick, other swastikas exist in Wharfedale.

La Tène culture was undoubtedly introduced into Yorkshire by Gaulish invaders during the third century B.C. Its characteristic chariot-burials have their closest parallels in Champagne, the Marne region, and especially in the Seine Valley at Nanterre near Paris. The anthropoid swords are identical with French examples, the knobbed bronze armlets similar to those from Samsois, Marne. The skeletons also go to show that the charioteers and iron swordsmen were new-comers to Yorkshire. The majority were dolichocephalic, with long and oval faces, brow ridges slight or absent, and statures ranging from 5 feet 2 inches to 5 feet 10 inches in the men, and from 4 feet 11 inches to 5 feet 7¾ inches in the women. Clearly these cannot be the descendants of the Bronze Age folk, who were both long- and round-headed, with powerful jaws and prominent brow-ridges.

The Gaulish charioteers overran East Yorkshire, the fourth invasion since the coming of long-barrow man. Unlike the Late Bronze Age invaders, they preferred the Wolds, and to a less extent the Limestone Hills, in this respect resembling the beaker-makers.

From the Wolds La Tène culture spread into other parts of the county whose inhabitants were still in the Bronze Age. The change from bronze to iron was no doubt gradual. At the Ulrome lake-dwelling La Tène ware was observed. In a rubbish-bed by the beckside at Low Mill

[1] The design ultimately derives from the Cretan swastikas of the Bronze Age. See Evans, *Palace of Minos at Knossos*, ii, 197–8, Fig. 107.

Garth, Thornton Dale, there was a piece of pottery like the final of Italian house-urns of Late Bronze or Early Hallstatt date; and a potsherd incised with a La Tène pattern, and certainly pre-Roman; there were pre-Roman potsherds of a light grey to black clay mixed with large pieces of hard-white grit; bone points like those found with the Grimthorpe sword; a penannular bronze brooch with knobbed ends; a large Roman fibula of a type belonging to the early part of the first century A.D., and several scraps of Samian ware; and a clay model of a coracle. Here we seem to have a site occupied from the close of the Bronze Age to the early Roman period.

Steyforth Hill on Stainburn Moor between Otley and Harrogate is another site which was continuously inhabited from the Bronze Age to the first century A.D. Leaf-shaped and barbed arrow-heads, pieces of Bronze Age pottery, black polished Iron Age ware, and a bronze brooch (A.D. 20–60) have been found there. Sites of this kind point to the gradual acquisition of Iron Age culture by the Bronze Age folk.

Settlement sites have not yet been recorded from the Wolds, despite their richness in La Tène remains. A close survey of the neighbourhood of the Danes' Graves would be well worth while, for the large community who buried their dead there must have left other indications of their presence. At Atwick, twelve to sixteen miles south-east of the Graves, numerous pit-dwellings of the Iron Age have been recorded. Usually they were about 5 feet deep, of elongated form, a few even being 40 feet long by 9 to 10 feet wide. They were filled with hardened blackish mud overlain by soil from 15 to 18 inches thick. In one at Rolston a southern entrance sloped gradually down to a central hearth made of rough stones (Fig. 20). Near by was a broken pot, with broken bones of the ox, horse, sheep or goat, pig, and red deer; heavy stone pounders and rude flint knives and flakes were scattered around. A peaty substance on the floor seems to have been the remains of a couch made of grass and rushes. Near the hearth lay the bones of a dog curled round as if asleep.

9

The atlas vertebra of a whale in another pit had been used as a stool. At the time of their discovery these pits were considered to be Neolithic, but their pottery proves that they belong to the Iron Age.

Recent research has shown that Iron Age sites are numerous and widespread in West Yorkshire. On the plateau of the Great Scar Limestone in Wharfedale Dr. Raistrick finds saucer-shaped barrows, often encircled by a trench, up to 30 yards in diameter. They have yielded iron knives, coarse pottery, bronze and iron ornaments, and multiple burials. Associated with these barrows are extensive lynchets and cultivation plots of the Celtic type. Twelve lynchet groups occur in Upper Wharfedale, one of

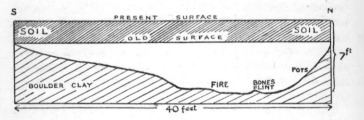

FIG. 20.—SECTION OF IRON AGE PIT-DWELLING, ROLSTON, HOLDERNESS

the best preserved is in the High Close Pasture north of Grassington. Here the lynchets enclose rectangular fields, amongst which a broad, short strip is most frequent. The fields average 360 to 400 feet in length, and 75 feet in breadth, that is about 0·65 of an acre. South-west of the lynchets stands the " Druids' Circle," an oval area 150 feet long by 75 feet wide. It consists of a bank surmounted by a single or double row of flat-topped stones about $1\frac{1}{2}$ feet high by 2 feet wide. The enclosed arena is below the level of the surrounding land. This may have been a communal meeting-place of the Iron Age folk, who cultivated these fields, and who lived in isolated huts, the circular foundations of which can be seen in Grass Wood adjoining High Close Pasture, and elsewhere. In them iron knives with deer-horn hafts like those from the barrows have been found; also spindle-whorls of stone, pottery and lead (one of Roman type), saddle-back querns and pounders, and charred barley, the most ancient evidence of this cereal in Yorkshire.

On the plateau of the Great Scar Limestone south of Arncliffe in Littondale, Celtic fields are associated with some unusually regular enclosures, rough masonry walls 5 feet wide at the base, mostly fallen, in places still 3 feet high. When mapped, they indicate rectangular and circular chambers ranged round a rectangular space with two entrances. The walls of one chamber had been built on the bee-hive principle. Along the east side a green sunken road led to a group of Celtic fields, and by it are the remains of two so-called 'dew-ponds', a feature characteristic of the Celtic field-system. These walls are undoubtedly the ruins of dwellings. Dr. Raistrick assigns them to the Late Iron Age because of their association with Celtic lynchets and because they are paralleled by hutments within a rectangular wall on Lea Green, Grassington.

The so-called Celtic wall near Settle probably goes back to the Iron Age. Originally it appears to have been continuous. Two lengths still stand, one about 18 yards long; the other 42 yards distant, being 27 yards long. They are built of massive horizontal slabs, decreasing in size towards the top, and very weathered.

From time to time we have discovered Celtic fields with their 'dew-ponds' on the Eastern Moorlands, where their regularity is in marked contrast to the irregular Bronze Age fields they so often adjoin. Excavation alone will definitely date them, for in this barricaded region the system may not have been introduced until post-Roman times. Bee-hive rotary querns have been found on or near Celtic fields in Kildale, and at the Hulleys near Cloughton Newlands north of Scarborough. This utensil, though undoubtedly first used during the Iron Age, is of little service for dating purposes, as it survived the Roman occupation.

Celtic fields have not yet been recorded from the Wolds,

the headquarters of La Tène culture. Modern agriculture has no doubt swept them and also those of the Bronze Age away. Air photography alone will reveal their traces.

A negative feature of the Yorkshire Iron Age is the absence of those iron currency bars which have often been found south of a line drawn from Northampton to Leominster. As a matter of fact the county was the northern limit of the area in which ancient British coins circulated in eastern England. These coins have been traced back through Gaulish types to the gold stater of Philip II of Macedon who died in 336 B.C. The ancient British tribes seem to have begun to mint them about 100 B.C., each tribe adopting a coinage of its own, that of Yorkshire being issued by the Brigantes who, as we learn from Roman historians, dominated the north of England at the time of the Roman conquest. Their coinage was the poorest and latest of its kind, with a low metallic standard and of extremely crude design.

In 1829, 18 gold coins and nearly 200 Roman, mostly of the Republic, were found at Castle Hill, Almondbury near Huddersfield. Two of them in the Yorkshire Museum, are inscribed on the convex side VO LI SIO and on the concave side DVM NO CO VEROS. Three others are ornamented with a peculiar wreath, a large beaded ring at each end, the degenerate survival of the laurel crowning the head of Philip II on his gold staters ; and on the other side an intertwined figure, the degenerate survival of the horse-driven chariot on the staters, together with the letters VEP COR F, which Professor Rhys believed to be the Latin for VEPOGENUS, SON OF CORREOS.

In 1893, 5 British silver coins and 18 Roman were discovered at Honley near Huddersfield. The British coins were inscribed VOLISIOS on the convex side in five and DVMNOVEROS on the concave in four instances. In the fifth the inscription reads CARTIOVE, which can only refer to Cartimandua, the notorious queen of the Brigantes, who betrayed Caractacus to the Romans about A.D. 51. Professor Oman has suggested that Volisios was a Brigan-

tian king who associated with himself as colleagues first
Dumnocoveros, perhaps his son, and later Cartimandua,
who must have been his daughter and heiress.

Thirteen of the Honley Roman coins were silver denarii ;
9 of these belong to the Republic (209–42 B.C.). The
latest coin in the hoard was a middle brass of Vespasian
(A.D. 72–3). In addition to the coins there was a native
first-century brooch, a bronze Roman seal box with a
hinged lid plated with silver, and two small bronze rein-
rings of La Tène type.

Between 1828–31, gold British coins and Roman
Republican (184 B.C.), and Imperial coins were found at
Lightcliffe near Halifax. Two bore the name Volisios,

FIG. 21.—BRITISH GOLD COIN, HORNSEA
Hornsea Museum

and these and a third a horse and chariot. As the latest
Roman coin was one of Caligula (37–41), this hoard must
have been hidden before the Honley hoard.

An uninscribed gold coin is recorded from Ackworth,
near Pontefract. Another coin found at Keighley bears
the name of Verica, a son of Commius, ruler of the British
Atrebates, inhabiting Hampshire and Berkshire, and a
branch of the Belgic tribe of the same name. Verica seems
to have reigned about the time of the Roman conquest.

Fig. 21 shows a gold British coin found at Hornsea.

The most outstanding field antiquity of the Early Iron
Age in Southern England, the more or less circular or oval
hill-fort, is rare in Yorkshire. It is absent from the Eastern
Moorlands, which had no attraction for the La Tène
invaders. Until the complex of earthworks on the Wolds
has been resolved its occurrence in that region remains
uncertain.

Though the type occurs in West Yorkshire, their age has usually not been definitely ascertained. The best attested is that of Wincobank, situated on a spur high above the Don valley between Sheffield and Rotherham. The double ramparts enclose an oval area of 2½ acres, destitute of any traces of habitation. The ramparts are made of earth, covering a dry wall of undressed stones with well-built facing, and a charred rubble core. Roman potsherds found very near the bottom of the ditch show that the fort cannot have been erected long before the Roman Conquest, possibly during the first century A.D. Two and a half miles to the north-east another well-preserved oval camp stands on high ground in Scholes Wood. The rampart is 16 feet high, encircled by a ditch, with a counter-scarp 7 feet high, and enclosing an area of one acre. Another earthwork, Stainbrough Low near Wentworth Castle in the same area, seems to have been of the same type, but a garden and building erected by Horace Walpole in 1789 have obliterated it. On the isolated hill of Brierley Common (275–300 feet) near South Kirby, there are the remains of an irregular oval work, the north and south sides of which are partly strengthened by ravines. The ramparts are from 8 to 10 feet high, with traces of an outer ditch, enclosing 4½ acres.

In the Huddersfield area are the stony remains of a circular or oval work on the end of a steep spur opposite the Roman fort at Slack. At Almondbury we have the famous Castle Hill earthworks, on a headland 900 feet high, very steep on three sides, with a narrow approach from the east. The whole work covers 8 acres, and is an elongated oval, consisting of an earthen bank and a dry fosse, with signs of an outer bank. There seems little reason to doubt that this is a British fort, as testified by the coin-hoard already described. Its original features have been marred by the erection within its western half of a Norman motte and bailey castle with its burgus. It commands the Roman road from Manchester to Slack, and appears to have been the Camunlodunum of Ptolemy (p. 147). The name means the hill-fort of Camunlos, a

Celtic war-god. Exactly when the fort was built, and how long it was occupied, can only be determined by excavation. On Cullingworth Moor, between Bingley and Haworth, there lies an oval earthwork (360 by 300 feet) called Castle Stead Ring. It has a rampart 6 feet high, a ditch 4 feet deep. Most of it has been swept away, but originally it covered $1\frac{3}{4}$ acres.

In the North Riding the finest example of this type of fort is the Castle Steads at Gayles, south of Dalton, about half-way between Richmond and Barnard Castle. It stands on a very steep-sided spur between two becks. Its shape is somewhat irregular ; the stony rampart running along the sides of and crossing the spur on the north and south encloses $3\frac{3}{4}$ acres. There is an outer ditch, and the remains of a counter scarp, mostly destroyed by landslips. It stands at an altitude of 800 feet, two miles from the Roman road between Catterick and Bowes, which it overlooks.

It is probable that the Yorkshire hill-forts of this type will ultimately prove to date from the first century, and that they were constructed to oppose the progress of the all-conquering Romans. In them we no doubt see the forts of the Brigantes referred to by Juvenal in his Satires.

The hill-forts were purely military, but on Ingleborough (2,350 feet) we have the remains of a fortified village unique in Yorkshire. On the flat grassy summit, about 15 acres in extent, there are numerous circular stone foundations of huts, usually with southerly entrances. Round the edge of the often vertical crags which crown the mountain-top the inhabitants of these huts created a massive stone rampart nearly 3,000 feet in length, and defining an irregular pear-shaped area. Myriads of millstone grit slabs have been piled up to form a high wall which has now collapsed. On the south-east upright slabs run along the inside, and on the north slabs laid horizontally with occasional vertical bonding slabs reveal the original structure. Here and there very large blocks line the inside. There are openings in the wall in the north, south-west and east. That on the north is about 50 feet wide, and flanked with large slabs.   This break corresponds with the extreme edge of a vertical crag.   Much of this ancient stronghold has been destroyed in building the huge modern cairn which mars the dignity of this sublime site.   Though late Romano-British potsherds have been found [1] on the site, the village is certainly Brigantian, the last stronghold of some indomitable chief and his followers, who resolutely refused to surrender to the Romans.

For Reference :   B.M. Guide to *Early Iron Age Antiquities*, 1925. W. Greenwell, *Early Iron Age Burials in Yorkshire*, Arch., vol. lx, 1906.   Greenwell and Gatty, *The Pit Dwellings of Holderness*, Man, x, 1910.   Mortimer's *Forty Years' Researches*, 354–64 ; *The Danes Graves*, P.Y.G.S., xiii, and R.Y.P.S., 1897.   T. Sheppard, *Chariot Burial at Hunmanby*, Y.A.J., xix, 1908.   Elgee, *Early Man*, chap. xviii.   E. Curwen, *Ancient Cultivations at Grassington*, Ant., ii, 1928.   A. Raistrick and S. E. Chapman, *The Lynchet Groups of Upper Wharfedale*, Ant., iii, 1929.   C. Hawkes, *Hill Forts*, Ant., v, 1931.   M. Kitson Clark and others, *Iron Age Sites in the Vale of Pickering*, Y.A.J., xxx, 1930.   E. S. Armitage and D. H. Montgomery, *Ancient Earthworks*, V.C.H.Y., ii, 1912.   J. A. Petch, *Early Man in the Huddersfield District*, Tolson Museum Publication, 1924.

---

[1] Information supplied by Dr. Raistrick.

CHAPTER IX

ROMAN YORKSHIRE

I

IN the abundance and variety of its Roman antiquities Yorkshire stands second to no other county. We find camps, signal-stations, fortresses; houses, villages, towns; iron-mines, lead-mines, potteries; baths, amphitheatres, temples; cemeteries, inscriptions, altars; and the thousand and one objects of daily life, from the shells gathered by children at the seaside to the jet pins which still adorn the dark hair of one whose beauty otherwise is dust.

To describe, or even to list these antiquities, is impossible. All that can be attempted is to note typical remains, especially field antiquities, and to outline the Roman occupation from a combined historical and geographical point of view, the only way in which to realise something of that imposing epoch.

Yorkshire corresponds to no natural or inevitable division of Roman Britain. On the contrary, its diversity of remains arises from the circumstance that the two principal aspects of the Roman province—the civil, more or less restricted to the lowlands, and the military, predominantly characteristic of the highlands—met and mingled in Yorkshire. Civil life spread over the Wolds and the Howardian Hills, reaching its most northerly limit in and around the Romano-British city of Isurium, now Aldborough. It even flowed up to the walls of the legionary fortress of Eboracum, now York, the base of the vast military zone ranging westwards over the Pennines to the legionary fortress of Chester, and northwards to Hadrian's Wall in Northumberland.

In the first century of the Christian era Yorkshire was shared by at least two Celtic-speaking tribes, the Parisi and the Brigantes. The former, who occupied the Wolds and Limestone Hills, were a branch of the Gaulish Parisii settled on the Seine, who had introduced La Tène culture into East Yorkshire during the Iron Age.

The Brigantes dominated West Yorkshire, Lancashire, Durham, and possibly more northerly regions. Their origins are not altogether clear, though they seem to have been an offshoot of the Brigantes or Brixantii of the Lake Constance region. In the first place they may have been the folk who introduced our Late Bronze Age culture, and who, in time, gradually absorbed or became overlords of the older population whom we have called the Urn Folk.

The Brigantes seem to have been culturally inferior to the Parisi, from whom they no doubt acquired the elements of La Tène culture, as revealed by the Grassington settlement described in the last chapter, and which may be regarded as a typical Brigantian village of the western dales. In areas like the Eastern Moorlands the inhabitants seem to have remained in a very primitive condition, judging from the extreme rarity of La Tène remains. But both Parisi and Brigantes were much below the status of the Belgic tribes of south-eastern Britain, who in addition to a superb creative genius of their own had also been powerfully influenced by Gaulish and Roman culture from over the sea.

Contact between the Brigantes and the Romans began early. By A.D. 47, or only four years after the Claudian invasion, P. Ostorius Scapula, the governor, had established a temporary Roman frontier by means of a line of forts along the Fosse Way from Axmouth to Lincoln. In 51 he defeated the Silures of Wales who were led by Caratacus, the defiant king of the Catuvellauni, a Belgic tribe of the south-east. Caratacus sought refuge with Cartimandua, the pro-Roman Brigantian queen, whose coins have been already described. Despite the disapproval of Venutius, her husband, she betrayed Caratacus, who was conveyed in chains to the Imperial City to make a Roman holiday.

His undaunted courage so impressed the Emperor Claudius that he was set at liberty.

Cartimandua's action created civil war amongst the Brigantes. Venutius, inflamed by Caratacus' example, attacked the Romans under Didius Gallus and Cæsius Nasica who speedily mastered the situation and made a peace which lasted for nearly seventeen years.

In 69 Cartimandua repudiated or divorced Venutius, and married his standard-bearer, Vellocatus. Backed by most of his tribesmen Venutius compelled her to seek a haven with the Romans, and we hear of her no more. The Brigantes were by now very definitely antagonistic to the invaders, and initiated a frontier war which raged intermittently for more than a century.

And so their subjugation became one of the Roman aims. In 71 Q. Petillius Cerialis, the governor of Britain, attacked them suddenly, fought many battles, and ravaged most of their territory. This he did in less than three years. He was succeeded by Frontinus, who spent his governorship (74-77) chiefly in a war with the Welsh Silures. But the next governor, G. Julius Agricola (77-85 or 6) consolidated the conquests of Cerialis, and even carried the Roman arms to the foot of the Grampians.

To this Flavian period, so-called after the Flavian Emperors Vespasian, Titus and Domitian (69-96), the earliest Roman works in Yorkshire belong. Under Cerialis the Roman frontier had pushed to Chester on the west and to York on the east, now the headquarters of the Ninth Legion. This ill-fated corps had had a long and distinguished history. For its services in N.W. Spain (not because its legionaries were Spaniards) it received, about 25 B.C., the title "Hispana". It formed part of the invading army into Britain under Claudius in 43. It was almost annihilated in Boudicca's rebellion in 61, when its commander, Cerialis, and the cavalry alone escaped.

From its former station at Lincoln the legion advanced into Yorkshire, no doubt by way of the ancient Humber crossing at Brough, where a field called the Burrs, the site of a large Roman station, possibly of Flavian origin, has yielded many relics. From Brough the advance was probably northwards over the Wolds along or near tracks which were defined in long-barrow times (p. 45). A Roman road, still more or less continuous, runs along the western margin of the Wolds from Brough to Malton, the pavement having been observed near South Cave (5 to 7 yards wide), Londesborough Park (8 yards wide, and wheel-rutted), and Millington Dale. Another road, not so well-marked, appears to have run from near N. Ferriby towards Etton, and thence west of Bainton, Tibthorpe (where a ridge was formerly visible), Wetwang, to Wharram-le-Street, Langton and Malton. Roman remains have occurred near these roads, and though their exact date is not known, it is not unlikely that Cerialis followed these lines (see map).

On the north bank of the Derwent at Malton there is a large Roman fort, the history of which the spade is revealing. There are indications of a pre-Agricolan occupation covering an area of not less than 22 acres, showing that originally it must have been a camp large enough to hold a legion. Coins of Vespasian, and pre-Agricolan pottery are recorded, also tile fragments stamped LEG. IX. HISP.

Another early invasion line followed the prehistoric route from Derbyshire along the Rother valley (p. 68). Between the junction of this river with the Don, but about a mile to the east, the Romans built a square fort with turf ramparts resting on gravel and clay, surrounded by a berm and outer ditch, and enclosing an area of 5½ acres (Fig. 22). This fort, known as Templeborough,[1] is almost certainly older than Agricola's campaign, possibly older than that of Cerialis, for pottery and coins indicate an occupation as early as 50, which no doubt continued throughout the Flavian period. A tile stamp of Legio IX has occurred, and others of the IV Cohort of the Gauls, the permanent garrison.

The Roman army comprised two classes of troops; the legionary and auxiliary. The legions were about 6,000 strong, citizens of the Empire; the auxilia from 500 to 1,000 men, recruited from recently conquered frontier

---

[1] Now covered by steel works.

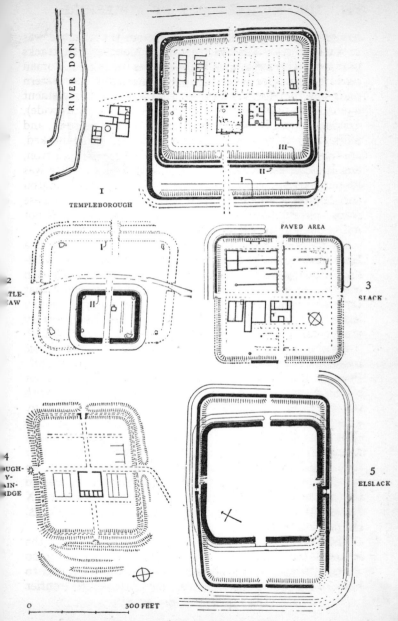

FIG. 22.—PLANS OF ROMAN FORTS

1 TEMPLEBOROUGH

RIVER DON

2 TLE-AW

3 SLACK

PAVED AREA

4 UGH-Y-IDGE

5 ELSLACK

0   300 FEET

tribes. The auxiliaries were given the brunt of the fighting, the legions being kept in the rear, for Roman blood was precious. The auxiliaries occupied frontier forts for their permanent quarters : the legions were stationed at a rearward base. Auxiliaries defended Hadrian's Wall ; the legion was stationed at York.

Templeborough stood on Riknild Street which, just south of the fort, was 18 feet wide, and made of two layers of sandstone footings and road metal. This Roman road ran more or less parallel to and north-west of the Fosse Way from Worcester to Lichfield, Derby, and Templeborough, beyond which its course is uncertain. North of the Don the line may have run almost due north to Aldborough, but further research is needed to confirm this. More probably Riknild Street continued along the Don until, just above the junction with the Dearne, it turned northwards by Hickleton along the so-called British way to fall into the Doncaster-Castleford Roman road. Whether this road was laid down by then we do not know. North of Castleford the road pursues a straight course on a ridge about 8 yards wide and often 5 feet high to Aberford, whence it can still be traced to Newton Kyme where, at Long Brough on the south bank of the Wharfe, there is a Roman fort ($10\frac{1}{2}$ acres) which was occupied from the later part of the first to the fourth century, and where a fine strip of the outer wall can be seen.[1] The Wharfe was crossed at St. Helen's Ford, north of which the road, known as Rudgate, and still in use, leads direct to Aldborough.

Whether Cerialis founded Aldborough, which stands on the south bank of the Ure, we cannot say ; a Ninth Legion tile can be seen in the museum there. Its Roman name, Isurium Brigantum, shows that it was the tribal or cantonal city of the Brigantes. That it was an important pre-Roman site is indicated by its proximity to the Devil's Arrows which, as we have seen, stand within the well-settled, prehistoric area of mid-Yorkshire (p. 77). From a military point of view, however, its position was far less

[1] Information supplied by Mr. F. G. Simpson.

vital than York ; and so, whilst Isurium became the most northerly of Romano-British towns, York, the foundations of which were laid by Cerialis, became the military capital of Roman Britain.

On advancing over the Wolds to Malton, and along Riknild Street to Aldborough, the Romans would arrive at the ancient route across Yorkshire at Fimber and Bramham. By exploring this route in either direction, they would inevitably come to a pause where the Ouse breaches the morainic ridge at York. To erect a fortress there had superlative advantages. It would command the main route between the east and west of Yorkshire, and effectively check tribal co-operation. Roman galleys could sail up the Humber, and anchor under its very walls ; and roads could be driven along the margins of the plain, the easiest and most direct lines to the north.

Eboracum lies in the angle formed by the meeting of the little River Fosse and the Ouse. As recent excavations have revealed, the first fort consisted of a clay rampart enclosing an area of unknown extent, on which stood timber barracks. Of Flavian type, further research will probably confirm the view that it is the work of Cerialis. Tile stamps and inscriptions prove that for about fifty years (71 to 120) York was the headquarters of the Ninth Legion.

There is meagre evidence of an advance into Yorkshire from Chester at this period. Two small, peculiarly-shaped camps at Meltham on the Pennines, south-west of Huddersfield, and at Kirklees in the Calder valley between Brighouse and Dewsbury, indicate an early reconnoitring expedition over the Pennines and down the Colne valley by Almondbury Castle Hill, in the direction of Aldborough or York. No paved road has been found on this line, so the forts must have been connected by an earthen track. That at Meltham is a little over an acre in extent, with an outer ditch on three sides, ramparts of loose stones and earth laid upon an artificial bed of clay, and a double wooden gate across a few yards of cobbled road. The Kirklees fort is similar but rather larger, with gravel ramparts and a double ditch on the east side.

It is a question whether Cerialis pushed further north than Malton and Aldborough. His successor, Agricola, however, subjugated the whole county, and established the main features of the Roman occupation so securely and skilfully, that with little modification they served until its close.

The first fort at Malton belongs to this period. It covered 8½ acres, enclosed by sandy clay ramparts and at least one ditch. The north-east gate was double-timbered, and the earliest buildings, like those of the previous camp, were of wattle and daub.

With Malton, and possibly also Brough, controlling East Yorkshire, and York firmly established as a legionary base, Agricola would be in a position to secure the mountainous region of West Yorkshire. Operating from Chester, the fortress of the XX Legion, he drove two roads through the Pennines. The first ran from Manchester north-eastwards over Stanedge (1,300 feet) and down the ridge north of the Colne valley to the Calder near Rastrick, beyond which it seems to have led towards Leeds and York. This road is three or four miles north of and parallel to the Meltham-Kirklees line, which it superseded because it traversed less arduous country.

The Agricolan age of this road is fully proved by excavations at the forts of Castleshaw and Slack (Fig. 22) which guard it, the first on a south-west spur of the Pennines below Saddleworth, the second eight miles to the north-east, above the Colne valley. Castleshaw fort (120 × 100 yards) covered 2½ acres, enclosed by a turf and clay rampart 18 feet wide, and no doubt carrying a stockade. The ditch lay close to the rampart, and from the north to the south-west corner was double. A tower, or a platform for artillery at each corner rested upon rough stones. The four gateways and the interior buildings were of wood. Agricolan potsherds were discovered. Within this fort there is a smaller one of later date.

Slack fort was larger (256 feet square, 3⅔ acres), with a turf rampart 20 feet wide, whose outer edge rested on stone foundations, surrounded by one or two ditches and a

PLATE IV

TOMBSTONE OF L. DUCCIUS RUFINUS,
A STANDARD-BEARER OF LEGIO IX HISPANA
FOUND AT MICKLEGATE, YORK, 1686
Yorkshire Museum

berm. The four gates were of timber, two being double, and all except the west provided with wood guard-rooms. On the eastern side there was no ditch south of the gate, but a paved parade ground. All the internal buildings, granaries, headquarters, workshop and barracks were of wood. Wood towers guarded the north, and possibly the west and south corners. Outside the fort was a two-roomed building for hot and cold baths. These features are of Agricolan date ; others, of a somewhat later period, will be noted in due course.

The second route followed by Agricola ran from Ribchester in Lancashire along the valley of the Ribble. The road enters Yorkshire near Rimington, and pursues an almost straight course to Skipton. The ridge, 16 feet wide, can be well seen near Barnoldswick. East of Thornton the paving is visible, whilst at Elslack station there stands a fort known as Burwens Castle (Fig. 22). The railway cuts through it, and excavation has proved that it was occupied until 85, and is therefore Agricolan, possessing all the features of a Flavian fort, a square clay rampart on stone foundations, with a double ditch 24 feet wide, a berm 2 to 3 feet wide, the inner ditch interrupted opposite the timber gateways. No interior buildings of this age were found ; but first-century pottery and coins also help to date it.

From Skipton the Elslack road continued almost direct to Aldborough. Its course is still well-marked, especially on Blubberhouses Moor, where there is a straight run of seven miles, known locally as Watling Street. Here it is made of large native boulders, and edged with larger boulders. It crossed the Nidd near Hampsthwaite Church, where the paving has been noted.[1] North-east of this crossing its course to Aldborough is obscure.

On the ridge north of Skipton the Elslack-Aldborough road branched eastwards to York, by way of Ilkley and Adel—both important Roman stations. Apart from casual finds (p. 154), of Adel we have little knowledge ; but Ilkley has been partly excavated, and shown to be of Flavian,

[1] *B.R.A.C.*, vi, 1928 ; Codrington, *Roman Roads*, 98.

probably Agricolan date. The fort stood on a plateau about 40 feet above the Wharfe, and about 100 yards from the river. It was flanked by watercourses, and was possibly $2\frac{1}{4}$ acres in area. Ilkley parish church and other buildings partly obliterate the site. The fort had the usual clay rampart on stone bedding, with wooden gateways, and most likely wooden buildings. Even at this early date a civil settlement sprang up outside the fort, and developed later into a considerable town (p. 166).

By planting forts at Ilkley and Elslack Agricola gained complete control of the old route through the Aire Gap. In fact from York to Ilkley, Elslack and Ribchester the Roman road almost coincides with the ancient cross-Yorkshire route.

West of Skipton the York-Ilkley road has been traced to Long Preston and beyond. Here, just east of the churchyard, are the remains of two forts, one within the other. The larger (500 feet square and 6 acres in extent) is slightly rhomboidal, with double ditches except on the south side above the steep slope to the stream. Trenches in the western rampart revealed a thin clay band based on cobbles, and a double-entranced gateway, with post-holes. On the east there were traces of an annexe for traders and camp-followers. Though a fragment of pottery (*circa* A.D. 300) was found near the gateway, nevertheless the general outlay suggests a Flavian, and possibly Agricolan origin. The inner fort was undoubtedly later. It covers 3 acres, consists of a square with rounded corners, cobble-stone rampart foundations enclosed by two large fosses.

West of Long Preston the road may have continued by Settle and Ingleton to the fort of Overborrow in Lancashire. But be that as it may, a Roman road undoubtedly went from near Settle up Ribblesdale, by Horton to Ribblehead, and thence round the north shoulder of Whernside and down the whole length of Dentdale. Dr. Villy, who first discovered this road, formerly known as Craven's Way, says that for long stretches over two miles on the heights it is a plain, heavily built cambered and kerbed road about

20 feet wide, with many flag-covered culverts, some still working.[1]

Craven's Way joined the main Roman road from Ribchester to Carlisle, which can be seen traversing the Forest of Bowland; and north of the Wenning where it was seven yards wide, and paved with broad flat stones resting on a thick bed of pebbly gravel; and in the Sedbergh district just east of the Lune, from Fordholme on the Rawthey to Gibbet Hill where it crossed Carlin Gill on the county boundary.

Branching from this road, or from that which may have run between Overborrow and Long Preston, there proceeded another splendidly defined road from Ingleton to Bainbridge in Wensleydale. The modern road along the Greta valley from Ingleton to Ribblehead coincides with the Roman line, for it essentially conforms to the Roman principles of lay-out. From Ribblehead the road runs somewhat irregularly, owing to the mountainous country, over Cam Fell to a height of 2,000 feet on the south-east side of Wether Fell. Thence the Old Cam High Road holds a straight course for four miles downhill to the Bainbridge fort. This road intersected Craven's Way near Ribblehead.

The Bainbridge fort stands on a hog-backed mound of boulder-clay between the junction of the Bain with the Ure, and its plan can still be traced (Fig. 22). Recent excavations show that it was probably occupied throughout Roman times. The earliest fort consisted of a clay rampart about 20 feet wide, laid on cobbles, and provided with a wood parapet and gateways. These features may very well be of Agricolan date.

A Roman road has been confirmed for a mile to the south of the fort, apparently aiming for Buckden in Wharfedale. Another road traversed Wensleydale westwards to Middleham (where Roman remains have occurred), but its exact line is uncertain. A third road is said to have gone north-eastwards over Askrigg Common to Low Rowe in Swaledale, and thence over the Fells and across Arken-

[1] *B.R.A.C.*, ix, 1929.

garthdale to fall into the main Roman road between the forts of Bowes and Greta Bridge. Its Roman origin has not yet been established.

That Agricola advanced northwards up the Vale of York is unquestionable, for this was the easiest line of march into Scotland. Haverfield considered it virtually certain that he built the Roman road from York to Corbridge-on-Tyne, and thence to Newstead-on-Tweed and Inveresk outside Edinburgh. From York this road ran in a north-westerly direction to Whixley, where it fell into the older Rudgate which, as we have seen, went to Aldborough. Northwards from Aldborough the road called Leeming Lane, still a great modern highway, pursues an unswerving course to Catterick where, at Thornborough on the south bank of the Swale, stood the Roman station Cataractonium, the history of which has not yet been investigated, but the Agricolan foundation of which may confidently be anticipated. From Cataractonium the road, here known as High or Watling Street, runs almost due north to the Tees, over which it was carried by a bridge some of whose foundation stones have been observed. The crossing was defended by a powerful fort at Piercebridge on the Durham side of the river. Leeming Lane and Watling Street constitute the finest continuous Roman road in the county. They were paved with large cobbles, many of which can be seen in old buildings, walls and yards alongside them.[1]

At Scots Corner the road branched to the north-west, over the Stainmore Pass to Carlisle. Near the corner the ridge is 8 yards wide, and 5 feet high in places. The modern road runs along the ridge to Greta Bridge where, in the field behind the Morritt Arms, stands a Roman fort (190 by 130 yards) between the junction of Tutta Beck and the Greta. From this fort the road climbs steadily westwards to the county boundary on Stainmore Pass. The modern highway closely follows the Roman, which in its turn is the successor of the old prehistoric route over the Pass (p. 67). At Bowes (975 feet) there is another Roman

[1] *Arch. J.*, vi, 213, 334.

fort, which, like that at Greta Bridge, has not been explored. Both may be of Agricolan origin.

At Rey Cross on the county boundary the road intersects a large camp, which stands at an elevation of 1,468 feet, and covers 20 acres. Each side is 300 feet long, and broken by numerous entrances, protected on the outside by isolated mounds or tituli. There are signs of a ditch, and the ramparts are of limestone. The size of the camp shows that it must have housed a legion. Its exact date is unknown, though its position and temporary character suggest that it preceded the permanent forts of Bowes and Brough-under-Stainmore in Westmorland.

The roads and forts which we have described were disposed so as to encircle the Pennine block between the Stainmore Pass and the Aire Gap, as well as to command the routes along those lines and the Vale of York. The forts were situated so as to command every dale together with their approaches, including the rivers.

It is quite possible that the Roman stations at Doncaster, Castleford and Tadcaster are of Flavian date, but of this we cannot be sure, as next to nothing is known of their history, and very little of their archaeology. The road from Lincoln to Doncaster, and thence to Castleford, Tadcaster and York, was planned to avoid the Humber crossing, which the Lincoln-Brough-York road entailed.

We do not know when the road from Brough to York was built, but it must have been early. It branched from the Brough-Malton road near South Newbald and ran thence as Humber Street to Market Weighton, Barmby Moor (15 feet wide, and made of concrete 1 foot thick), over the Derwent at Kexby, and so to York.

From near Barmby another road went north-westwards to Stamford Bridge on the Derwent, where it met Garrowby Street, the Roman road which ran eastwards from York along the morainic ridge, and thence over the Wolds in the direction of Bridlington. The map clearly shows that Garrowby Street is a continuation of the Ribchester-Elslack-Ilkley-Adel-Tadcaster-York road, which throughout its course clings closely to our old cross-Yorkshire route (p. 69).

Mook Street branched from Garrowby Street, about 1½ miles from Stamford Bridge, and fell into the Brough-Malton road on the high ground north of Thornethorpe.

From Stamford Bridge ran an important road northwards along the eastern margin of the Vale of York. Its course can be traced by lengths of modern road and parish boundaries in a curve via Sand Hutton, Flaxton and Stillington to Easingwold. Thence it seems to coincide with the modern highway to Thirsk, north of which it passed through Thornton-le-Street (Roman remains), two miles west of Northallerton (Roman remains) to the Tees at Middleton-one-Row, and through Durham to Chester-le-Street and Hadrian's Wall at Newcastle. This part of its course is made up of lanes, parish boundaries, hedgerows and the like. The ridge can be seen at Hallikeld Bridge, east of Brompton near Northallerton.

This road, more or less parallel to the York-Piercebridge road, offered an alternative route to the Wall, but its date of construction is not known. It is unusual in not being fortified, unless, indeed, forts await discovery. Perhaps Thornton-le-Street was a fort. There are signs that a road from Aldborough joined it at Thornton-le-Street—a suggestive northward prolongation of Riknild Street. The small station at Northallerton seems to have stood on a cross-road to Catterick. Another road, the Malton Street, certainly led from Aldborough to Malton. Its course is not clearly traceable, but Roman remains have occurred at intervals.

Returning from this brief survey of our undated Roman roads to the period under discussion, we have next to note that Agricola, after subjugating the natives, then proceeded to Romanize them ; so that, forsaking their own mode of life, they gradually adopted that of their conquerors. For instance, Roman influence percolated amongst the villagers of Grassington, where we find datable pottery, and what is said to be a Dacian sword.

To what extent the Romanization spread at this time

we have no evidence. In 83, one Demetrius of Tarsus, a grammarian, was teaching in Britain, as Plutarch tells us in his tract "On the Cessation of Oracles". His name occurs on two small silver-gilt bronze tablets, found at York. They were punctured with two inscriptions in Greek capitals, which read as follows :—(1) The scribe Demetrius to the gods of the Imperial Praetorium ; (2) Demetrius to Oceanus and Tethys. Haverfield says that Plutarch's Demetrius can be confidently identified with the York Demetrius.

At this time the West Yorkshire lead was being mined. Two "pigs" found in 1734 on Hayshaw Moor between Pateley Bridge and Ilkley were inscribed IMP. CAES. DOMITIANO AVG. COS. VII, and the side of one BRIG. (Briganticum).[1] The seventh consulship of Domitian fell in 81, when Agricola was still in Britain.

The occurrence of these pigs points to the existence of a road from Ilkley to Pateley Bridge, where at Castlesteads there formerly stood a rectangular Roman station. Leslie Armstrong informs us that Roman pottery was found there.

The lead was mined at Greenhow Hill, between Pateley Bridge and Grassington, and the old workings can still be seen. A third pig, bearing Trajan's name, dated 98, comes from this area. By Hadrian's time the Swaledale lead was being worked, as is testified by a pig found at the Hurst Mines, and inscribed ADRIAN (117–38).

Derbyshire lead was imported into Yorkshire. In 1700 a pig inscribed BR. EX. ARG.[2] was found at Brough-on-Humber, and another from South Cave, now in the Hull Museum, is stamped C. IVL. PROTI. BRIT. : LVT. EX. ARG. : (Property) of C. Julius Protus, British (lead) from Lutudarum (in Derbyshire), silver extracted.

An analysis of pigs not stamped 'exargenta' shows that they had nevertheless been desilverised. The Yorkshire pigs bear the Emperor's name, as the state held all mineral rights. In Derbyshire, however, private persons, chiefly Greek freedmen (Protus is a name of Greek origin), held mineral leases.

[1] *C.I.L.*, 1207. [2] *C.I.L.*, 1217.

II

In 85 or 86 Agricola's governorship ended, and he returned to Rome, where, if we can believe the insinuation of Tacitus, he was poisoned by Domitian. About the same time a legion, the II Adjutrix, was recalled to the Danube. Seizing their opportunity the Brigantes revolted under King Arviragus, as Juvenal mentions in his " Satires ". How this revolt affected Yorkshire we cannot say. Domitian was assassinated in 96 ; and after Nerva's brief reign (96–98) Trajan became emperor for about twenty years (98–117).

Under Trajan, the Flavian forts began to be reconstructed in stone, work that continued under his successor Hadrian (117–138). It was undertaken to strengthen and consolidate the frontier region. To distinguish between Trajanic and Hadrianic work is not always possible. At Malton the earlier ditch was filled, the rampart cut back, in order to erect a stone wall in front of which two great ditches were dug—work that seems to be mainly Trajanic. At Castleshaw a diminutive fort (160 × 190 feet) with a turf rampart and at least one stone building was erected inside the Flavian fort. Its occupation may be dated 100–120. At Slack the internal buildings only were partially reconstructed in stone, and the baths enlarged. Tiles stamped COH. IIII. BRE. found in both forts record the garrison as the IV Cohort of the Breuci from the Roman province of Pannonia between the rivers Drave and Save, in what is now north-west Jugo-Slavia. The tile-kilns were discovered in 1590 at Grimscar, a few miles northeast of Slack, and are dated about 104. A tile stamp of the IX Legion is also recorded from Slack. Other Yorkshire forts were no doubt strengthened during Trajan's reign, but the evidence is not positive.

The best-preserved and most striking remains of the Trajanic period are the four camps situated on the exposed, waterless brink of the Tabular Hills at Cawthorn, four miles north of Pickering (Fig. 23). They have been thoroughly explored by the Yorkshire Archaeological

Society, with the following results, as summarised by Richmond who carried out most of the work :

A and C were erected first. This is shown by the way in which D cuts into C and B into A. Further, the presence of low turf mounds—the foundations of tents or huts—and cooking-ovens in C show that it was occupied by troops for a time. A revealed no traces of contemporary occupation, and has therefore been regarded as an exercise camp for the troops quartered in C.

A similar relationship holds between B and D. D, which

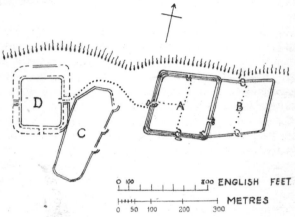

FIG. 23.—PLAN OF ROMAN CAMPS, CAWTHORN, N.R.

has incomplete double ditches outside a large turf rampart, contained no trace of occupation. From it a gravel-road, curving round C, led through A to the west gate of B. B contained Trajanic potsherds, turf-mounds and stone-ovens which prove its occupation by troops. Outside B and within A a turf tribunal, ovens, and a latrine ditch were proved to be the work of B's troops, because they encroached on the defences of A. When exercising, B's troops used camp D.

The occupation camps B and C consist of a single turf rampart and outer ditch with gateways protected by curved rampart extensions or *claviculae*. Few objects were found, a circumstance bespeaking a brief occupation.

We think it not unlikely that the troops encamped at Cawthorn were engaged in constructing the road known as Wade's Causeway or the Old Wife's Trod, which traverses the moors in a north-easterly direction from the camps. Its exact relationship to the camps has not yet been unravelled. It appears to have run from York or Stamford Bridge, over the Howardian Hills, on the heights of which the pavement has been observed south of Appleton-le-Street. At this village it crossed the road between Malton and Aldborough. Thence it struck across the Vale of Pickering by the low hills of Barugh and Riseborough (Roman pottery) to Cawthorn where, at the beginning of last century, it could be seen in the village. On the moors north of the camps its course is easily traceable. A mile and a half of it, on Wheeldale Moor, has been uncovered, revealing a pavement of flat slabs resting on a layer of gravel or rubbish. Originally gravel or earth filled up the spaces between the slabs, which were often kept in position by flat stones set on edge along the sides of the road. Culverts and side gutters can be seen. It is from 16 to 17 feet wide, and raised well above the surface.

On the west side of Goathland Dale, owing to the hilly country, the road is winding. On Lease Rigg, above Grosmont, there formerly stood a rhomboidal camp, similar to B at Cawthorn, and a sure proof that the road and camps are contemporaneous. At Grosmont the road crossed the Esk, beyond which its course is obscure. It seems to have been aiming for Eskmouth, the only considerable river-mouth between the Tees and the Humber. Traces of Roman occupation have been found at Whitby.

In Trajan's reign Eboracum became a stone-walled fortress of considerably more than 53 acres, with stone towers and gateways. The walling has been traced along the outer margin of the Flavian rampart on the north-east and south-east sides. On the other sides the fortress

PLATE V

ROMAN INSCRIPTION AT BOWES, N.R.
Found in 1929

DEDICATION STONE OF THE TEMPLE OF SERAPIS, EBORACUM
Found in Friar's Garden, York, 1770
Yorkshire Museum

seems to have gone beyond the present wall which is of
fourth-century date. At a depth of 28 feet in King's
Square close to the south-east gate the following imperfect
inscription was found :

iMP · CAESAR · divi
nERVAE · FIL · Nerva tra
ia NVS · AVG · GERm · dac ·
pONTIFEX · MAXIMVs tribun ·
poTESTATIS · XII · IMP · Vi p.p.
pER · LEG · VIIII · HIsp · [1]

The letters, 6 to $3\frac{1}{4}$ inches long, are beautifully cut. The
complete stone may have measured $7\frac{1}{2}$ by $3\frac{1}{2}$ feet. The
lost letters are in small type. The inscription reads :—
The Emperor Caesar Nerva Trajan, son of the deified
Nerva, Augustus, Germanicus, Dacicus, Chief Pontiff,
invested the twelfth time with Tribunician Power, saluted
Imperator the sixth time, Father of his Country, had this
erected by the IX Legion Hispana.

This record commemorates an important public building
—perhaps the south-east wall and gateway—over which
it may have been placed. It dates from 110.

Other IX Legion inscriptions have been found at York,
amongst them the memorial stone of L. Duccius Rufinus,
of the Voltinian tribe of Vienna (Gaul), aged 28, a signifer,
or standard-bearer of the IX Legion (Plate IV). His
effigy shows him with the signum in his right hand. This
monument was found in Micklegate, a curved street which
joins another, Trinity Lane, a lay-out suggesting that they
mark the site of an amphitheatre, that necessary adjunct
to every important Roman station.

From the Mount there comes an altar dedicated to the
woodland god, Silvanus, by L. Celerinius Vitalis, a
cornicularius (or orderly-room clerk) of the IX Legion.

At the Mount Villas there was also a tomb made
of tiles stamped LEG. IX. HISP. In this type of
tomb cremated ashes were often placed in earthenware
urns.

[1] *C.I.L.*, 241.

This tomb is one of many that have been found on or near the Mount, which is on the line of the Tadcaster road, by which there was a Roman cemetery. According to custom, the tombs may have extended along either side of the road for miles, for at Askham Richard church, 4 to 5 miles from York, there is a massive sarcophagus. The cemetery also extended north-westwards to where the railway station now stands. Other cemeteries lay between Bootham and the Ouse, the Ouse and Fosse, and the north-east wall and Fosse (Fig. 27).

Trajan's beneficent reign ended in 117. Soon after the accession of Hadrian the IX Legion was annihilated. The disaster probably happened during a Caledonian revolt, aided and abetted by the Brigantes. To crush this revolt Hadrian came over to Britain, and the VI Legion was despatched from the Lower Rhine. Replacing the unhappy IX it was stationed at Eboracum for nearly three centuries. It will be convenient, therefore, to survey its inscriptions here.

The legion appears to have been founded between 44 B.C. and A.D. 14. For distinguished service in Spain the Emperor Augustus entitled it " Victrix ", victorious. From about A.D. 70 to 120 it was located on the Rhine, and for its services in Gaul it received the titles of " Pia ", loyal, and " Fidelis ", faithful.

Tiles stamped LEG. VI are numerous at York. Three tombs built of these tiles have been found, one of which enclosed eight or ten glass vessels. At Dalton Parlours, near Collingham on the Wharfe, the flue-tiles of a hypocaust or heating-chamber of a villa bore the legionary stamp. This villa was discovered in 1854, and a tessellated pavement with the head of Medusa or Gorgon can be seen in the Yorkshire Museum.

The legion's tilery was probably on the site of the modern brickyard at New Earswick. Here have been found the remains of a fossed wall, large quantities of coarse bowls, dishes, jugs, flagons, jars, amphorae, and mortaria ; Samian, Rhenish, and Castor ware ; flanged roofing-tiles, bricks (one with the legionary stamp),querns, etc. It dates from the second and lasts well into the fourth century.

A massive stone coffin found in the Castle Yard, York, bears this inscription :

```
                    D · M ·
         AVR · SVPERO · CENT
      LEG · VI · QVI · VIXIT · ANIS
   XXXVIII · M · IIII · D · XIII · AVRE
      LIA · CENSORINA · COIVNX
         MEMORIAM  POSSVIT ¹
```

"To the Gods of the Underworld (dis manibus). To Aurelius Superus, a centurion of the VI Legion who lived 38 years, 4 months, and 13 days, Aurelia Censorina, his wife, erected this memorial."

The skull of Aurelius Superus has been preserved in the Yorkshire Museum.

The Mount has also disclosed a memorial to the wife, Flavia Augustina, aged 39 years, 7 months, 11 days ; the son, Augustinus, aged 1 year 3 days ; and the daughter, aged 1 year, 9 months, and 15 days, of C. Acrisius, a soldier of the VI Legion Victorious. Carved on the stone are the figures of husband and wife, and the two children. The words "et sibi" show that the memorial was also erected to himself.[2]

Another and a better-known coffin inscription found near the railway bridge in Holgate Lane runs thus :

```
      D · M · SIMPLICIAE · FLORENTINE ·
         ANIME · INNOCENTISSIME ·
      QVE · VIXIT · MENSES · DECEM ·
   FELICIVS · SIMPLEX · PATER · FECIT ·
               LEG · VI · V · ³
```

"To Simplicia Florentina, a most innocent soul, who lived 10 months, Felicius Simplex, her father, of the VI Legion Victorious, erected this."

We now turn from tombstones to dedicatory altars and tablets, which throw a great light upon the religion of the

---

¹ *C.I.L.*, 246. ² *C.I.L.*, 245. ³ *C.I.L.*, 247.

legionaries. The following inscription was found in Tanner Row near the Mount :

DEO · SANCTO ·
SERAPI ·
TEMPLVM · ASO
LO · FECIT ·
CL · HIERONY
MIANVS · LEG ·
LEG · VI · VICT · [1]   [Plate V.]

" To the Holy God Serapis, Claudius Hieronymianus, Legate of the VI Legion Victorious, erected this temple himself."   [Early third century.]

Serapis is the Greek rendering of Osiris-Apis, the bull-god of Memphis.   The Serapis cult was an oriental salvationist religion like Mithraism and Christianity.

Where Tanner Row joins Railway Street, the bases of twelve columns (3 feet in diameter) were uncovered.   They are in all likelihood the remains of a temple, though whether that erected by the Legate, or another devoted to Jupiter, we cannot say.

Near St. Martin's Church in Micklegate was found the celebrated Mithraic tablet.   Mithras is in the act of slaying the bull, a dog leaps at its breast.   Torch-bearers stand on either side, and figures at the base depict the devotee's initiation, purification, and translation to the spirit world. Mithras, symbolised by the sun, overcomes evil (the bull). Originally Persian, the Mithraic faith became widespread throughout the Roman world, and at one time proved a serious rival to Christianity.   Its mysterious rites were celebrated in caves (one has been found near Housesteads —Borcovicum—on Hadrian's Wall).   It was essentially the religion of the Roman army, as Kipling realises in his " Song to Mithras " which begins :

" Mithras, God of the Morning, our trumpets awaken the Wall ;
Rome is above the nations, but Thou art over all."

We may here note that inscriptions to Hercules, and to the Divinity of the Emperors found near the junction of

[1] *C.I.L.*, 240.

Ousegate and Fossgate point to the existence there of temples to those deities. Spartianus also mentions a temple of Bellona at Eboracum, the site of which is unknown. It no doubt stood outside the fortress walls, where the others, together with the cemeteries, were also situated.

The worship of the Three Mother Goddesses, or Deae Matrae also prevailed, as testified by the following altar inscription from Micklegate :

MAT · AF · ITA · GA·
M · MINV · MVDE ·
MIL · LEG · VI · VIC ·
GVBER · LEG · VI ·
V · S · L · L · M · [1]

" To the Mothers of Africa, Italy and Gaul, M. Minucius Mudenus, soldier of the VI Legion Victorious, to the Guardians of the VI Legion, joyfully, willingly and faithfully kept his vow " (*Votum solvit laetus libens merito*).

Two other altars to the Mother Goddesses have been found in York ; inscribed altars at Doncaster [2] and Aldborough [3] ; an uninscribed one at Adel. The home of this cult appears to have been in the Mediterranean region whence the legionaries carried it into Britain and Germany. But this worship, as we have seen, goes back far into the past ; being ultimately derivable from the Earth-Mother or Mothers of the Bronze Age, already represented in Yorkshire by the three chalk " drums " of Folkton, the stone triangles, and many standing stones. The cult persisted into the Middle Ages, and the three witches in Macbeth express its final degeneration.

Inscriptions of the VI Legion are numerous on the Wall, which they built with the assistance of other legions, notably the II Augusta, who were moved from the fortress at Caerleon-on-Usk. The name of this legion is to be seen on the tombstone of a tesserarius, a soldier in charge of the centurial pass-words. It was found at Ilkley.[4]

---

[1] *C.I.L.*, 238.   [2] *C.I.L.*, 198.   [3] *C.I.L.*, 260.
    [4] *Y.A.J.*, xxviii, 315.

An altar found on the site of the Roman baths, now the L.N.E.R. station, reads :

DEAE
FORTVNAE
SOSIA
IVNCINA
Q · ANTONI
ISAVRICI
LEG · AVG · [1]

" To the Goddess Fortune Sosia Juncina (wife) of Q. Antonius Isauricus, legate of Augustus (i.e. governor of Britain)."

This is the only known reference to this legate.

Similar dedications often occur on bath-sites, no doubt because games of chance were played there.

Another altar was found in the bath-house at Slack, with the following dedication :

FORTVNAE
SACRVM
C · ANTO · MODES
Ɔ · LEG · VI · VIC · P · F·
V · S · L · M · [2]

" Sacred to Fortune : Caius Antonius Modestus, a centurion of the VI Legion Victorious, Loyal and Faithful, willingly fulfilled his vow " (Ɔ stands for centurion.)

Another legionary inscription in Durham Cathedral Library was found on a Roman site near Castle Hills, Northallerton, when the railway was constructed in 1838. It reads :

INSTANTE
FL · HYGIN ·
LEG · VI · V ·

and means either " Erected under the supervision of Flavius Hyginus, of the VI Legion Victorious ", or " Erected by the VI Legion Victorious, under the supervision of F. H." This record does not necessarily mean that the

[1] *C.I.L.*, 233.   [2] *C.I.L.*, 199.

whole legion was employed at Northallerton, but that a detachment was sent from York, probably to build a small fort, as indicated by the remains of stone-walling.

In Hadrian's reign the forts of Slack and Castleshaw were abandoned. This event probably took place about 125, the date assigned to the altar from Slack, just described. Their garrisons were either engaged on the Wall —an inscription of the IV Cohort of the Breuci has been found at Ebchester in Durham [1]—or in constructing the great Roman road from Manchester to Ilkley, over Blackstone Edge. This road replaced the earlier Slack-Castleshaw road laid down by Agricola, possibly because it traversed fewer long, steep hills. On Blackstone Edge the pavement can be seen as it was in Roman times. It is bounded by large stone kerbs, 16 feet apart, deeply embedded in the ground. A series of large slabs runs down the middle. On the steepest slope they have been worn into a deep hollow by skid-pans.

The Blackstone Edge road ran to Ilkley, crossing the Calder near Sowerby, and the Aire near Keighley, where it intersected another that ran from Elslack in the direction of Castleford. Between the Edge and Sowerby it sent off a branch via Greetland—probably the site of a fort—to join the Slack-York road near Rastrick (see map).

This road indicates the growing importance of Ilkley. Its Flavian fortress was probably destroyed at the same time as the IX Legion. A stone rampart wall and stone guard-chambers were erected by the middle of the second century, possibly under Hadrian or Antoninus Pius. The II Cohort of the Lingones, a Gaulish tribe from the district of Langres on the Marne (p. 147), constituted its garrison.

Greta Bridge fort was occupied at this time, as is indicated by Hadrianic coins and pottery fragments of Trajan-Hadrianic date, found recently when the Morritt Arms Hotel was rebuilt. The fort covers about three acres, with double stone-cored ramparts on the south, girded by a ditch, and broken by a gateway 25 feet wide. The east side falls in a double scarp to the Greta, the ditch of the

---

[1] *C.I.L.*, 458, early third century.

west rampart is occupied by a lane, and the hotel and its grounds encroach on the northern defences.

At Bowes an imperfect inscription seen in 1599 by Camden on a large stone used as a communion table, but now lost, contained the names of Hadrian; the imperial legate, S. Julius Severus (about 130); and the IV Cohort of the Frisians or Frisiavones [1] who were no doubt engaged in building work commemorated by the inscription. The fort covered about 3 acres. The stone core of the rampart is best preserved on the south side.

Another instructive record of the Hadrianic period is the military diploma found in 1760 at Stannington, 4 miles west of Sheffield, and now in the British Museum. It originally consisted of a pair of engraved bronze plates joined together, but it is now fragmentary. It was a certificate of discharge from the army, granting civil privileges to the veteran soldier, and citizenship on his wife and children. A copy of the diploma was filed on the wall behind the temple of Minerva at Rome. This was the inscription: "The Emperor Hadrian, son of the deified Trajan, surnamed of Parthia, grandson of the deified Nerva, head of the Sacred College, in the 8th. year of his reign, 3 times Consul, Proconsul, has given to the cavalry and infantry who have served in the 6 wings; 1st. Spanish, the Asturian, the Picentine, Petrian, (and others); and in the 21 cohorts; 1st. Spanish, 1st. Frisiavones, 1st. Hamian archers, 1st. Lunuci, 1st. Vangiones 1,000 strong, 1st. Baetasian, 1st. Dalmatian, 1st. Aquitanian, 1st. Menapian, 1st. Eugerni, Trajan's Ulpian, Roman citizens, 1st. Vardulli, 1st. Batavian, 1st. Tungrian, 2nd. Lingones, 2nd. Asturian, 2nd. Dongones, 2nd. Nervii, 3rd. Bracaraugustan, 3rd. and 6th. Nervii and others, being in Britain under Platorius Nepos, and discharged honourably after 25 years or more of service, the Roman citizenship for themselves, their children and their descendants; also the recognition of their marriage with those who are their wives at the date of this grant, or in the case of the unmarried, any wives

[1] *C.I.L.*, 275. The inscription iiiiF has been emended to ITHR or iiiiB (reucorum), *J.R.S.*, xxii, 56.

PLATE VI

ROMAN MULTANGULAR TOWER, YORK

The South-West Bastion of the Early Fourth-Century Fortress of Eboracum

they may subsequently marry, provided they only have one each. Dated the XVI Kalends of October in the consulship of Gaius Julius Gallus and G. Valerius Severus (124), and addressed to the son of Albanus, of the I Cohort of the Sunuci, Commander Marcus Juncus Claudianus." [1]

This diploma gives a good idea of the cosmopolitan character of the Roman auxiliaries.

In the Hadrianic Age Eboracum finally became what it afterwards remained, the legionary base for the region extending northwards to the frontier Wall. From Eboracum the Wall could be more quickly and easily reached than from Chester, henceforth of secondary military importance. Reinforcements and drafts from the VI Legion could be despatched to any threatened point, or to assist the auxiliaries stationed at the numerous forts defending the Wall. Behind this formidable military zone the peaceful and cultured life of the rest of the province stood secure.

III

Of the age of the four Antonines (138–92) Yorkshire has yielded little evidence. About 140 the Wall of Pius between the Forth and Clyde was constructed to serve as a further check to Caledonian incursions. In 155 the legate Julius Verus crushed a Brigantian revolt, and in 160 the legate Statius Priscus effected their final subjugation.

An inscription seen by Camden and Horsley in a buttress of Ilkley Church and dedicated by Caecilius Lucanus, prefect of the II Cohort of the Lingones, to the third Antonine, Lucius Aelius Verus (161–9), is unique in Britain in that it addresses the Emperor as Jovi dilecti (beloved Jove). [2]

About 160 Claudius Ptolemy, the famous Alexandrian astronomer and geographer, compiled his *Geographical Narration*, a list of over 8,000 places, with their latitudes and longitudes. In the British section he tells us that the Brigantian territory extended from sea to sea, and that amongst i[t]s cities were Cataractonium, Isurium, Olicana (presumably Ilkley), Eboracum and Camunlodunum

[1] *C.I.L.*, 1195.   [2] *C.I.L.*, 209.

(probably Castle Hill, Almondbury). He also names several capes and bays on the coast, of which Abi fluvia ostia, Humber-mouth, alone has been certainly identified. Round one of them, Gabrantvicum Opportunum Sinus, lived the Parisi. The location of their city Petuaria remains unsettled, though it may have been in the Wold area. In his *Syntaxis Mathematicae* (ii) Ptolemy states that the 24th parallel ran through Cataractonium. His are the oldest known literary records relating to Yorkshire.

In 1929 Antonine pottery, wall foundations, quern-stones, animal bones, iron-nails and tile-fragments were found near Bainesse Farm, close to the Roman road, a mile and a half south of Cataractonium. Other discoveries have been made here, including an almost perfect bronze steelyard. In the eighteenth century building foundations and a pair of iron-gates were unearthed, and in digging the foundations for the farmhouse a square arched vault built of bricks stamped BSAR was opened. On the handle of an amphora were these words:

II AVR · HERACLE
PAT · ET · FIL · F · BAR · [1]

Aurelius Heracletus, father and son, were evidently potters, living at some town the contraction for which is Bar. Their trade was extensive, for similar inscriptions have been found at Colchester and Rome.

The vault must have been sepulchral, resembling that which can still be seen at 104, the Mount, York. Its walls are of stone, supporting a brick barrel-roof. A grit sarcophagus, with a blue stone cover, 7 feet long, is sunk into the floor which it almost fills. In it lay a complete skeleton, and alongside it an urn holding cremated bones.[2]

Whether the Bainesse site is that of a villa we cannot say. Of Cataractonium itself what little is known may be summarised here. The fortress measures 240 by 175 yards, or nearly 9 acres. Its east wall, uncovered in 1851, is still visible, restored with its original stones, one or two of which are said to have been inscribed. Fragments of glass,

[1] *C.I.L.*, 1331 (20).   [2] *Arch.*, xvi, 340.

tiles, pottery, amphorae, Samian ware, fibulae, bronze ornaments, coins (including a gold coin of Nero), bronze scale armour, and columns have been found. There were also two stone lions, and an altar to the Deae Syria.[1] In 1620 an altar was found dedicated to Hermes,[2] as the god of roads and footpaths (191).

In the reign of Severus (193–211) the Caledonians devastated northern Britain ; for the governor, Clodius Albinus, who, on the death of the fourth Antonine Commodus (192), had here been proclaimed Emperor, weakened the frontier garrisons by withdrawing troops to Gaul, where he was defeated and slain in the battle of Lugdunum (197). The new governor, L. Virius Lupus (c. 197–200), bought off a threatened Caledonian invasion, and began reconstructive work, of which we have two Yorkshire records. One from Ilkley, seen by Camden, is now lost [3] ; the other, on an altar from Bowes, is at Trinity College, Cambridge.[4] It runs thus :

DEAE · FORTVNAE ·	Deae Fortunae
VIRIVS · LVPVS ·	Virius Lupus
LEG · AVG · PR · PR ·	Legatus Augusti Propraetori
BALINEVM · VI ·	Balineum VI
IGNIS · EXVST	Ignis Exustum
VM · COH · I · THR	Cohors Prima Thracum
ACVM · REST	Restituit
TVIT · CVRAN	Curante
TE · VAL · FRON	Valerio Frontone
TONE · PRAEF ·	Praefecto
EQ · ALAE · VETTO ·	Equitum Alae Vettonum.

It tells us that the baths, destroyed by fire, had been restored by the I Cohort of the Thracians, under Valerius Fronto, praefect of the horse of the Ala Vettonum (from near the mouth of the Rhine, and probably garrisoned at Binchester, in Durham, where other inscriptions have occurred), when Virius Lupus was governor.

This is another of the many Fortune altars from bath sites. The Bowes bath, as usual, lay outside the fort. It was floored with large grooved tiles, and bore traces of destruction by fire, and subsequent reconstruction. An

[1] *C.I.L.*, 272.   [2] *C.I.L.*, 271.   [3] *C.I.L.*, 210.   [4] *C.I.L.*, 273.

aqueduct brought water to the fort from Laverpool, a name which still retains that of the station, Lavatrae. Samian and other pottery, sandals, coins of Nero, Vespasian, Faustina, Severus, and the later Empire, gold and brass medals of Nero and Antoninus Pius are recorded from Bowes.

In 205 the Caledonians broke through Hadrian's Wall, seriously damaging it. Eboracum, too, suffered heavily, and recent excavations have revealed evidences of rebuilding in Severus' reign. The governor, L. Alfenus Senecio, unable to cope with the crisis, appealed to the Emperor, who, despite his three-score years, came to Britain, established his headquarters at York, and invaded Scotland. Of this phase we have two inscriptions from Bainbridge, others from Greta Bridge and Bowes, all bearing the name of Senecio and recording reconstruction or building-work between 205–10. Three are dedicated to Severus and his two sons, M. Aurelius Bassianus Antoninus V (Caracalla) and P. Septimius Geta Antoninus VI. Geta's name is obliterated, in accordance with the instructions of Caracalla who murdered him in 211, after the death of Severus.

One Bainbridge inscription records the construction of a vallum with an " arm " formed of rubble by the VI Cohort of the Nervians, and a legionary detachment under the supervision of L. Vispius.[1] The second inscription is lost.[2] In the Greta Bridge inscription [3] Geta's name can still be made out in spite of the erasure. It was found near the north gateway in 1793, and has been built into the north garden wall of Windlestone House.

The Bowes inscription (Plate V), now in the church, was found in the Vicarage Garden in 1929. Nearly 6 feet long and 3 feet wide, it reads :

IMPP · CAESS · L · SEPTIM ·
SEVERO · PIO · PERTINACI ·
ARAB · ADIAB · PART · MAXI ·
ET · M · AVR · ANTON · PIO · AVGG ·
/ / / / / / / / / / / /   IVS ·
SV · · ALFENI · SENECIONIS · LEG ·
AVGG · PR · PR · COH · I · THRAC · EQ ·

---

[1] *C.I.L.*, 269.   [2] *C.I.L.*, 270.   [3] *C.I.L.*, 279.

"To the Emperors and Caesars, Lucius Septimius Severus Pius Pertinax, conqueror of Arabia and Adiabene, greatest conqueror of Parthia, and Marcus Aurelius Antoninus Pius Augustus (Geta's name obliterated) this building was erected by order of Lucius Alfenus Senecio, imperial propraetorian legate, by the I Mounted Thracian Cohort."

During the greater part of the second century there seems to have been little military occupation at Malton, though the gateways may have been rebuilt and strengthened, and massive roadways laid down under Severus, or possibly Constantius Chlorus (c. 296–306). In 1753 an inscription found in the Pye Pits near the Castle Lodge outside the fort to the north-west reads:

D · M ·
AVR · MA
CRINVS · EX
EQ · SING · AVG [1] (equiti singulari augusti).

"To Aurelius Macrinus of the Imperial Horse."

As a reward for its services, Severus bestowed the title of Severianus on the VI Legion, as tiles from York stamped LEG. VI. SEV. testify.

The Antonine Itinerary mainly dates from the reign of Caracalla. This, a traveller's road-book, gives the distances in Roman miles (1,000 paces or $\frac{4}{5}$ English mile) between stations on Roman roads. The British section is subdivided into 15 consecutively numbered *Iters*, five of which pass through Yorkshire. Their importance lies in the fact that they are our sole authority for the Roman names of many stations.

Iter I starts at High Rochester in Northumberland, and follows the road through Corbridge and county Durham to Piercebridge (unnamed), the Yorkshire section reading:

Cataractoni			Catterick
Isurium	XXIIII	MPM	Aldborough
Eburacum, Leg. VI. V.	XVII	,,	York
Derventione	VII	,,	?
Delgovicia	XIII	,,	?
Praetorio	XXV	,,	?

[1] *C.I.L.*, 264.

We find a close agreement in the distance XXIIII mpm. (milia passuum minus, i.e. 1,000 paces less fractions) between Cataractonium, undoubtedly Catterick, and Aldborough ; and in XVII mpm. between Aldborough and York.   Therefore Aldborough is Isurium.

Derventio is usually placed at Stamford Bridge on the Derwent, 7 mpm. from York.   Though an important road junction and a strategic point, as we shall later realise, no remains of a Roman station have been found there. Roman urns and coins have been recorded from Scorby, half-way between Stamford and Kexby, where the York-Brough road crossed the Derwent.   If Malton on the Derwent was Derventio, then the distance must be increased to XVII mpm.   It is conceivable that X has been accidentally omitted by the scribes.   Delgovicia may have been near the site of a Roman cemetery and other signs of occupation between Fimber and Wetwang, XIII mpm. from Stamford or Malton.   Praetorium seems to have been the governor's summer residence, somewhere in East Yorkshire.

Iters V and VIII contain the following items :

V		
Dano		Doncaster
Legeolio	XVI mpm.	Castleford
Eburaco	XXI	York
Isubrigantum	XVII	Aldborough
Cataractone	XXIIII	Catterick
Levatris	XVIII	Bowes

VIII		
Eburaco		
Lagecio	XXI	Castleford
Dano	XVI	Doncaster

Note the spelling of Legiolium and the name Isubrigantum, the only record showing that this station was the tribal and cantonal city of the Brigantes.

Iter II ran from Birrens near Middlebie in Scotland via Carlisle, York, Chester, Wroxeter, London to Richborough in Kent.   Here is the Yorkshire section :

Lavatris		Bowes
Cataractone	XVI	Catterick
Isurium	XXIIII	Aldborough
Eburacum	XVII	York
Calcaria	VIII	?
Camboduno	XX	?
Mamucio	XVIII	Manchester

Calcaria is usually equated with Tadcaster, but as Newton Kyme fort is also VIII mpm. from York it may not be so. Both stand on the Magnesian Limestone, hence the name Calcaria could be applied to either.

Cambodunum is still a puzzle. Horsley suggested that if it was XXX mpm. from Calcaria and XXIII from Manchester, the station would be at Greetland in the Calder valley. Here, above a large double bend in the river and on an irregular spur, features which correspond with the meaning of Cambodunum, crooked hill, an altar now in Trinity College was found in 1597.

Front	*Side*
D · VICT · BRIG ·	ANTONINO ·
ET · NVM · AVGG ·	II · ET · GETA ·
T · AVR · AVRELIAN	COS ·
VS · D · D · PRO · SE ·	
ET · SVIS · S · MAC · [1]	

" To the Goddess of Victory of the Brigantian land, and to the Divinity of the Emperors, Titus Aurelius Aurelianus offers this gift without blemish on behalf of himself and his family."

The side reads, " In the second consulship of Antoninus and the first of Geta." This altar dates from 205, and may come from the site of a fort.

At Longwood in the same neighbourhood there occurred an altar dedicated to Brigantia and the Divinity of the Emperor by Titus Aurelius Quintus at his own expense.

DEO ·
BREGANTI ·
ET · N · AVG ·
T · AVR · QVINTVS
D · D · P · ET · S · S ·

---

[1] *C.I.L.*, 200.

It probably comes from a small temple of a type frequent in the countryside, and dates from after the middle of the second century (Fig. 24). It reflects the fusion of native and Roman ideas then taking place. Altars to Brigantia have also been found at Adel [1] and Castleford.[2]

IV

From the death of Severus until the close of the third century Yorkshire and the frontier generally seem to have been more peaceful. The Romanization of the county must have progressed considerably, attaining its maximum development under Constantine the Great (306–37).

For the year 237 we have the first datable record of York as a colonia. This occurs upon an altar found at Bordeaux in 1921, dedicated to the protecting goddess Boudiga by Marcus Aurelius Lunaris, Sevir Augustalis of the colonies of Eboracum and Lindum in the province of Lower Britain. This altar he vowed to erect on leaving Eboracum. He fulfilled his vow in the consulship of Perpetuus and Cornelianus (237).

The colonia was a settlement of ex-service men or veterans who were granted lands, and who were liable to be called upon as reserves (p. 146). They settled outside the fortress, chiefly south-west of the Ouse. They were governed by a council of decuriones, drawn from the ordo or upper classes of Eboracum.

In the Yorkshire Museum there is a sarcophagus inscribed:

D · M ·
FLAVI · BELLATORIS · DEC · COL · EBORACEN · VIXIT ·
ANNIS · XXVIIII · MENS · ·

" To Flavius Bellator, Decurion of the Colonia of Eboracum, lived 29 years, .. months."

Between the Ordo and the people were the Seviri Augustales, who were elected by the decuriones, and who promoted the cult of Emperor worship. Such were M. A.

[1] *C.I.L.*, 203. [2] *Arch. J.*, xlix, 191 ; *Y.A.J.*, xxiii, 395–8.

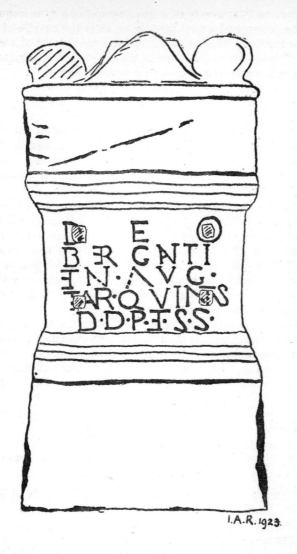

FIG. 24.—ROMAN ALTAR, LONGWOOD, W.R.

Lunaris and M. Verecundus Diogenes. The latter's sarcophagus, inscribed with his name and office, is recorded by
Camden. The massive coffin of his wife, Julia Fortunata,
a native of Sardinia, is in the Yorkshire Museum.

Between 238–44 the VI Legion was granted yet another
honourable title, Gordianus, after the reigning Emperor,
as recorded on a York tile stamp.

The period 249–83 has yielded
eight milestones. Those of the
earlier and later periods have not yet
been discovered, though they must
have been numerous. A milestone
from Duel Cross (Fig. 25), 3 miles
north of Aldborough, is inscribed,
IMP. CAES. MESSIVS. Q. DECIO.
TRA. PIO. FELICI. AVG. XX.
C. S.[1] It dates from the reign of
Decius, 249–51, and records a distance of 20 Roman miles. A fragmentary milestone was found at
Aldborough.[2]

Another Decius milestone comes
from Beancroft Road, Castleford.
In 251–3 it was inverted, and the
names of Gallus and Volusius were
inscribed upon it. Another, recording these two Emperors, occurred at
Greta Bridge.[3]

FIG. 25.—ROMAN MILE-
STONE, DUEL CROSS,
ALDBOROUGH, W.R.

Aldborough Museum

A milestone dug up in Carlton
Street, Castleford, gives the distance
between Eboracum and Legiolium
and is dedicated to Florianus, who reigned for 3 months
in 275.

Another milestone found in 1924 near Vale House, on
the Roman road over Stainmore, inscribed IMP. C. M.
ANNIO. FLORIANO. PF. AVG. was, according to Collingwood, altered with a minimum of re-cutting and no erasure
to IMP. C. M. AVRELIO. PROBO. PF. AVG. Probus

[1] *C.I.L.*, 1180.   [2] *C.I.L.*, 1181.   [3] *C.I.L.*, 1182.

reigned from 276–82, and was succeeded by Carus (282–3) whose name occurs on a milestone found close to the last-named, and inscribed, IMP. C. M. AVR. CARO. PF. AVG. M.[1] No distances are given on these two stones. On a third from the same place the inscription has been erased. An eighth milestone formerly stood at Spital on Stainmore.[2]

By the examination of gateposts and garden-rollers we may discover more milestones.

In the reign of Carus we first hear of the Saxons, who, emerging from the North Sea mists, began to harass the coasts of Britain and Gaul. With the accession of Dio-cletian (284–305), these raids had become so dangerous that a special naval department was instituted with its headquarters at Boulogne, and of which Carausius was the first chief, entitled Count of the Saxon Shore. He at once utilised the fleet to further his own ambitions. Proclaiming himself Emperor of Britain (287), he so successfully defied the central authority, that Diocletian and his co-Emperor Maximianus were reluctantly compelled to acknowledge his position. The coins of Carausius have often been found in Yorkshire, and were specially numerous at Malton.

Carausius was murdered by Allectus in 293 who reigned as Emperor of Britain until defeated and slain by Con-stantius Chlorus, Caesar of the West, in 296.

These internal disturbances led, as usual, to the with-drawal of troops from the frontier. The Malton excavations clearly prove that this fort was abandoned after the death of Carausius, its garrison no doubt serving in the south under Allectus in his war with Chlorus. The granaries were deliberately fired, before the garrison left, as masses of burnt grain prove. Both Carausius and Constantius appear to have conducted campaigns against the Cale-donians ; and we know there was a revolt amongst the Brigantes of the Western Yorkshire dales.[3]

The evidences of this revolt have been brought together

---

[1] These two milestones are in the County Hall, Northallerton.
[2] *C.I.L.*, 1182.
[3] *Y.A.J.*, xxvii, 1923.

by Richmond who dates it from 300–4, but it may have begun rather earlier. The occupation of the Ilkley fort came to an end about the same time as the reign of Carausius, and the Commandant's house was destroyed. A villa at Gargrave, between Elslack and Long Preston, was sacked at the end of the third century, as testified by the absence of later pottery in the burnt and ruined outbuildings. This villa was of the courtyard type; that is, with a yard completely surrounded by buildings, as is not unusual in our farms of to-day.

A large villa was destroyed at Castle Dykes, about halfway between Ripon and West Tanfield. It stood within a rectangular enclosure of double mound and central ditch on three sides, and a marsh or moat on the north side. In 1866 two rooms were found fitted with hypocausts; the tessellated pavements were littered with wall-plaster. These rooms appear to have formed the end of a wing. In 1874 further excavations revealed a villa of the bipartite corridor type, with extensive baths. This villa had been twice destroyed. After the first destruction it was rebuilt on a new plan and enclosed by the said defensive works. Such precautions were unavailing, for the villa was finally sacked, burnt, and its occupants slain. Coins of Gallus, Volusianus, Postumus, and Constantius; and pottery of the close of the third century date the disaster.

During this revolt a Roman iron industry which had developed in and around the Spen valley between Calderdale and Bradford also came to an untimely end. Near Bierley iron slag heaps have been found associated with coins of Diocletian, Carausius, Constantius and Constantine (287–306), but nothing later. Coin hoards from Cleckheaton (218–68, near Roman stone foundations), Thurstonland (222–93, near Roman millstone), Clifton (253–70), Hove Edge (287–305), and Elland Hall Wood (253–93), all prove unsettled conditions at the end of the third century.[1]

The largest hoard, dating from the same period, found

[1] Richmond, *Huddersfield in Roman Times*.

at Methall near Warter, E.R., contained the following coins :

Valerianus	2
Gallienus	202
Salonina	11
Postumus	11
Victorinus	282
Marius	3
Tetricus I	1,087
,, II	233
,, I or II	87
Claudius Gothicus	160
Quintilius	9
Aurelianus	3
(illegible)	452
	2,542

The disturbed conditions at the end of the third century are vividly revealed by the Romano-British remains from

FIG. 26.—ROMAN ' DRAGON ' OR ' S ' BROOCH, NORTON, E.R.
British Museum

the Victoria Cave at Settle, and the Dowkerbottom Cave between Arncliffe and Kilnsey in Wharfedale. According to the coins, they were occupied from about 253 to 340. Associated with them were many fine examples of Romano-British enamelled metal-work, such as S-shaped bronze brooches with a dragon-head at each end (Fig. 26), essentially a northern product ; harp-shaped brooches, head-stud brooches, a common second-century type derived from pre-Roman Brigantian brooches ; bronze plates embossed with Celtic designs ; bronze wire brooches, and penannular brooches of Welsh type.   Other objects include bone spoons with perforated bowls, bone pins, skewers and bodkins, broad iron knives, jet and glass armlets, the ivory boss of a sword-handle, jet and glass beads, finger-rings, spindle-whorls of lead and pot, and fragments of Samian ware.   These caves were either the dens of robbers or places of refuge.

Richmond has suggested that the Elslack and Temple-borough forts were reoccupied in order to crush the revolt. That this was really serious is further shown by evidence that has come to light since his account was published. Miller's York excavations prove that even the legionary fortress was partly destroyed towards the end of the third century.   The catastrophe could only have been brought about by a weakening or withdrawal of the VI Legion by Allectus in his campaign against Chlorus (296).   The natives, possibly exasperated by the exactions of the upstart Emperors of Britain, seized the opportunity thus offered for retaliation.

After defeating Allectus, Chlorus hastened north, quelled the revolt and rebuilt the walls of York, the best-preserved feature of which is the Multangular Tower (Plate VI).   It formed the west bastion, a ten-sided structure 25 feet high, built of rubble faced with Magnesian Limestone ashlar and bonded with bricks.   The foundations stand on a concrete bed laid on oak piles.   Internally the bastion had been divided by a centre wall, and there are indications of two timber floors at 8 feet and $17\frac{1}{2}$ feet above the Roman ground-level.   The bastion is pierced with embrasures, now partly blocked up.

Traces of the south bastion were discovered in 1852 in Feasegate.   The wall joining these two bastions ran par-allel to and 300 to 400 feet from the Ouse for a distance of 468 yards.   The part adjoining the Multangular Tower still remains.   Between 1917 and 1923 a polygonal wall tower was explored half-way between the Tower and Stone-gate.   The foundations of the south-west gate through which the Tadcaster Road entered the fortress along Stonegate have been observed in St. Helen's Square, and wall foundations in New Street between St. Helen's Square and Feasegate (Fig. 27).

The foundations of the north-west wall, 550 yards long, lie under an earthen mound on which stands the existing mediaeval wall from the Multangular Tower to the Deanery

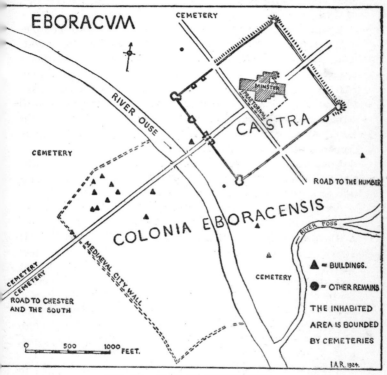

FIG. 27.—PLAN OF ROMAN YORK

Gardens. The mediaeval Bootham Bar occupies the site of the north-west gateway.

As no traces of older south-west and north-west walls have been observed, it is probable that Chlorus erected entirely new walls on these sides. On the north-east and south-east, however, he simply repaired the older walls.

Nothing is visible except near Monk Bar where the exterior face is exposed. The north-east gateway lay further to the north-west than Monk Bar. King's Square, where the Trajan inscription was found, marks the position of the south-east gateway. Here and there turret foundations have been observed. The fortress walls in the fourth century enclosed a space of rather more than 53 acres, presumably smaller than the Trajan-Hadrianic fort.

Constantius Chlorus died at York on July 25, 306. Tradition relates that he was buried under the church, destroyed in 1585, of St. Helen's-on-the-Wall. St. Helen was his wife, and the mother of Constantine the Great, who on the death of his father was proclaimed Caesar of Britain and Gaul at Eboracum. He became Emperor of the West in 307, and at his death in 337 he had been Emperor of both East and West for 14 years.

With the accession of Constantine Yorkshire and the north generally entered on a period of comparative peace and prosperity for nearly half a century. It was the lull before the final storm which tore Britain from the Empire. It will accordingly be convenient to glance briefly at aspects of Roman Yorkshire not included in the foregoing survey.

V

The altars already described give some idea of the varied religious beliefs of Roman Yorkshire. We also have altars to Mars at Greta Bridge,[1] Norton [2] and York ; to Hercules at York,[3] and a statue presumably of this god armed with a club from Nappa in Wensleydale ; to Britannia at York [4] ; to Jove greatest and best, and to the spirits of the household and hospitality, also at York.[5]

There were river deities, as testified by an altar to Verbeia [6] (the Wharfe) at Ilkley, and to Elauna [7] (the Lune) at Greta Bridge.

Christianity had gained a foothold in Yorkshire by the time of Constantine. In 314 Eborius, Bishop of Eboracum,

---

[1] *C.I.L.*, 276–7. [2] *C.I.L.*, 263a. [3] *C.I.L.*, 236. [4] *C.I.L.*, 232.
[5] *C.I.L.*, 237. [6] *C.I.L.*, 208. [7] *C.I.L.*, 278.

PLATE VII

Leeds Museum

In situ
ROMAN MOSAIC PAVEMENTS, ALDBOROUGH, W.R.

attended the Council of Arles. Bishopshill, York, is con-
jectured to have been the site of the Romano-Christian
church. A bone slip found with jet armlets and a beautiful one-handled glass vessel in a woman's coffin at York
bore a pierced Christian invocation, S(or)OR AVE VIVAS
IN DEO (Hail sister! thou art alive in God). Terra-
cotta lamps and a bronze foot-rule from York bear the
Chi-Rho monogram. A bone tablet on the breast of a
skeleton is inscribed, DOMINE VICTOR VINCAS FELIX.

The chief centre of civil life in Yorkshire was Isurium
Brigantum, the now old-world village of Aldborough. Little
is known of its history, though it undoubtedly originated
as a IX Legion camp adjoining Brigantian settlements
and the Devil's Arrows. Long before the end of the second
century, when we first hear of it as Isubrigantum (p. 152),
it had become a flourishing Romano-British town, the
most northerly administrative tribal centre in Britain
(Fig. 28).

The city covered about 60 acres, a little more than one-
sixth the area of Roman London. It was surrounded by
walls built of local red sandstone, the foundations of which,
11 to 16 feet wide and 5 feet high, can still be traced.
They were provided with watch-towers, the base of two
occurring near the south-west angle, whilst the remains
of a bastion have been uncovered at the north-east corner.

Stones belonging to the east and west gates are now in
the Manor garden; those of the north gate, two large
square blocks of millstone grit, remain *in situ*. The road
leading from it was 30 feet wide, and paved with large
cobble-stones.

The inhabitants, who may have numbered about 3,000,
lived in houses built of timber resting on stone foundations.
Two of the corridor type were discovered just north of
the church, and close to the west wall near the south-west
angle. The floors were usually paved with small squares
or tesserae of differently coloured stone and brick to form
tessellated and mosaic pavements. Since the days of
Leland (1534) Aldborough has been famous for its mosaic
pavements. Many have been destroyed; one is buried

under the vicarage, and another under the wooden floor of a cottage near the old Manor House, the site of a corridor pavement not on view to the public. Other pave-

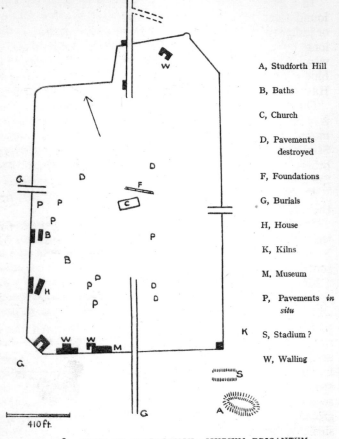

A, Studforth Hill

B, Baths

C, Church

D, Pavements destroyed

F, Foundations

G, Burials

H, House

K, Kilns

M, Museum

P, Pavements *in situ*

S, Stadium ?

W, Walling

410 ft.

FIG. 28.—PLAN OF ALDBOROUGH—ISURIUM BRIGANTUM

ments are preserved in Leeds Museum, Aldborough Museum, and the Manor House. In the garden of the Aldborough Arms there are two square pavements supported by the pillars of a hypocaust or heating chamber.

One shows a panther or leopard under a palm-tree, the second an eight-pointed star surrounded by an elaborate border (Plate VII).

In a garden between the Inn and the Museum are half-foundations of a building formerly considered a basilica or judgment hall, but by Haverfield a villa. It was 52 feet long by 24 wide, with an apsidal end, the pavement of which contains two Greek words meaning " Have pity ", in blue glass, near a figure in long robes which, according to Haverfield, probably represents a muse on Mount Helicon.

Outside the south-east corner are two earthworks. One is a knoll called Studforth Hill, the other an elongated mound known as the Stadium. Some authorities regard Studforth Hill as the remains of a Roman amphitheatre, others as the site of a motte and bailey castle.[1] The Stadium is thought to be part of a Roman race-course.

At the south-west corner is a large Roman quarry, but the carvings on its face are not Roman.

The remains of baths have been located south of the west gate. Cemeteries lay outside the walls alongside the York and Ilkley roads, whilst at the Red Hills near the south-east angle two kilns marked the site of a pottery.

Many small objects have been dug up, such as bone spoons, hairpins, combs, and dice ; jet finger-rings ; plain and ribbed blue, pink, yellow and green glass beads ; polished signet stones ; intagliated carnelian and onyx stones ; gold ear-rings ; silver spoons ; enamelled brooches and other bronzes, tweezers, thimbles, bells, scrapers used in the bath ; iron knives, keys, tongs, shears, ladles, spades and the like. Bee-hive and flat querns can be seen in nearly every garden, showing that most households ground their own flour. Oyster, whelk, cockle and mussel shells occur in profusion, especially near the baths, where they suggest there was an oyster bar. Unimportant inscriptions have been recorded. Samian and other pottery abounds. The coins range from Augustus (23 B.C.–A.D. 14) to Valentinian II (390), those of the third and fourth centuries being most numerous. They indicate a more

[1] *V.C.H.Y.*, ii, 45.

or less continuous occupation until the last decades of the fourth century.

North of Isurium the evidences of civil life and the Romanization of the natives become increasingly rare. Besides the villa at Castle Dykes there was another at Well (pavement in the church). A hypocaust at Middleham in Wensleydale marks the site of the most northerly Roman country-house in Britain. At Swinton near Masham massive Roman sarcophagi have been found, and at Round Hill in Arnagill, six miles west, a hoard of bronze patellae. A similar hoard comes from Stittenham between York and Malton. These vessels were imported, and no doubt represent the stock-in-trade of dealers. At Fremington Hagg near Reeth in Swaledale many Roman bronze articles, and silver-plated fibulae now in the Yorkshire Museum, occurred. Part of a huge hoard of bronze vessels, in the Yorkshire Museum, comes from Knaresborough, and two small vessels inscribed, P. Cipii Polybi, are recorded from Castle Howard.[1]

On Grewelthorpe Moor, ten miles west of Ripon, the body, probably of a Romano-Briton, was found in peat in 1850. It was tanned and dried, and fully clothed in a green cloak, a scarlet garment, yellow stockings and leather sandals. No care was taken to preserve this unique discovery, and the body was interred in Kirby Malzeard churchyard. A sandal and part of the stockings are in the Yorkshire Museum.

Small village sites like that recently discovered at Wetherby on the Wharfe are indicated by pottery, querns and burials. The chief civil settlements, however, flourished outside the fortress walls of York, Ilkley and Malton, where they had developed from the annexes reserved for camp-followers, traders, ex-service men and the like. From these and from the forts themselves innumerable objects have been recovered, of which only a few can be briefly referred to. Ilkley has yielded the fragments of nearly 100 Samian ware vessels of the last

[1] *C.I.L.*, 1293. P. Cipius Polybius, a first-century manufacturer of Campania.

PLATE VIII

ROMAN GLASS VESSELS FOUND IN YORK

The large vessel on the left held the burnt ashes of Corellia, 13 years of age, the daughter of Q. Corellius Fortis

Yorkshire Museum

two decades of the first and almost the whole of the second century; a bronze Silenus mask from the handle of a vessel of Italian workmanship of the first century; an iron spear-head; and a broken bone article like a paper-knife, inscribed Conicilli, a Celtic name.

From York there comes an overwhelming mass of Samian, Castor, and other kinds of pottery; a superb series of glass vessels, chiefly out of coffins, one of which contained the calcined bones of Corellia, 13 years of age, the daughter of Quintus Corellius Fortis.[1] There are numerous small bronze figures of birds, animals, humans; gold, silver, glass and bronze finger-rings; bone, silver, gold and glass pins; bronze compasses and foot-rules; enamelled fibulae and other ornaments of Romano-Celtic type; earthenware ink-pots and bronze pens (styli); mosaic pavements from Micklegate Bar, Tanner Row and Toft Green; coffins of stone, lead and wood, in some of which the body had been imbedded in liquid plaster; bases of glass and Samian vessels used by children in playing hop-scotch; ivory, bone and glass counters; terra-cotta lamps, domestic and funerary, some marked Fortis, a manufacturer of Mutina in N. Italy; earthenware candle-sticks, lead lamp-stands and the like.

Plate IX shows a life-size statue, found in 1880, in the garden of St. Mary's Convent. The stone consists of light-coloured grit, and the statue is one of our finest examples of Romano-British sculpture. It represents a Roman soldier with his helmet, shield and sword. When discovered, it was broken in two or three places, and parts of the right arm and the feet were missing. There was no pedestal nor inscription. The face is said to bear a likeness to that of Geta whose bust is in the Vatican. It will be remembered that Caracalla murdered Geta, and ordered his statues to be removed and broken. We cannot however be certain that this is a statue of Geta, as the dress is not that of the Emperor. It might conceivably be a statue of Mars, for with it were found an altar to Mars, another to the Matres Domesticae,

[1] C.I.L., 250.

and a third was inscribed DEO VETERI. This inscription refers to a Rhineland god whose name was Huiter.

Characteristic of York are jet necklaces, armlets, pendants, rings, beads and hairpins from the coffins of the ladies who wore them. From a sarcophagus found when building the railway station there came the lady's hair with jet pins still thrust into her tresses, the most fascinating treasure of the Yorkshire Museum. Carved jet medallions have occurred, two with Medusa heads, one with the heads of a man and wife ; another of an old lady ; a larger example has three heads which may represent Diocletian, Carausius, and Maximianus. These and jet articles from other sites in Yorkshire and elsewhere prove a considerable traffic with the coast between Peak and Runswick Bay, where the finest Whitby jet could be gathered on the shore. Its abundance in Britain is mentioned by Solinus who wrote about 218.

The civil settlement of Malton stood chiefly on the south bank of the Derwent at Norton, formerly the site of a camp about 100 feet square. Numerous remains have occurred here, especially alongside the roads to Stamford Bridge and across the Wolds. An inscription found in the churchyard in 1814 reads :

FELICITER · SIT
GENIO · LOCI
SERVVLE · VTERE
FELIX · TABERN
AM · AVREFI
CINAM [1]

" Greeting to the Spirit of this place. My servant, good luck to your goldsmith's shop."

This inscription is indicative of the prosperity of a region bestrewn with country houses. Two have recently been excavated at Langton, and fourth-century pottery and coins as late as Valens or Valentinian have been found. At Musley Banks and Rowborough tessellated pavements have been uncovered. Further west at Hovingham, pavements, bath and hypocaust, and coins from Antoninus

[1] *C.I.L.*, 265.

Pius (138–61) to Constantine (337) were discovered in 1745. Still further west at Burton House Farm on the slope of the Howardian Hills near Oulston, a fine corridor mosaic, now in the Yorkshire Museum, 35 feet by 10½ feet, parallel to and on the west side of a series of rooms, occurred. Villas also existed at Harpham near Driffield ; Bishop Burton ; and at Millington, where the foundations of a circular and two oblong buildings, pavements, tiles and a coin hoard occurred. Half a mile to the east was a cemetery of oval shallow graves containing doubled-up skeletons and two Roman vases. Hypocausts are recorded from Langtoft and Etton. Coin hoards and pottery finds still further mark the Romanization of the Wolds and Holderness.

Pottery kilns were established at Norton, Knapton, and above all at Castle Howard. Here there were four kilns, each consisting of three parts :

1. A stokehole about 6 feet across with a ramp opposite the flue openings.

2. A flue passage from the stokehole to the furnace, 1 to 1½ feet wide and 2 feet high, floored with clay or limestone slabs, walled with undressed stones set in clay, and roofed with larger slabs.

3. The furnace pit covered by a clay platform pierced by holes through which the heat and gases passed into the oven in which the pots were fired.

Vessels of many kinds were made, the most common being straight-sided flanged bowls and dishes ; straight-sided dishes ; hammer-head mortaria ; storage jars ; deep wide-mouthed bowls. It appears probable that the kilns were worked from the end of the third or early in the fourth century, with an increasing output up to about 370.

Another large pottery has recently been explored at Pot Hill, Throlam Farm, near Holme-on-Spalding Moor. The ware has a general resemblance to that at Castle Howard, but it has not been found either at York or Malton. It must therefore have supplied other sites, possibly Brough-on-Humber, during the second half of the third century until about 280.

What is known of the Roman stations of Castleford and Doncaster may be noticed here. Castleford stood below the junction of the Aire and Calder, on the high ground occupied by the church and old rectory. Urns, pottery, pavements, inscriptions and coins have occurred.

Doncaster stood on the south bank of the Don on a pre-historic site situated at the first ford above the vast swamps of its lower reaches. Samian and other pottery, coins, and an altar have been recorded. From the Notitia Dignitatum, a late fourth-century [1] list of officials, stations, and garrisons throughout the Empire, we learn that Danum was garrisoned by cavalry from Crispiana in Pannonia (equitum Crispianorum). No inscription confirming this has been discovered in Doncaster, but a tombstone to Egeria Lecta, aged 30, and a child of 3, erected by her husband Antonius of the Pannonian Cohort serving in Britain, was found at All Saints' Church, York.

It is doubtful whether there was ever a fort at Tadcaster, but the Wharfe was bridged there, and a villa has been discovered at Kirkby Wharfe, south of Tadcaster.

To enumerate the many Roman objects found throughout the county is out of the question Attention may be called to a bronze eagle from Keighley; a bronze arm-purse from a barrow on Farndale West Moor ; and a third-century bronze helmet from Guisbrough. We must now turn to the final phases of the Roman occupation.

VI

After the death of Constantine in 337 Britain became increasingly subject to assaults from the Irish, then called Scots, on the west ; the Picts or Caledonians on the north ; and the Saxons on the east. In 343 the Emperor Constans took the field in person against the northern barbarians. He was the last emperor to set foot in York. In 364 Picts, Irish and Saxons invaded Britain. Three years later they

[1] Anachronisms in the British section make it more likely to belong to a period antecedent to the army reforms of Constantine.— *J.R.S.*, xxii, 55.

swept over the greater part of the country—an overwhelming catastrophe which shook Roman Britain to the core. Of its effects in Yorkshire we shall know more when Aldborough, Catterick, Brough and other sites come to be excavated. As the latest coins in one of the Langton villas date from Valens or Valentinian I (364–78), its destruction may be attributed to this invasion.

To retrieve the disaster Valentinian despatched a large army under Theodosius who recovered the north and

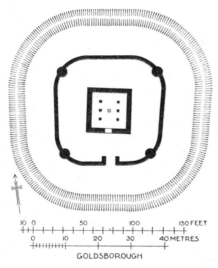

GOLDSBOROUGH

FIG. 29.—ROMAN COASTGUARD FORT, GOLDSBOROUGH, N.R.

reorganised its defences. Exactly what he did to the permanent fortresses we do not know. There is little doubt that he initiated the erection of coast-guard forts between Huntcliff and Filey Brigg, the last military works constructed by the Romans in Britain.

The excavations of W. Hornsby and F. G. Simpson have established their uniform design. The most perfect stands in Goldsborough Pasture, at an altitude of 425 feet, and half a mile from the sea at Kettleness, the south point of Runswick Bay (Fig. 29). The outer wall, 4 feet thick at the base which alone has survived, enclosed an area 105 feet square, with rounded corners strengthened by circular bastions or turrets (10 feet diameter). The south wall was broken by a gateway leading into an open unpaved court-yard about 10 yards wide, surrounding a square central building where massive stone foundations 5½ feet thick had three offsets or steps on the outside. Such strong founda-tions must have supported a heavy wooden tower 90 to 100 feet high, divided into two or three storeys, the lowest floor being held up by strong posts resting in socketed stones. The fort was encircled by a ditch separated from the outer walls by a wide berm. Near the south-east bastion and within the courtyard was an unwalled well 8½ feet deep, in which three human skulls, one that of a handsome woman under 30, the bones of two breeds of oxen and of two kinds of dog, and a small piece of cloth were found. In the south-east corner of the tower there had been an open hearth over which the skeleton of a short thickset man lay face downwards, the left hand, upon which was a bronze ring, behind his back ; the right touching the south wall. Near his feet lay the skeleton of a taller man, also face downwards, and beneath him the skeleton of a large and powerful dog, the head against the man's throat, the paws across his shoulders. Near the feet were two silver coins of Eugenius (392–4) and Honorius (395–423). The only other coin found was a Valentinian.

Other objects were a deer-horn pick, iron knives, jet, bone and bronze finger-rings, bronze bangles, a bronze brooch of twisted strands, pottery spindle-whorls, millstones, and a small granite tablet which appears to have been part of a druggist's equipment. Bones of pigs, oxen, goats, deer, hares, rabbits, small birds and fish, and shells of crabs, mussels, limpets, whelks and periwinkles littered the floor of the central building.

At an altitude of 365 feet on Huntcliff near Saltburn stood a similar fort, more than half of which has fallen into the sea. Between the south gate and the surviving wall of a central building was an unlined well nearly 14 feet deep. The upper part to a depth of 6 feet was filled

PLATE IX

LIFE-SIZE STATUE OF ROMAN SOLDIER
Found at St. Mary's Convent, York, 1880
Yorkshire Museum

with earth, clay and stones with mortar still adherent. In the next 3 feet were smaller stones and pebbles, charred wood, potsherds, many bones of men, women and children, including eleven skulls ; and a coin. Then below a sandstone slab lay three more skulls ; and at the bottom potsherds, two wooden bowls, the oak draw-wheel, a leather sandal, and a yard of brown woollen cloth.

The minor objects resembled those from Goldsborough. The 25 coins ranged as follows :—1 Constantine family (330–342) ; 1 Constantius II (337–361) ; 6 Valentinian I (364–375) ; 6 Valens (364–378) ; 8 Gratian (367–383) ; 1 Valentinian II, 1 Theodosius, 1 Arcadius (388–392).

Potsherds were numerous, mostly belonging to a ware common over the north of England in the late fourth century. Collingwood proposed that it should be called Huntcliff ware. Its colour ranges from black to smoky-reddish or greyish-brown ; it is hard and gritty ; and the chief vessels are peculiar neck-rim jars, jars with oblique rims, and jars with plain recurved rims. It was the development of a pre-Roman ware which was manufactured throughout the Roman occupation, little influenced by Roman styles until its widespread use in the fourth century.

A third fort on Scarborough Castle Hill was almost identical in plan with that at Goldsborough, the east wall alone having been destroyed by coast erosion. It yielded nothing sensational, and its arrangements had been considerably disturbed by pre- and post-Norman Conquest buildings.

A fourth fort on the Carr Naze, north of Filey, was imperfectly excavated in 1857. The remains were similar to those already described. Five symmetrically placed square stones with two off-sets and a socketed top served like those at Goldsborough to hold the stout oak beams —charred remains of which occurred—which supported the lowest floor of the watch-tower. The stones can be seen on Filey Promenade.

A fifth fort stood at Peak, the southern headland of

Robin Hood's Bay. In 1774 the following inscription was found amidst stone foundations :

> JVSTINIANVS P · P ·
> VINDICIANVS
> MASBIERIVPR
> M CASTRVM FECIT
> A · C ·[1]

The third and last lines have not been deciphered ; the rest tells us that Justinianus the Commander and Vindicianus built the fort. Justinian is recorded by Zosimus as having gone to Gaul in 407 with Constantine, a common soldier who had been elected Emperor in 406–7 by the troops in Britain. The name Vindicianus also appears on a massive sarcophagus full of bones found at a depth of 3 feet at East Ness, 8 miles north-west of Malton, and inscribed :

> TITIA PINTA VIXIT ANN XXXVIII
> ET VAL ADIVTORI VIXIT ANN XX
> ET VARIOLO VIXIT ANN XV VAL
> VINDICIANVS CONIVGI ET FILIIS
> FC [2]

" Erected by Valerius Vindicianus to his wife Titia Pinta, aged 38 ; and to his sons Valerius Adjutor, aged 20, and Variolus, aged 15."

The coast-guard forts clearly belong to one system dating from about 370 to 394, and possibly a few years later. Fire or smoke signals from their tall outlook towers spread the news of invading Saxon fleets up and down the coast and to inland garrisons. Such a garrison was undoubtedly stationed at Malton, which was continuously occupied from 300 to 375, as dense masses of Huntcliff ware testify. If Malton was Derventio, then at this time, as we learn from the Notitia Dignitatum, it was garrisoned by local troops known as the Petuarienses, after Petuaria, the chief town of the Parisi of the Wolds (p. 122). The same document also tells that Bowes (Lavatrae) was garrisoned by scouts

[1] *C.I.L.*, 268.   [2] *C.I.L.*, 266.

(exploratores), and that the VI Cohort of the Nervians occupied Virosidum. This may be Bainbridge in Wensleydale, where fourth-century occupation has been found, and where the cohort is mentioned on a third-century inscription (p. 150). Further excavations are needed to ascertain what other Yorkshire forts were occupied in the last half of the fourth century, and to identify other stations named in the Notitia.

The last years of Roman Yorkshire were coming to a close. In 383 Magnus Maximus, a Spaniard, in command in Britain, emulated Clodius Albinus and Carausius. Proclaiming himself Emperor, he depleted the garrisons ; and, at the head of an army thus formed, fought for his title on the Continent until in 388 he was defeated and killed by Theodosius II. The Wall had by then been abandoned, for no coins later than 383 have been found there. Barbarian invasions inevitably followed, and in 388 the province was ravaged. In 395 General Stilicho cleared the province, and reorganised the army.

The distressed state of Yorkshire is revealed by coin-hoards from Catterick (many of late Emperors in bronze vessel) ; Richmond (silver, Constantius to Valentinian and later Emperors) ; Northallerton (late Emperors) ; Whorlton (silver in silver vase, Constantius to Honorius) ; Wilton-in-Cleveland (silver and one gold, Valens to Honorius).

In 402 Stilicho withdrew British troops in order to cope with the pressing Continental situation. Five years later the last usurper, a common soldier, Constantine III, crossed the Channel with all available troops, leaving the country to defend itself as best it could against the three-fold attacks of the Irish, Caledonians and Saxons. Our last glimpse of Roman Yorkshire reveals the overthrow of the coast-guard forts, the firing of their watch-towers, the slaughter of their occupants, the corpses of men, women, children and dogs flung pell-mell into the wells —the handiest of graves, and the inhabitants of the countryside put to the sword.

For Reference : T. N. Dickons, *Roman Yorkshire*, 1899. Gordon Home, *Roman York*, 1924. C. Wellbeloved, *Eburacum*, 1842.

R. G. Collingwood, *Archaeology of Roman Britain*, 1930, and *Roman Britain* (Oxford University Press). F. Haverfield, *The Romanization of Roman Britain*, and *Lectures on Roman Britain*. *B.M. Guide to Roman Britain*, 1926. A. R. Burn, *The Romans in Britain* (an anthology of inscriptions), 1932. T. Codrington, *Roman Roads in Britain*, 1928. Sir G. Macdonald, *Roman Britain*, 1914–28, British Academy Supplementary Papers, vi, 1931.

Also see references mentioned in the Gazetteer.

CHAPTER X

ANGLIAN YORKSHIRE

HISTORICALLY and archaeologically, the century following the separation of Britain from the Roman Empire is a blank. We can only surmise that the Romanized Britons of Yorkshire must have been involved in a more or less chronic war with northern barbarians and Anglian sea-rovers. York, Aldborough, Malton, Ilkley, and other centres of civilized life may have been abandoned or sacked. Whatever was the fate of their inhabitants, we know that the Britons of the Pennines and Eastern Moorlands were, generally speaking, unmolested; for in these areas Anglian remains are scarce, and Celtic or British place-names numerous. To-day, even, Yorkshire dalesmen employ Celtic numerals when counting their sheep: in Cleveland *pethera* is 4 (Welsh, *pedwar*); *pimps* is 5 (Welsh, *pump*; Cornish, *pimp*); *bumpit*, 15 (Welsh, *pymtheg*); *pethera bumpit*, 19 (Welsh, *pedwar ar bymtheg*).

For the sixth century we have both historical and archaeological records, including the *Ecclesiastical History of the English Nation*, by the Venerable Bede, a monk of Jarrow (700). He tells us that the Teutonic immigrants comprised the Saxons, the Jutes and the Angles. The original home of the Angles appears to have been Slesvig, then known as Angel, between the Sle and the Flensborg Fiord. According to Bede, the whole nation migrated to this country, and many of them settled in East Yorkshire where remains of this invasion are abundant.

In early Anglian times the country east of the Pennines and north of the Humber was divided into at least four regions, no doubt based on older, possibly tribal, divisions, for all bore names of British origin. Loidis and

Elmet comprised the regions round Leeds and Sherburn-in-Elmet respectively, but their extent is not precisely known. Deira, perhaps originally restricted to the Wolds and Holderness (p. 4), ultimately included most of Yorkshire, and became the southern province of the Anglian kingdom of Northumbria of which Bernicia beyond the Tees constituted the northern province.

The first recorded king of Deira was Aella (585–8). His daughter married Ethelric, youngest son of Ida, King of Bernicia, who, on the death of his father and father-in-law, became King of the whole of Northumbria. He was succeeded by Ethelfrith (593–617) and by Edwin (617–33). In 625 Edwin married the Kentish princess Ethelburga, who was a Christian, and who brought with her the Roman missionary Paulinus to convert the Angles. Edwin eventually embraced the faith (626–7), and Paulinus, the first Anglian Bishop of York, erected a wooden church on the site of the Minster. In 633 Edwin was defeated and slain by Cadwallon, a British King of Mercia, in the battle of Hatfield near Doncaster. For a time Christianity in Northumbria received a set-back, only to be more firmly re-established by Oswald (died 642), Oswin, King of Deria (644–71), and Oswy, King of Northumbria (651–70). The middle of the seventh century may be therefore taken as the end of the pagan period.

The most frequent pagan remains are cemeteries in which bodies or urns containing cremations were buried in more or less parallel rows just below the surface. Their non-Christian character is proved by the many associated objects for the use of the dead. With the coming of Christianity this age-long custom was discarded. Christian burials are therefore far less informative than pagan.

Nearly all Anglian urns are hand-made, of a grey, brown, or shiny black colour. Some are ornamented with raised arches, ribs or bosses ; and most with indented designs including swastikas, triskeles, wheels, stars, triangles, circles, lines and the like. Small plain vessels, cup or gourd-shaped, usually occurring with inhumations, held food or drink for the use of the dead (Fig. 30).

The continental affinities of our Yorkshire urns have yet to be worked out. Generally speaking, urns from the Anglian districts of England resemble those of the 4th and 5th centuries in Schleswig and Hanover, thus confirming Bede's statement as to the original home of the Angles.

The occurrence of 40 urns and 4 food-vessels at Heworth close to York, 5 urns outside Micklegate Bar, and 6 (in one of which was a bone comb, iron shears, and a silver Roman coin) on the Mount shows that the break, if any, between Romano-British and Anglian York must have been brief. The Angles often wore Roman coins as ornaments. Gold coins of Honorius and Arcadius mounted as pendants were

DRIFFIELD, 5″, 5¼″   GARTON, 5¼″

FIG. 30.—ANGLIAN FOOD-VESSELS, E.R.
Mortimer Museum, Hull

found within half a mile of one another at Kirkby Knowle, N.R.

From the Mount there comes a beautiful fluted glass bowl (5½″ wide) with a flat base, dating from the sixth century, and imported from the Meuse-Rhine region, the centre of manufacture.

One of five urns from a cemetery at Broughton near Malton held a bone needle and comb. At Sancton near Market Weighton more than two dozen urns and vessels occurred in a field near the church. In a few there were objects, some burnt, such as amber and glass beads, bone combs and spindle-whorls, bronze pins, tweezers, clasps, iron shears, knives, and a sickle-like tool. Amongst many bronze brooches there was one disk-shaped, one penannular and torc-like, nine annular,—a common Yorkshire type—and two long brooches, one dating from about 550 and the other from the early part of the 6th century.

The evolution of the long brooches, typical Anglian ornaments, from those of South Russia, whence the Goths brought them to Scandinavia and Germany, cannot be described here. In Germany the foot of the brooch developed into a simple horse-head design; two such brooches have been found at Rudston and date from the late 5th century.

Another Anglian cemetery was situated on Hob Hill, at Saltburn. It contained at least 35 urns, much broken

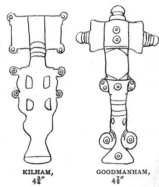

KILHAM,
4¾"

GOODMANHAM,
4⅞"

FIG. 31.—ANGLIAN BROOCHES, E.R.

British Museum

by later Anglian inhumations. Associated with them were many fine beads of amber, crystal, jet, glass, paste, and triplet " pearls " lined with gold; a massive bronze-gilt long brooch (4½"), late 6th century; and a large iron throwing-axe of the francisca type, the only one so far found in Yorkshire, rare in England, and as the name implies, a favourite weapon of the Franks, with whom the Angles came in contact on the continent (Fig. 32).

Urns have also been found at Swine in Holderness, Nafferton near Driffield, and at Robin Hood's Bay with beads, tweezers, small square-headed and annular brooches of the 6th century.

Square-headed brooches have been found elsewhere; their original home was Denmark, but some show South Russian influence, as in one from Kilham (Fig. 31). From the same place there also comes a radiated brooch, the knobs set with garnets; it is typical of the 5th century.

Much more frequent and extensive are cemeteries with inhumations. Whether this change in burial-custom reflects an influx of new-comers or the earliest influence of Christianity is uncertain.

Usually the dead were interred in a crouched or extended

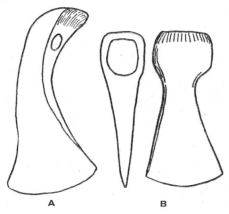

FIG. 32.—ANGLIAN AND VIKING AXES

A, Saltburn 7½″, *Middlesbrough Museum.* B, York, 6½″, *Yorkshire Museum*

position in shallow graves, often in wooden coffins. Cist-burial was also practised, the best example coming from Spaunton, on the Limestone Hills near Pickering. In it lay the extended skeleton of a round-headed man, accompanied by a small Anglian food-vessel and beads.[1]

At Hebden Bank near Easthorpe, on the road between Malton and Coneythorpe, a cist contained a woman's perfect skeleton, a pair of gold ear-rings, an amber necklace, a small food-vessel, and a bone comb.

At Hessle a cist was made of chalk slabs. Greenwell

[1] In Y.M.

records several Anglian stone cists from near Yearsley, whilst at Castle Howard others, probably of very early Anglian date, occurred in close association with the Roman pottery kilns (p. 169).

One of the largest East Yorkshire cemeteries was situated in the northern fosse of an entrenchment at Garton, near Driffield. There were 60 graves arranged in rows two to four deep, and in two groups nearly 50 feet apart. One group was pagan with the heads north-west. Bones of sheep, goats and oxen occurred. A young woman had been interred with a small wooden vessel bound with iron hoops, an annular silver brooch on the right shoulder ; a necklace of bronze, glass and amethyst beads ; a gold pendant with a central garnet ; a bronze hairpin ; two silver ear-rings ; a bronze thread box ; an annular brooch, a bronze buckle, bone comb, chalk and bone spindle-whorls, and two coloured glass objects resembling Roman draughtsmen or counters. The second group, containing few gravegoods and with the heads to the west, was no doubt a Christian burial-place.

Anglian burials are frequent in the neighbourhood of Driffield, some having been found in King's Mill Road in the town itself, and in one of which there was a small reddish vessel with Frankish affinities.

In a cemetery on Acklam Wold there occurred a circular gold pendant with a cruciform filigree design, with carbuncles between the arms and in the centre ; an iron sword nearly a yard long, knives and sharpening irons or steels, and an iron ladle with a long handle. Another ladle comes from Pontefract. They appear to be of Scandinavian origin.

In 1857 the following finds were made at the Seamer Quarry near Scarborough : a small urn, a lozenge-shaped gold pendant, gold pin, two small gold ornaments supposed to be part of the necklace to which the pendant was attached, a plaited band of fine silver wire, a considerable quantity of broken pottery, a piece of a glass vessel, iron fragments, staples and large nails, a grave containing a crouched skeleton, a large bronze ring, and a small iron knife.

The Angles often interred their dead in Bronze Age round-barrows, and at Rudston they even used a long-barrow. The "men-in-armour" found in the beaker barrow at Ferry Fryston (p. 62) and Pudding Pie Hill, a large round-barrow at Sowerby near Thirsk, were Anglian warriors who had been buried with their arms, for shield-bosses and spears are recorded from both.

In the Kelleythorpe barrow described on p. 53 nearly 50 Anglian interments occurred. The bodies, some contracted, others extended, had been laid in shallow graves, their heads towards the centre. In one grave a woman had been buried with an ivory bracelet on her wrist, a broad annular brooch on each shoulder, bronze strap-ends on the right shoulder, 55 amber and glass beads of a neck-lace two feet long, a bronze hairpin, a bone spindle-whorl, and a pair of girdle-hangers. Like the small domestic shears so often found in Anglian graves, the girdle-hanger was an article of feminine attire. It may represent the bunch of keys worn by Roman matrons : it may have served to lift a latch after passing it through the keyhole. It seems to have been later a symbol of domestic authority.

Other articles from the graves include square-headed brooches, annular and long brooches, a bracteate or thin gold plate embossed with a distorted, dissected animal design, resembling others from Kent and West Gothland of the 6–7th centuries ; double combs in cases ; domestic shears ; and a strike-a-light with buckle attachment.

One warrior's grave was too short for his spear, which had been broken in two. The remains of his wooden shield lay above his right elbow. In another grave there was an unbroken spear 6¼ feet long, the iron-socketed head of which was 18″ long.

The spear was a commoner weapon than the sword in Yorkshire. One from the bed of the Ouse at Kelfield, 8 miles south of York, is of the rare Carolingian type. It is 17 inches long, massive and with wings at the base of the socket. It is said to be a hunting weapon of Continental origin and may date from the 9th or 10th century.

Cheesecake Hill between Driffield and Nafferton was

another Bronze Age barrow which had been used as an Anglian cemetery. This contained several coarse urns with cremations, and many inhumations, including those of warriors with their shields, large and small knives, spear-heads (one 2½′ long), socketed arrow-heads, etc. A woman had been buried with a pair of long brooches dating about 550, and a circular brooch with gold-foil filling, rather like the saucer brooches of the West Saxons, a type not found in our county.

That the barrow had been a cemetery for many generations is shown by the discovery in an east and west grave of a perforated bronze-gilt fish worn as a brooch and as a Christian emblem. Fish ornaments were popular in early Christian times.

In and near a barrow (94 feet by 3 feet high) at Uncleby, adjoining Kirkby Underdale on the Wolds, at least 70 interments had been made. The bodies had, as usual, been laid in rows running east and west and about a yard apart. There were none on the north side; 18 on the south side had the head pointing N. and N.W.; on the east side the heads were higher than the feet; whilst the opposite held good for the west side. Only 8 bodies were extended. No coffins had been used; charcoal occurred with all; the aged were always women; the men were young.

Grave furniture was abundant and varied. Weapons included a sword, sword-knives or scram saxes (10½–18″ long), 12 square-ended steels, but no spear-heads. Beads were scarce, but a young woman possessed a necklace of amethysts, quartz and glass beads. Cylindrical bronze thread-boxes, one still containing two kinds of thread and a spindle-whorl, had also been buried with women. Long brooches were absent; an annular brooch with animal head designs is typical of 7th-century Teutonic art. A gold disc also occurred. Many objects have Kentish affinities, from which we may infer the presence of influences that came in with the Kentish princess, Ethelburga.

In a large barrow on Sunny Bank west of Hawnby in Ryedale, a young woman of rank had been buried with her ornaments. Round her waist was a leather girdle with a gold clasp ornamented with an X pattern and garnets, and fastened with gold rivets. Her hair had been secured with gold and silver pins. There were several silver-wire rings, the ends twisted together, blue glass beads, an iron knife, and a stone spindle-whorl.

At her head there stood a thin bronze bowl with three handles or escutcheons, and its decayed wooden cover ornamented with strips of bronze arranged in a diamond pattern and fastened with a bronze hasp. A similar bowl (13½″) with separate tripod stand and movable U-shaped handles was found at a woman's hips in the Uncleby barrow. Their use is obscure though the handles show that they were suspended. A more ornate example was dug up with two earthenware vessels in the Castle Yard, York. It has three escutcheons shaped like birds with tinned wings, the strip between them silvered. The hammered-up base has an inner and outer embossed silver disc ornamented with an interlacing pattern of an annular wreath of two knots. The same design is to be seen in the Irish Book of Kells (c. 750) and on Scotch and Irish sculptured stones. This, and enamelled examples peculiar to England, relate the bowls to those of the Iron Age, the art of which survived through Roman times in England, and especially in Ireland.

The only known Anglian interment in a Bronze Age barrow on the Eastern Moorlands can be directly associated with an historical event. Bede tells us that in 626 "there came into the province (Northumbria) a certain assassin called Eumer, sent by the King of the West Saxons, whose name was Cuichelm, in hopes at once to deprive King Edwin of his kingdom and his life. He had a two-edged dagger dipped in poison, to the end that if the wound were not sufficient to kill the king, it might be performed by the venom. He came to the King on the first day of Easter, at the river Derwent, where then stood the regal city, and being admitted as if to deliver a letter from his master, whilst he was in an artful manner delivering his pretended embassy, he started on a sudden, and drawing the dagger from under his garment, assaulted the King ; which Lilla, the King's beloved minister, observing, having no buckler at hand to secure the King from death, interposed his own body to receive the stroke ; but the wretch struck so home that he wounded the King through the Knight's body. Being then attacked on all sides with swords, he in that confusion also slew another soldier whose name was Forthhere." The regal city on the Derwent has not yet been identified. Lilla was undoubtedly buried in Lilla Howe, on the moors east of Goathland, and 8 miles from the important Anglian centre at Whitby. In the Howe there have been found several gold rings, a gold brooch, 4 silver ornaments like strap-tags, and two roundels of gold-ornamented scrolls in filigree work.

Even Christian Angles were occasionally buried in barrows. In the Howe Hill, Carthorpe, there were burials ; some crouched, with a few knives, a bronze buckle and beads. The scarcity of relics, and the western position of the heads indicate the transition from pagan to Christian. Skeletons with their heads to the west, and without relics, were also found in the Ferry Fryston barrow.

More striking were the contents of a barrow on Lamel Hill in the grounds of the Retreat near Walmgate Bar, York. The barrow was 375 feet round, and almost circular, with a height ranging from $14\frac{1}{2}$ to $22\frac{1}{2}$ feet, the top being flat. At a depth of $10\frac{1}{2}$ to $12\frac{1}{2}$ feet there were 20 to 30 skeletons laid as regularly as in a churchyard, and the detached bones of as many more. At the centre, and a few inches above these skeletons, stood a Roman pot ($12\frac{1}{4}''$), hard, coarse, well-baked, unglazed, a dirty brick-red colour, with black patches. Near it lay a skeleton 6 feet 4 inches long.

Unfortunately the upper part of the mound had been much disturbed. It contained many scattered bones, often in small heaps.

Thurnam, who excavated the barrow, estimated that originally it must have covered 200 to 300 interments, chiefly of middle-aged persons. There were 2 infants under two years of age, a child of eight, and 2 or 3 from twelve to fifteen. Many of the people were six to six feet four inches tall ; one was not less than six feet eight inches. The skull form was chiefly long. These features are typical of the Nordic race, of which the Angles were a branch.

A similar barrow was excavated a little south of Dinnington, near the county border between Rotherham and Worksop. Made of stones, it was 42 paces long from east to west, 35 broad, and 7 to 8 feet high. It covered at least 22 skeletons, many of old persons, and all in the crouched position, except one at full length with the head pointing N.W. Twelve lay in the centre, close together, some 12 feet deep, one only 2½ feet. At the east end there was a skeleton set apart from the others.

As there were no associated objects the mound was difficult to date. Rolleston, its excavator, compares it to similar mounds in Luxemburg and Thurgau. Most of the skulls possessed features characteristic of the Roman cranium ; others were long ; one had Frankish affinities. It is not unlikely that the mound dates from the Anglian period.

As we should expect from its position and advantages, the Wolds were the earliest and main centre of pagan Anglian settlements. They are particularly numerous along the south side of the Great Wold Valley ; they are also frequent along the western margin, but rare on the northern. In Holderness cemeteries have occurred only at Swine and Hornsea. In North-east Yorkshire the Anglians favoured the coast and the Limestone Hills, but less so than the Wolds. The Moors were entirely avoided. In the Vale of York remains have occurred here and there, notably at York, Thirsk and Selby. West of the Vale they are exceedingly scarce ; burials have been noted only near Ferry Fryston (W.R.) and Carthorpe (N.R.). A line of isolated finds extends from Pontefract to Catterick, west of which they are unknown.

Two of the isolated finds are gold finger-rings. One weighing 1 oz. 6 dwt., found on Bramham Moor in 1754, is now in Copenhagen Museum. It is ornamented with a black alloy (niello), and bears a Runic inscription which has not yet been satisfactorily interpreted.

The second ring (312 grains), ploughed up between Sherburn and Aberford, is in the British Museum (Fig. 33). The outside is engraved, and partly filled with niello. On the bezel are a lamb, and the letters A and D with a stroke through it, the Saxon TH, forming the initials of the Greek words "Lamb of God." On the inside of the bezel is the inscription EATHELSWITH REG(I)NA in large double letters, except the last two. The engraver seems to have over-estimated the space, and so has left out the I in Regina and written NA in single lines. Eathelswith was the daughter of Ethelwulf, sister of Alfred the Great, and wife of Burhred, King of Mercia, whom she married in 852. She was thirty-two years older than Alfred, died on her way to Rome in 888-9, and was buried at Pavia. It is

FIG. 33.—QUEEN ETHELSWITH'S RING FOUND BETWEEN SHERBURN AND ABERFORD, W.R.

British Museum

probable that she had offered the ring at some Yorkshire shrine.

By the middle of the 7th century Christianity had made considerable progress. In 601 Pope Gregory instructed the Roman missionaries, amongst whom was Paulinus, that idols only, not temples, should be destroyed. Holy water was to be sprinkled on them, altars erected, and relics placed. The erstwhile heathen were to build huts of boughs round the temples thus transformed, that in them they might kill their cattle and feast to the praise of God. In this way Gregory sought to wean the pagans from their religion by a policy of gradual change.

In 627 Coifi, Edwin's heathen chief priest, on his conversion, himself ordered the destruction by fire of a temple and idols at Goodmanham, near which many pagan

Anglian remains have occurred (Fig. 31). The present church no doubt stands on the site of the heathen temple. Fimber church was erected upon a Bronze Age barrow that had served as an Anglian burial-place. The same holds good for Rudston, where the great monolith has defied destruction.

Paulinus built the first Yorkshire churches at York and Campodunum, usually identified with Doncaster, but more probably Cambodunum, the Roman site at Greetland in the Calder valley (p. 153). After the battle of Hatfield, 633, Campodunum Church was destroyed, and according to Bede the stone altar erected there by Paulinus was to be found a century later at the abbey in the forest of Elmet where Thridwulf was then abbot. The site of this abbey is unknown, though both Sherburn and Barwick in Elmet have been suggested. Collingwood suspects it to be Dewsbury where, before the Reformation, there was a strong tradition that Paulinus preached and celebrated mass.

Owing to the influence of King Oswald, who had been educated by the monks of Iona, the Irish form of Christianity became established in Northumbria, and it was supported both by Oswin and Oswy. In 664 a synod met at Whitby, where it was decided that Irish usages must give place to Roman.

At this time many Anglian monasteries were founded. That at Ingethlingum, now Gilling near Richmond, was built shortly after 642, to atone for the murder of King Oswin by King Oswy at that place. Prayers were offered up daily for the souls of the two kings. Except for late Anglian and Danish cross-fragments no structural remains of this monastery have survived.

The monastery at Lestinga, now Lastingham, on the edge of the moors 6 miles north-west of Pickering, was founded by Ethelwald, son of King Oswald, for his own use and burial. At Ethelwald's request the site was chosen by Cedd, bishop of the East Saxons, ' among craggy and distant mountains, which looked more like lurking-places for robbers and retreats for wild beasts than habitations for men ; to the end that, according to the prophecy of Isaiah, ' in the habitations where before dragons dwelt, might be grass with reeds and rushes ' ; that is, that the fruits of good works should spring up, where before beasts were wont to dwell, or men to live after the manner of beasts '. Bede's description reveals why the Anglians, heathen and Christian alike, never settled within the Eastern Moorlands.

Cedd and his brother Cynybil first purified the site of its former crimes by fasting daily through Lent until the evening, when they ate a little bread and an egg, and drank a little watered milk. The monastery was then built, but St. Cedd died there of a pestilence. He was first buried in the open, later, on the right hand of the altar in a stone church built in the monastery in honour of the Virgin. Of this monastery, in which the Irish form of Christianity was practised, there are a few remains in the crypt of the present church, including a jamb with vine scroll-work, lintels, part of the head of a great cross, and other stones of later Anglian and Anglo-Danish type. Two old wells in the village are named after St. Cedd and his brother St. Chad.

In 657 the great monastery at Streoneshalh, now Whitby, was founded by St. Hilda, the daughter of King Edwin's nephew Hereric, who embraced the faith when thirteen years of age, after hearing Paulinus preach. It was one of the six Deiran monasteries endowed by King Oswy after his victory over Penda of Mercia at Winwoodfield near Leeds. The monastery, which was situated on the East Cliff, included both monks and nuns, and was ruled by St. Hilda for seventeen years. Bede tells us that King Oswy and his queen, King Edwin, Oswy's daughter Elfleda, and many other noble persons were buried there.

During the recent restoration of the present abbey rude stone foundations, probably those of an Anglian building, were discovered north of the Abbey Church. Its walls were built of wattle and daub, fragments of which are exhibited in Whitby Museum. Two enamelled escutcheons from hanging bowls (p. 185), two beautiful openwork gilt

bronze discs with fine interlaced ornament (all probably
7–8th century Hiberno-Saxon work) ; a green glass cameo,
and a fragment of lapis lazuli inlaid with gold, were also
found.

Many years ago the kitchen-midden of the Anglian
monastery was found to be at the foot of the East Cliff
between the Black Horse Yard and the Church steps. It
consisted of a pile of bones of the shorthorn ox, sheep, red
and roe deer, goat, and pig ; and the shells of the oyster,
cockle, whelk, winkle and limpet. There were two combs,
one of walrus ivory fixed between two pieces of deer-bone,
bearing the invocation, " May God look on us. May God
Almighty help our race ", inscribed in 7th-century runes
(Fig. 34) ; the other of bronze, with an ornamented open-
work back, a rare 8th-century type. A leaden bulla of
Pope Boniface was also found.

These combs were used during monastic ceremonies,
when it was customary to comb the hair of the officiating
clergy before Mass, Vespers, and other Orders. Hence the
religious inscription on the ivory comb which may have
been in the hands of St. Hilda herself. Pope Boniface,
who exhorted King Edwin and Queen Ethelburga to become
Christians, presented the queen with a silver mirror and a
gilt ivory comb.

In the year of her death St. Hilda built a small monastery at Hackness near Scarborough. It was here that the
nun Begu had a vision of the translation of St. Hilda to
heaven at the very hour of her death. Historians of the
nineteenth century were disposed to doubt this, together
with many other miraculous occurrences related by Bede,
saying that he did not rise above the prevailing credulity
of his age. This verdict we cannot now regard as final,
for the spiritual exaltation and sublime faith of these
Anglian Christians may well have endowed them with
powers transcending the limitations of the material
world.

In Hackness church there are fragments of a great
8th-century cross with regular scrolls, symmetrical plaits,
figures and beasts, typical Anglian sculpture. It bears

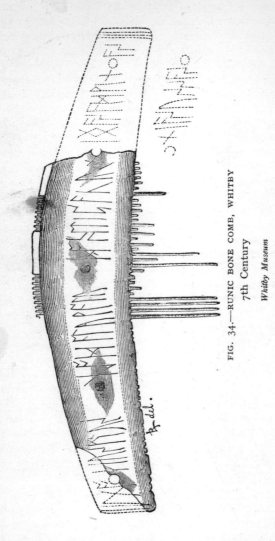

FIG. 34.—RUNIC BONE COMB, WHITBY

7th Century

Whitby Museum

inscriptions in Anglian runes, twig-runes, and Oghms, which have not yet been deciphered ; and one in Latin to the memory of Oethelburga, a former Abbess and a grand-niece of St. Hilda. The impost of the chancel arch is late Anglo-Saxon or Norman. A nave, probably built immediately before the Norman Conquest, is represented by the present nave within the arcades, the walls of which are two feet thick, a pre-Conquest feature.

Under St. Hilda at Streoneshalh many eminent men were trained for Holy Mother Church. Here lived Cædmon, our first English poet. His name is Celtic, however, and so he may have been a Briton. From it John went forth, to found a monastery at Beverley, of which nothing survives. Bones and an Anglian dagger, found when the Minster nave was repaved in the 18th century, have been attributed to St. John and King Athelstan respectively. This king, before his victory over the Danes at Brunanburh in 937, paid a pilgrimage to St. John's shrine, and placed his dagger on the altar as a pledge of the privileges he would grant to the church, if victorious.

Wilfrid also left the abbey for Ripon, where a monastery had been founded in 660 by Alchfrith, King of Deira, who filled it with Scottish monks. These, however, he removed in 661. Whereupon Wilfrid instituted the Benedictine rule in a building on another site, and the crypt of it can be seen under Ripon Cathedral (Fig. 35). It consists of a small, oblong chamber with very thick walls containing niches for lamps, holy water (N. wall) and cruets (E. of N. wall). Originally it enshrined the relics of a saint whose bones were found at the east end. The skull and humerus are preserved in the cathedral library. The pilgrims entered the chamber by one of the long passages, and left by the other.

Of other Anglian remains at Ripon there is the shaft of a stone cross inscribed ' Adhuse the priest ' (in Yorkshire Museum), two stones in the S.E. corner of the cathedral transept, and the head of a cross with birds and plaits of the Anglo-Danish period. In the cathedral library there is a fragment of a late 9th-century illuminated missal,

14

and an iron spur. Curiously enough, Ripon spurs have always been famous.

The establishment of Anglian monasteries and churches gave birth to a school of sculpture which filled them with crosses, grave-slabs, and other works of beauty. Owing to the ravages of the Danes, the Puritans, and other iconoclasts, few pieces survive intact ; nevertheless, over a thousand fragments of this and the later Anglo-Danish sculpture occur in Yorkshire. They have been described

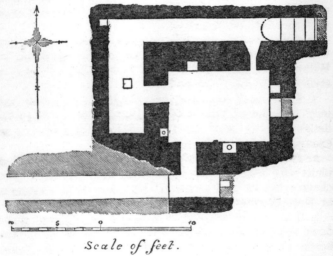

Scale of feet.

FIG. 35.—PLAN OF ANGLIAN CRYPT, RIPON CATHEDRAL, W.R.

and illustrated by Collingwood in a series of papers on which the following account is based.

Anglian sculpture flourished from about the beginning of the 8th to the middle of the 9th century when, after the Viking conquest and settlement, an Anglo-Danish style prevailed up to the Norman conquest, and even later. In its earliest and finest form Anglian sculpture consisted chiefly of free-armed crosses, elaborately decorated in high relief with symmetrical interlacing or plait-work, combined with human or animal figures. These crosses were further embellished with bright colours, and many were set with jewels. The ardent faith of the Angles expressed itself pre-eminently in these astonishing monuments.

The style has affinities with 7th- and 8th-century Italian sculpture. The beginning of plait-work is to be found in Roman tessellated pavements, and in the 6th and 7th centuries it was a frequent motif in Italian art, where scroll-work is also to be seen. Under such influence Anglian sculpture evolved, inspired and guided by men of the calibre of Bede, Wilfrid and Benedict, who were in constant touch with Gaul and Italy, and introduced foreign craftsmen into Northumbria.

In lower Wensleydale there arose a native school, which flourished for nearly a century, encouraged no doubt by Wilfrid's monastery at Ripon. Three main varieties of style characterised the school :

1. Free-armed crosses without a wheel or nimbus, and only ornamented with a long-handled lens or lorgnette design, one on each arm. The Ripon cross is a good example.

2. Free-armed crosses with chevron border, symmetrical plaits and bosses, and lorgnette design ; the shaft with chevron border and scrolls of the vine, as in fragments at Northallerton church.

3. Tall crosses with head in centre, scrolls and plaits down edge of shaft with carved birds, beasts or human figures on the sides, as displayed in four stones at Easby near Richmond, on one of which there is a panel of Christ enthroned between angels.

These types are all linked together by similarities in design and treatment. Graceful birds and beasts of the same school occur at Croft, Otley, Cundall, Aldborough (with human figures), Tanfield, Melsonby, and elsewhere. At Croft in particular the sculpture is of the highest art ; the wonderful beauty of the design and the delicacy of execution are amazing. At Wensley a slab inscribed Donfrid is carved with a cross, between the arms of which there are dragons. A similar cross-slab has the name Eadberecht inscribed between the arms. Symeon of

Durham's chronicle, under 740, mentions Eadberctus, who is probably the same person.

Collingwood arranges the human figures of this school in a series, beginning with the Easby Christ, and noble saints on cross-fragments at Otley, through the apostles at Collingham, to the less successful work on the three crosses in Ilkley churchyard. The tallest and most perfect has the four evangelists on one side, and Christ with monsters underneath him on the other.

In Masham churchyard there is the cylindrical pillar, nearly 7 feet high, of a colossal cross. It is carved in three courses of panels, but it is sadly weathered. The highest panel represents Christ and his apostles ; the middle may relate the story of a saint ; the lowest portrays imaginatively conceived creatures.

Another exceptionally beautiful cross existed at Dewsbury (Fig. 36) ; but only six fragments remain, the monument apparently having been destroyed by the Puritans. Leland saw it in the reign of Henry VIII, and records its inscription, " Paulinus hic praedicavit et celebravit." Collingwood has made a restoration, a model of which, together with quite a number of local crosses, all coloured, can be seen in the Huddersfield Museum. They are a joy to behold. The Dewsbury cross must have been 18 feet high, and dates from the middle of the 9th century.

Rather later than the Dewsbury cross are fragments at Thornhill on the opposite side of the Calder valley. Two pieces of a grave-slab, an unusual type of Anglian monument, bear an imperfect inscription that " so-and-so set this in memory of Osberht, a monument over his grave. Pray for his soul ". It is said to be the tombstone of King Osberht, killed by the Danes at York, March 21, 867.

Part of another cross-shaft at Thornhill has the following inscription in Anglian runes : " Gilsuith reared (this cross) to Berhtsuith, a monument (on) her grave. Pray for her soul." These are ladies' names of the later part of the 9th century. Two other Anglian runic cross inscriptions are preserved here. One reads, " Ethelberht set up (this)

FIG. 36.—ANGLIAN CROSS, DEWSBURY
(restored by W. G. Collingwood)

Huddersfield Museum

in memory of Ethelwini. Pray (for him)." The other, " Eadred set (this) up to Eata. . . ."

Towards the end of the 9th century crucifix crosses became fairly common, one of the best executed being at Kirkburton (W.R.). In Kirkdale church there is a sandstone crucifix 5 ft. 3 in. high, by 22 in. across the arms, by 16 in. across the shaft. The head has a forked beard, and the umbilicus is exaggerated. Another cross of the same period is built into the west wall. Of early Anglian age is the " King Ethelwald " grave slab in the same wall. On it is carved a cross, with a central hole for a jewel, flanked by knops and leaves at the ends of spiral stems in low relief. It is said to have borne King Ethelwald's name in runes, which, if they ever existed, are no longer legible. Kirkdale is only 5 miles from Lastingham, where King Ethelwald wished to be buried.

A late Anglian monument is the " St. Cedd " slab (5′ 8″ long). It belongs to a much later period than St. Cedd. The carving covers the slab, and consists of intricate interlacing and circles. The design is by no means symmetrical, and is not inevitable as in the best Anglian work. An interlocking border is very much damaged. The narrow sides of the slab are decorated with a fringe of tassels ; the whole monument appears to perpetuate the pall.

At Yarm-on-Tees, found in a cottage and serving there as `a mangle-weight, now in the Durham Library, is part of a late Anglian cross-shaft, decorated with interlocked and bold knot-work, and bearing an inscription which reads :

. . . .
RIBEREHC
T + SAC +
ALLA + SIGN
UMAEFTER
HISBREODERA
GISETAE +

" (Pray for) Heriberecht. Alla set up (this cross) a monument after (in memory of) his brothers."

In the churchyard at Hauxwell is a late Anglian cross-shaft covered with interlacing rope-work, smoothly cut, but on one side the intricate pattern of over and under becomes confused.

In the Anglian period the York mints were founded. The Royal mint issued coins more or less continuously until the reign of William III; the Archiepiscopal mint until the reign of Henry VIII. The earliest coins may have been uninscribed; but two copper coins from Bolton Percy inscribed ECGFRAIDE (obverse) and EVDΛINI

I. ST. PETER'S PENNY, OF YORK

II. NORTHUMBRIAN SCEAT OF EADBERHT
(737–758)

FIG. 37.—ANGLIAN AND VIKING COINS (enlarged) MINTED AT YORK
British Museum

(reverse) may be those of Ecgfrid, King of Northumbria (670–85), or Offa's son, Ecgfrid (796), EVDΛINI being a moneyer's name of the late 8th century.

Small silver coins or sceattas (cf. German *schatz*, treasure) were issued at York by King Eadberht (737–57) and his brother Ecgberht, the first archbishop (734–66). The regal coins have a horned animal on the reverse, and the King's name on the obverse (Fig. 37). One was found at the New Gas Works, York. Ecgberht's coins bear his name and A or AR (archbishop). There are three types :

1. A mitred figure holding a crozier in each hand, and Ecgberht on the obverse ; Eadberht on the reverse.

2. A mitred figure carrying a crozier in one hand and a staff in the other (example from the Mount).

3. A central cross surrounded by name, and the name (blundered) of King Athelwald (760–6) or Alchred (765–74).

Silver sceattas with the King's name and an animal reverse were minted until 789. They have rarely been found in Yorkshire, for they were essentially a southern coin type. One of Edilred I (774–7, 790–6) comes from Hornsea. Another minted at York or Chester-le-Street is a St. Cuthbert's penny inscribed S(sepulchrum), S(an)C (t) I CVD (berht). Cuthbert pennies of Elfwald (778–9) are also recorded.

The Northumbrian coin was the styca (cf. German *stück*, piece), usually of copper. The earliest from the Royal mint are of Osred II (789–90), and the latest of Osberht (850–67), when their issue came to an end with the Danish conquest. They usually have a central cross of varied form, often within a circle surrounded by an inscription beginning with a cross. The King's name was on the obverse and the moneyer's on the reverse. Eardwulf (796–806) employed twelve moneyers ; Eanred (807–41) thirty-two ; Ethelrid II (841–50) thirty-five ; Redwulf (844) fourteen, and Osberht sixteen. This gives us a good list of Anglian personal names. Two names, Broder and Wintrid, on coins of Eanred are in runes, and there are 168 varieties of this king's name and title. Leofdegn, a moneyer of Ethelrid, is shown with a hound. An uninscribed styca has a bird on one face and a bust on the other.

The earliest archiepiscopal stycas appear to be those of Eanbald II (796–808), who issued both copper and silver coins inscribed AR, ARE, AREP, and with his three moneyers' names (Cunwulf, Eadwulf, and Edilveard) on the reverse. Archbishop Vigmund (837–54) minted copper stycas, of which there are 559 in the Yorkshire Museum ; also gold and silver coins. One gold coin has a full-faced tonsured bust inscribed VIGMVND AREP on the obverse and MVNVS DIVINVM on the reverse. It resembles the gold solidus of Louis le Debonnaire (d. 814). Vigmund employed seven moneyers.

Wulfhere, the last Anglian archbishop, and the first under the Danes (854–901), minted copper stycas with retrograde inscriptions.

A hoard containing at least 10,000 stycas was found in 1842, at a depth of 5½ feet in St. Leonard's Place, not far from Bootham Bar, York. 3,500 have been described, and range from Eandred to Osberht, of both mints, the hoard dating from 860–70. The coins are made of copper mixed with varying amounts of zinc, silver, gold, lead and tin, a mixture supposed to be due to melting down late Roman coins made of gold or copper washed with silver.

Another hoard was found in 1695 near Aikey Hill, Ripon. It contained stycas of Eanred and Athelred, and seems to have been deposited at the same time as the preceding hoard.

In the Yorkshire Museum there is a lead cross (2″), found with two stycas of the same kings in Clifford Street, York. Its front is impressed with both faces of a styca of Osberht.

A large hoard of stycas was found in 1846 at Woodhill Close, in the township of Hornington in Bolton Percy parish, near Ulleskelf on the Wharfe. It consisted of 6,000 coins, so rusted together that only a few could be identified. Amongst them are 70 of Eanred, 267 of Athelred, 5 of Redwulf, 18 of Osberht, a few of Eanbald, 47 of Vigmund, and 5 of Wulfhere. It therefore dates from the second half of the 9th century, and, like the others, must have been hidden at the Danish conquest.

After reading this chapter the reader will be of opinion that the Dark Ages is surely a misnomer for these important centuries—when indeed Roman civilisation was over-thrown, but when English civilisation became rooted in the land, when paganism gave way to a sustained and well-ordered Christian faith, which enriched our county with surprisingly ornate sculpture, buildings and libraries, and men and women of European fame.

For references see end of next chapter.

CHAPTER XI

THE VIKING AGE

AFTER the middle of the ninth century the Anglian culture and development of Yorkshire were ruthlessly checked, and completely transformed first by the Danes and later by the Norwegians, both of whom are commonly known as Vikings. Not satisfied with mere plunder, they colonised the county so thoroughly that Viking land divisions, Viking courts, and Viking social organisation superseded those of the Angles. York became the capital of a state ruled by Viking kings who, for nearly a hundred years, resisted the efforts of Wessex to subdue them. Even after their kingdom had been reduced to a vassal state under Edred in 954, the old defiant spirit flared up from time to time, until William the Conqueror cowed it by his relentless harrying of the North in 1069.

The earliest recorded Viking raid occurred in 787, when three Danish ships harried the Dorset coast. As early, if not earlier, visits to Yorkshire are proved by the unique wooden images found at a depth of six feet in blue clay at Roos Carr near Withernsea in Holderness, and now in the Hull Museum (Plate X).

Five surviving figures are from 13½ to 16 inches high, and 1 to 1½ inches wide. Carved out of fir wood, they represent warriors with long, thin legs, heads slightly wider than the bodies, and with eyes of white quartz or limestone. The left arms are bent, and each originally carried a small roughly circular shield (2½"). The right arms are perforated to hold upright clubs, none of which has survived. Larger shields, 4 to 5 inches in diameter, covered their bodies. The legs were fixed in holes bored in a wooden boat, 20 inches long, rudely shaped like a serpent, the eyes

PLATE X

EARLY VIKING IMAGES AND BOAT (20″)
ROOS CARR, E.R.
Hull Museum

VIKING BRONZE BROOCH (4¼″)
NEAR BEDALE, N.R.
Edinburgh Museum

of which are of white quartz.   Three figures belong to this boat, which is constructed to hold four ; two to another boat now lost.

The boat and its figures are undoubtedly a contemporary model of a Viking longship, the prow of which was often carved into a serpent or dragon's head, and the warrior crew of which hung their shields outside the gunwales. The images have been dated as earlier than the Viking conquest in 867 on account of their poor workmanship, for at the conquest period Viking woodwork had attained its finest development.   Similar but larger wooden figures have been found singly at Ballachuish on the west coast of Scotland, in England, Ireland, Brandenburg, and Denmark.

At the end of the eighth and beginning of the ninth century Viking raids became more numerous and daring. Attracted by the wealth of the Anglian monasteries, the Vikings looted and destroyed that at Lindisfarne in 793. Alcuin, then at the court of Charlemagne, wrote of this catastrophe : " Never before in the 350 years that we and our forefathers have dwelt in this fair land has such a horror appeared in Britain as this that we have just suffered from the heathen."   The monasteries of Monkwearmouth and Jarrow were ravaged in 794.   Between 832 and 865 the Danish Vikings invaded and devastated eastern and southern England.   In 866 a great Danish army wintered in East Anglia.   Its leaders were the brothers Halfdan, Ivar, and Ubbe, who came to conquer and to settle.   For in 867, Ivar, nicknamed the Boneless, marched into Deira and captured York.   His task was rendered easier by a civil war between the Anglian kings Ella and Osbert for the throne of Northumbria.   Alarmed at the Danish invasion the two kings sunk their differences, only to suffer defeat and death at the hands of Ivar in a fierce battle in York.   According to Symeon of Durham, the victors next plundered the province, and ravaged the monasteries at Streoneshalh, Hackness, Lastingham and Crayke.   The religion of Thor and Odin triumphed over that of Christ.

In 871 Ivar became King of all the Vikings in Ireland

and Britain, his Irish title having been conferred by Olaf the White, whom he had assisted in the conquest of Ireland in 856, and who returned to Norway in 871. Ivar died in 873, his brother Halfdan succeeding him as King of York, and Eysteinn, Olaf's son, as King of Dublin.

With York as his headquarters Halfdan warred for the possession of Mercia and Wessex. In 871 he was defeated by Aethelred and Alfred at Ashdown, near Reading. In the same year he fought in the nine pitched battles against Alfred, and concluded a peace with him. In 874 he conquered Mercia. The following winter he passed on the Tyne, and in 875 he ravaged Bernicia, a province, however, that never became thoroughly Danish, as the scarcity of Danish place-names proves.

Returning to York in 876 he divided the lands of Deira amongst his followers, who began systematically to cultivate them. But nothing appears to be known of the Danish field-system. That of the Angles was the acre-strip (220 yards long by 20 yards wide). On the Wolds and in the western dales acre-strips can still be seen on hill-sides, where they form terraces or lynchets one above the other ; in flatter areas they have been obliterated by subsequent methods of cultivation.

The most likely region in which to discover the Viking field-system is the north-eastern dales, in which the Angles never settled, but which were cleared and cultivated by both Danes and Norwegians.

Under the Danes Yorkshire was divided into thridings, now the North, East and West Ridings. Each was represented by a third of the members of the Thing or Shire court which met at York. Each also had its own court, that of the North Riding under a maple tree near Thirsk, that of the East at Crackhow, near Windyates in Gardham, between Market Weighton and Beverley, and that of the West perhaps at York.

The Ridings were subdivided into small hundreds containing twelve carucates or ploughlands held by 100 families ; and large hundreds containing 120 carucates. At the Domesday survey in 1086, the East Riding com-

prised 18 hundreds.[1] Another administrative division was
the Wapentake ; the North and West Ridings contained
seven and eleven wapentakes respectively. Each wapentake (O.N. *vápnatak*, weapon-grasping) had its own court,
where the inhabitants met to grasp the weapons of the
King's representative in token of fealty in peace and war.
The wapentake courts met at convenient centres such as
a hill (Langbargh, N.R.) ; a tree (Skyrack or Shire oak,
W.R.) ; a well (Hallikeld, N.R.) ; a cross (Ewcross, W.R.) ;
a bridge (Agbrigg, W.R.) ; the Scamridge Dikes (Dic,
N.R.), etc. These meeting-places gave their name to the
wapentakes.

Smaller local courts within the wapentakes were known
as Things, a typical Viking institution. Most Things were
held in the open air, usually upon low hills. The sites of
many are known from place-names. In the North Riding
we find Thing-howe (now Fingay Hill) in Hallikeld wapentake ; Thingwall (O.N. *Thing + .völlr* = word), name
obsolete but near Whitby ; Tindall Holme near Scarborough, and Tinghowdale near Guisborough.

To unravel the factors which originally determined the
site of the Viking courts and the area of their hundreds
and wapentakes, and to follow the changes these have
undergone until to-day, is here out of the question. Such
an investigation will undoubtedly throw great light on
ancient and modern Yorkshire.

After settling his followers in Yorkshire Halfdan in 877
attempted to capture Dublin, feeling that as Ivar's brother
he had a rightful claim to the throne of that city, then held
by Eysteinn, Olaf's son. This king, with the help of the
Irish king Aed Finnlaith, compelled Halfdan and his small
force of Danes to abandon their enterprise. Halfdan then
sailed up the coast of Ireland, but he eventually met defeat
and death in a fight with Norwegians in Strangford Loch
(877).

This expedition initiated a struggle between York and
Dublin that dragged on for more than fifty years. Essentially it was a quarrel between the descendants of Ivar

[1] In 1284, we find the Riding subdivided into six wapentakes.

and Halfdan to weld Dublin and York into a single kingdom, a quarrel intensified by the antagonism of the Norwegians who dominated Dublin and the Danes who dominated Yorkshire.

Guthred or Knut, as he is sometimes called, ascended the York throne after the death of Halfdan. In 883 he became a Christian, no doubt following the example of Guthrum, King of the southern Danelaw, who, after his defeat by Alfred, embraced Christianity at Wedmore near Glastonbury. Archbishop Wulfhere, who had fled when York was captured by Ivar in 867, returned to his see. The Christianisation of the Yorkshire Danes must date from about this time, but we have no records of its progress.

Knut died in 894, and was succeeded by Siefred, who fought against Alfred in Wessex, and died in 896.

The next king of whom we have any knowledge is, strangely enough, Aethelwald, nephew of Alfred the Great, who reigned for two years (900–2). He made a bid for the throne of Wessex which had fallen to Edward, son of Alfred the Great ; but, losing his courage, he stole away by night and fled to Northumbria. Owing to the state of anarchy in York the Danes decided to hail him as their king. As such he waged war against Wessex, until killed in battle.

Chaos reigned for fifteen years ; but in 917 we hear of the York ruler paying homage to Aethelfleda, the Lady of the Mercians, who, with her brother Edward, had waged successful campaigns against the southern Danelaw. She died in the same year, and in 918 the throne of York was seized by Ragnvald of Dublin. This event alarmed the Christian Danes of Yorkshire, who resented both his paganism and his Norwegian followers. In 920 Ragnvald was obliged to render homage to Edward of Wessex. By this arrangement the Danes held their lands and escaped the tyranny of the Norwegians, whilst Ragnvald retained his throne. Thus, for a time, Yorkshire became part of a loosely united England.

Ragnvald was succeeded in 925 by his brother Sigtryg Gale, King of Dublin, almost at the same time that Aethelstan ascended the English throne. Sigtryg acknowledged the supremacy of Aethelstan and married his sister. In 926 he died ; Aethelstan invaded Northumbria, expelled Godfred, Sigtryg's son, and annexed it. He thereby became King of all England.

In 933, however, Constantine King of the Scots espoused the cause of Olaf Cuaran, son of Sigtryg, who was regarded as the heir to the York throne. Aethelstan quelled this revolt by a campaign in Scotland, but in 937 war again broke out, the York succession being the main cause. It is related that Olaf, at the head of an army of Scots and Vikings, raided Yorkshire by way of the Humber. Their success was short-lived, for they were decisively defeated by Aethelstan at the battle of Brunanburgh, on the Solway Firth.

Aethelstan appears to have appointed Eric Bloodaxe, son of Harald Fairhair, King of Norway, as earl of the vassal state of Northumbria. The English king died in 940, to be succeeded by Edmund, his half-brother, a mere youth. In 941 Olaf Godfredson, King of Dublin, expelled Eric and seized the York throne. Olaf died in 942, and Olaf Cuaran, his cousin from Dublin, ascended the throne. In 943 he submitted to Edmund, and became a Christian. The Yorkshire Norwegians objected to this, and drove him from York, enthroning his cousin Ragnvald Godfredson. Edmund thereupon invaded Yorkshire, captured York, and became overlord of Northumbria until his death in 946.

In 947 Wulfstan, Archbishop of York, fomented a revolt. Bloodaxe was reinstated as king. To punish this audacity Eadred, King of Wessex, ravaged Northumbria, and burned Ripon monastery. Ultimately the Danes submitted. Bloodaxe was deposed, and peace agreed to at Topcliffe-on-Swale.

In 949 Olaf Cuaran, abetted by Wulfstan, made himself king of York for the second time. In 952 Eadred imprisoned Wulfstan, so the scared Northumbrians expelled Olaf and restored Bloodaxe. Bloodaxe was the last Viking King of York, for in 954 Eadred conquered Yorkshire, and finally reduced Northumbria to a vassal state. He made Oswulf of Bamborough the first earl of Northumbria, of whom there were ten before the Norman Conquest, but whose history does not concern us.

Under the Vikings York attained an importance as great as any it had enjoyed since Roman times. Once more this was due to its position. Fleets of longships from Denmark and Norway could anchor under its walls, and communication with Dublin was expedited by means of the Roman route through the Aire Gap, so much easier and shorter than voyaging round Cape Wrath or by way of the English Channel.

To this day York bears the stamp of its Viking inhabitants to a far greater extent than that of its Roman founders. Its name is directly derived from that bestowed by the Vikings, Yorvick. Its old street-names are of Viking origin. For instance, Fishergate comes from *fiskare*, fisherman, and *gata*, a road or street ; Goodramgate from *Gothormr*, a man's name ; Coney Street from *konungr*, king ; Skeldergate from *skjaldari*, a shield-maker ; Coppergate from *koppare*, a joiner or turner ; Blake Street from *bleikr*, pale, white ; Stonegate from *steinn*, stone ; Micklegate from *mikill*, large, great. It will be noticed from many of the old names that people of like trades lived in the same street. We have records of other instances, such as Haymangergate from *heymangari*, a hay-salesman ; Ketmangeregate from *kiötmangare*, a fleshmonger ; Plouswayngate from *plógsveinn*, a ploughman.[1] Some of the old streets, such as Stonegate, no doubt coincided with those of Roman York. King's Court or Square may derive its name from the residence of the Anglian and Viking kings.

The city has yielded numerous Viking objects. In Clifford Street there were Viking workshops, the refuse and waste from which were thrown down the bank that sloped towards the river. Here in 1884 were found amber in the rough, or wrought into rings, beads and ear-rings ;

[1] For details see Lindkvist, *Middle-English Place Names of Scandinavian Origin*, Upsala, 1912.

jet rings ; a piece of molten glass, glass beads, and several glass roundlets, believed to be for smoothing linen ; a loom-weight with an interlaced pattern running along it, spindle-whorls and a spindle ; smoothing-stones, whet-stones ; iron knives and prickers ; a large series of combs of every shape, and in every stage of manufacture ; pins and needles in endless variety, ornamented with dragon-esque designs ; girdle-holders and bracers ; two wooden spoons, one with a rough interlaced pattern and two runes, the other with highly-finished plait-work ; two deer-horn hammers, and many ornamented deer-horns ; two wooden mallets, and bone skates. From the same street comes a fine example of a Viking stone carved with two bound dragons separated by plait-work. A bronze scabbard chape engraved with a distorted animal in the Jellinge style, associated with fragments of a bone casket and an iron axe-head, many kinds of which have been found in the city, comes from Ness Gate, hard by. Chapes similar to the one just mentioned are frequent in Scandinavia, with a decoration like that on a famous memorial stone at the royal graves at Jellinge in Jutland, which is dated at 975–80. Glass roundlets have been found in other parts of the city, and also in Denmark and Scotland. Bone combs, made of pieces joined by iron rivets, in their cases, have parallels in Scandinavia, and even in Russia, through which ran a Viking trade route.

The Vikings were skilful workers, and many bone imple-ments have been found in the city, often beautifully decorated with grotesque animal and interlacing designs such as we find in their sculpture. Five bone draughtsmen, carved with a ring and dot pattern, remind us that the Vikings were fond of games.

Circular pewter brooches, and one of silver enclosing a copy of a Valentinian coin have been assigned to the eleventh century.

To the Viking Age probably belong tree-trunk coffins furnished with end boards let into grooves. One from St. Saviour's Gate held a man's skeleton and a wooden paddle, a discovery suggesting that, like the Early Bronze Age tree-trunk coffins, they represent boat burial. Others have been found in Parliament Street, on the site of an ancient graveyard, where there was also a broken cross, with interlaced ribbon work and a bead moulding on three sides. Similar coffins have been found at Selby.

Another paddle blade, 18 inches long and 6 inches wide, with holes for affixing the shaft, was found ten feet deep in Coppergate. Associated with it were leather boots and gaiters, leather knife sheaths with impressed patterns similar to a bronze example from Gothland, and part of a large black pot with a broad flat handle, ornamented with grooves and saucer-shape depressions. If this pot actually was associated with the other finds, it is one of the very few pieces of Viking pottery known in England.

Under the Vikings the issue of copper stycas from the York mints ceased, silver coins taking their place. They were based on Scandinavian and Frankish types. The earliest known are those of Guthred-Cnut, who minted silver pence and half-pence. They bear an equal-armed or patriarchal cross, with the letters C.N.V.T. at the ends of the arms, and R.E.X. between the limbs. On the other side, + EBRAICE CIVITAS or + EB . IAI . CEC . IV, usually accompanied by a small central cross, and more rarely by the Carolus monogram. $K\diamond S$, introduced on to Frankish coins by Charlemagne.

Siefred issued coins of similar design, and pennies bearing his and Guthred's names indicate that these kings reigned together for a short time in 893–4. The succeeding kings carried on the same tradition with minor variations. The Danish standard is shown on some, a winged raven on coins of Olaf Cuaran, a sword on coins of Eric Bloodaxe, and the king's head, the Carolus monogram, the open hand, the hammer, and the bow and arrow on coins of Ragnvald II.

The Wessex kings Edward the Elder, Aethelstan and Edmund, as overlords of Northumbria, issued coins from the York mint.

A silver penny in the collection of Mr. G. D. Lumb bears on its obverse a cross patée within an inner circle, around which is the lettering EADVVEARD REX. On the reverse is York Minster, and the inscription WA . LT . ER . EO (fric), the moneyer's name, and York. The minster is depicted as a stone façade, with three entrances, and an arcade and pinnacles above, surmounted by a turret where in all probability a lantern was suspended to guide travellers through the Forest of Galtres.[1]

Aethelstan's coins were inscribed EƷDELSTAN REX TO BRIT (King of all Britain).

Little is known of the archiepiscopal coinage during the Viking period. No coins were struck for seven years, as Wulfere fled when the Danes captured the city (867). On his return he appears to have issued silver pennies of Cnut and Siefred. The reverses are usually inscribed MIRABILIA FECIT or DNS DS REX (Dominus Deus Rex). St. Peter's pence are the most characteristic coins issued by the archbishop's mint. Some of these silver coins are heavy, others light. The heavy coins usually bear a sword, and the letters SCI PE TR MO on one side, and EBORACE, variously spelt, on the other. The light coins have no sword in the field (Fig. 37).

St. Eadmund silver pennies were also struck, but they are not peculiar to York as are the St. Peter's pence.

After Northumbria had become a vassal state the Kings of all England minted coins at York. The king's head is stamped on Edgar's coins (959–75). One is inscribed EADGAR REX ANGLOW and DVN . MO EOFORPIC. Ethelred II's coins show his head and a sceptre in front, or his head crowned with a radiated helmet ; the reverses have a hand or a cross, sometimes with the letters CRVX in the angles. He employed 36 moneyers.

Canute's coins, 1016–35, bear a crowned bust and a long cross within quatrefoils. The reverses of Harald I's coins, 1035–40, have a cross of four ovals, and a fleur-de-lys in each angle. Hardicanute's coins, 1040–2, have a cross on the reverse, with a circle enclosing a pellet in the centre.

[1] *Y.A.J.*, xxx, 309–10.

Edward the Confessor, 1042–66, issued eight types from York ; the finest show him enthroned, and the cross and martlets on the reverse.

Harald II issued coins inscribed PAX at York, although he was only King of England for a few months.

In 1884 some hundreds of silver pennies of the Confessor, all struck at York except twelve, and a few of the Conqueror, were found on Bishophill in a cup with an incurved mouth and a dab of light yellow glaze on the lip. The cup and 174 coins are in the Yorkshire Museum.

In 1807 a lead box containing about 270 silver coins, and fragments of silver ornaments two pounds in weight, was ploughed up near Lobster House Inn in the parish of Bossall, between York and Malton. There were coins of Alfred, Edward the Elder, Aethelstan, and Viking coins with reverses EBORACE, the open hand, the Carolus monogram, and the bow and arrow. A silver bracelet was ornamented with patterns of Oriental origin, no doubt introduced via the Baltic, where in the tenth century the Viking trade route from Ireland and England met that from the east through Russia.

A hoard of silver coins in a small lead chest found at a depth of about three feet near Goldsborough Church (W.R.) well illustrates the far-flung range of Viking commerce. The coins included half an " offering-penny " of Alfred (871–901) and a coin of his son Edward (901–25). The remaining coins were Cufic, a name derived from that of a city near Babylon, which was the residence of the Caliphs before Bagdad was built. They were issued by the following princes of the Samanian dynasty :

1. Nasr ben Ahmed, one struck at Samarcand 889.

2. Ismail ben Ahmed, four struck at Tashkend, 893, 898, 899, 903, and three at Samarcand in 895, 897, 899 ; also many others not so legible.

3. Ahmed ben Ismail, two, 910.

4. Nasr ben Ahmed, one with the Caliph's name, Al Moktader Billah, whose rule ended in 932.

Associated with the coins were silver ingots, fragments of silver bracelets and brooches, including a typically

British brooch, the pin of which is $7\frac{3}{4}''$ long, and terminates at the hinged end in a thistle head from which springs a hoop, also ending in a thistle head on either side the pin, the diameter of the hoop being one-third the length of the pin. Even larger specimens have been found in Cumberland and Ireland, and they have occasionally occurred in Norway and Sweden. Both coins and ornaments are in the British Museum.

A Viking plaited gold bracelet was dug up in a potato field at Rudding Park, Wetherby (W.R.).

A bronze trefoil brooch (c. 900) comes from Pickering. It has a contorted ribbon-like animal on each lobe, the heads meeting in the centre of the brooch.

The most important Viking burials in Yorkshire were those found in Kildale Church (N.R.) in 1867. Seven or eight skeletons lay a few inches beneath mediaeval graveslabs, within the north wall of the nave. They lay east and west, the head of one being at the feet of another. Three of them had a sword lying obliquely across the leg-bones, the hilt at the right hip, and a two-edged dagger. A fourth had an iron axe-head on the right instep, the helve probably reaching to the right hand. There were also a small bone-handled knife, and fragments of spurs. In the chancel lay a fifth skeleton, associated with a perfect sword 33 inches long ; an ornamented bronze buckle ; a dagger with silver wire bound round the hilt ; a pair of tweezers ; the beam and pan of a pair of scales ; and a wooden frame with a movable panel, enclosing a small lead plate, probably a weight. The sword and scales would symbolise the warrior and the merchant, for more than any other folk the Vikings combined these professions. Scales have been found in Dublin and often in Norway. It is a crying shame that these instructive relics were stolen from the case in the church where they were preserved.

A man's skeleton at a depth of one to two feet in the middle of the Roman road, Leeming Lane, near Bedale, had a long square spear-head thrust through the breast, and on each shoulder a bronze brooch of the tortoise type, and of Norwegian origin (Plate X). The outer shell consists of an intricate open-work pattern, the seven bosses of which are connected by strands of twisted wire. Through the pattern the polished inner dome can be seen. Montelius, the famous Swedish archaeologist, dated this type 900-50.

At Camp Hill House near Carthorpe, 4 miles south of Bedale, a Viking burial with spear-head and sword with curved guard and pommel, now in the British Museum, was found a few years before 1865.

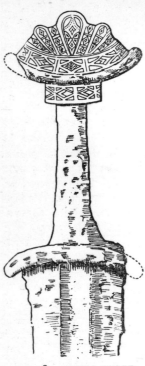

FIG. 38.—VIKING SWORD-HILT, WENSLEY, N.R.
½

From Pippin Castle, 5 miles west of Harrogate, comes an iron axe-head with a small projection or *kick* near the middle of the under edge of the blade. This feature distinguishes a type most frequent on the west coast of Norway, and in use during the ninth and early tenth centuries. In the same mound were beams of oak, two small horseshoes, and a saw blade, all bearing marks of fire, and part of a Runic stone which may have been a hog-back. A burial in Wensley churchyard yielded a sword of Viking type (*c.* A.D. 875) with a lobed pommel ornamented with nielloed silver plates, sickle, and spear (Fig. 38).

It will be seen from the foregoing account that many Viking relics are Norwegian. The Norwegians began to colonise Yorkshire under the rule of the Dublin Kings at York. Some, indeed, came directly from Norway to occupy the Whitby district, which, like York, is one of the most Scandinavian parts of England. The majority came from western Scotland, Man, and above all Ireland via the

Pennine passes to settle in Craven, the western dales, and to a less extent in Cleveland and on the Wolds. This colonisation is revealed by Norwegian names for natural features such as Gill (ravine), Foss or Force (waterfall), Slack (small shallow valley), Fell (mountain), Thwaite (clearing) ; and others of Gaelic origin such as Airy Hill from *airighe*, a hill-pasture ; Arras, Argos, Arram, Argam from *ergh*, a Scandinavianised form of the same word. The movement from Ireland is further proved by Irton and Irby, which contain old Norse Ire, a Viking who had been in Ireland, and by Irish personal names found in Duggleby (Dubghail), Lackenby (Lochan).

After settling in Yorkshire the Scandinavians, who in their homelands were not builders in stone, began to try their hands at sculpture. Being ignorant of the art they chose rough stones such as they could easily procure, and these they were obliged to chip and hack out, rather than chisel. Their space-filling decorations were pellets and ring-bands ; they used step patterns and the $T \underline{\perp} T$ design ; spirals, cables and chains. They introduced grotesque figures like those in Irish ornament, serpents and dragons for the most part. The development of their sculpture was aided by the work of their predecessors ; but never did they arrive at the fastidious delicacy and intricacy, or the graceful, harmonious assurance of the Anglian school of sculpture.

The Celtic or wheel-head cross is one of their most characteristic monuments. Collingwood has proved that it originated in Man, and was subsequently influenced by Irish, Scottish and Anglian tradition. The crosses were made out of slabs of stone, pierced at one end so as to form the four arms, which never became free therefore, like the Anglian crosses, but remained attached to a circumscribing rim, doubtless of symbolic significance. As the Vikings developed skill their work became more shapely, their methods more daring. No longer did the rim or wheel confine the cross. That sacred emblem became more conspicuous. Gradually its arms became all but free, as the wheel retreated towards the centre.

Wheel-head crosses, deplorably broken for the most part, are more abundant in Yorkshire, especially in the North Riding, than anywhere else. Their introduction must be attributed to the movement from the west, via Stainmore and the Aire Gap. We have early examples showing Manx influence. One of these is in the church porch at Topcliffe. It is neatly carved, with rounded edges. The wheel circumscribes the cross ; but, though hollowed out, is not pierced. The ornament consists of two contour lines, with a pellet in the centre of the cross. At Kirby Wharfe a wheel-head cross is decorated with an interlacing pattern used by Gaut Bjarnarson, the Manx carver, in 930–50. At York in the Hospitium is a fragmentary wheel-head cross said to come from St. Mary's, Castlegate. This cross is a hundred years earlier in date than the dedication stone hereinafter described. At Otley, in the tower, is part of a wheel-head, roughly hacked with a rounded strap and ring-twist. This church is rich in pre-Conquest remains, especially in those belonging to the transition between Anglian and Viking styles.

One of our most complete crosses, made of local limestone, is that at Stonegrave (N.R.). It is nearly 6 feet high, and possibly the work of a Scottish carver. The front of the shaft is quaintly decorated with the Latin cross and two human figures, and the space is filled with basket-plait, rudely but fascinatingly intricate. The crosshead is simply decorated with an interlacing pattern.

A tenth-century wheel-head cross at North Frodingham (E.R.) has projecting arms in the Hebridean style, and resembles St. Martin's cross at Iona. From St. Mary's, Castlegate, now in the Museum, there is another with beasts on the cross arms, a parallel for which we find at Kildalton in Islay. A cross-shaft at Lythe (N.R.) is engraved with wrestlers, a Scottish subject.

There are quite a number of pierced wheel-head crosses, including an almost complete example, in the vicarage porch, Kirby Moorside. It is made of cream sandstone, with a deeply-hacked interlacing pattern, and a pellet at the centre of the arms.

Another good example can be seen in the ringing chamber at Middleton. On the shaft is a bound dragon, with fangs, and a claw-like tail (Fig. 39).

At Thornton Steward is the fragmentary head of a cross, with a crucifix and rough key pattern on one side,

A   **B**

FIG. 39.—WHEEL-HEAD CROSSES, N.R.
A, Middleton.   B, Brompton.

and Christ enthroned, with pellets and key-pattern, on the other.

In Kirk Levington Church are four wheel-heads, two being crucifixes, one of these having served for " W.S's " tombstone in 1698. On this head there are only openings in the upper angles.

One of our most illuminating monuments is the cross in Leeds Church, restored from fragments. It dates from the late tenth century, and was certainly wheel-headed. The shaft probably incorporates incidents from Viking mythology. On one side is Völund the Smith, and the Swan Maiden, on the other either Sigurd or St. John.

Rey Cross was also a wheel-head cross, though only the base and shaft are standing on Stainmore. We can just make out a hacked pattern of diverging straps and pellets on the west side. Rey means boundary, and this cross was erected by Edmund (d. 946) to fix the boundary between Scottish Cumberland and England, after he became overlord of Northumbria.

In Nunburnholme (E.R.) churchyard is a tenth-century cross-shaft, more finely executed than the one at Leeds, but smaller. An archway is engraved on each face, and above it is scroll-work, with an arm outstretched from each corner, grasping the arch. Beneath one of these arches is a bearded Viking, with a helmet, long coat, collar, and sword, seated on a tilted stool, naïvely gesticulating with one hand, and holding his sword with the other. Beneath another is the Virgin and Child with a book; beneath a third possibly an Abbess, beneath the fourth a saint with nimbus, book and satchel. Below these figures are bound dragons, and human groups more roughly executed.

The carvings on the Nunburnholme cross are not unlike those on the Franks' casket in the British Museum. This is a carved ivory box of Northumbrian, and possibly Yorkshire origin. It bears carvings similar in design and execution, such as the Madonna under an arch, and the warrior holding a sword.

There is a cross-shaft of the same period at Hawsker, covered with a dragonesque device, criss-cross and knot-work.

Two variants of the wheel-head cross should be noted. The penannular head occurs at Kirby Wharfe, Burnsall, and High Hoyland (W.R.). They belong to the tenth and eleventh centuries. Of rather later date is the hammer-head cross, of which a striking and perfect example can be seen at Middlesmoor (W.R.). It is dedicated to St. Chad, being inscribed CROS · SCE · CEADA.

More numerous are the unpierced wheel-head crosses. A perfect example, where the wheel has become reduced to four cylinders lying in the angles, can be seen at the east end of the north aisle of Middleton Church near Pickering. It is 5 feet high, of light brown sandstone, carved with unsymmetrical and striking plait-work.

At Ellerburn Church, in the same district, there is a cross-head and part of its shaft built into the outside south wall. On the shaft is a spirited gagged dragon. The head consists of a beautifully balanced design of plait-work and pellets which are effectively introduced into the angles between the arms.

In the church at Stanwick is a cross-head of light buff, coarse sandstone, rudely hacked, with a central boss on each side, and on one side a crucifix, with three fingers only on each hand.

When Brompton Church (N.R.) was restored in 1867 many Viking sculptured stones were discovered. They included twelve crosses, one of which is practically perfect. It stands near the organ, is 43 inches high, and ornamented with plait-work. The arms reach well beyond the wheel, which fills the arm-angles (Fig. 39).

A similar one, 5 feet high, stands in the porch, and is a good example of hacked work, perhaps finished off with a chisel.

Three other wheel-heads of like style are in Durham Cathedral Library. In the fragment of another cross of the same type there is a central boss not panelled in a square like the others. There are also the fragments of two pierced wheels, decorated with pellets.

The shaft in the porch is of rather later date. On one side are two cocks, symbolising watchfulness or Peter's denial, and beneath them two grotesque figures. Another side seems to bear an angel, a third side a human figure, while the fourth is scroll-work.

Even more characteristic than the crosses of Brompton

are the eleven hog-back tombstones, six of which have been removed to the Cathedral Library, Durham. The Vikings, like many other folk, regarded the grave as a habitation, a tradition of pagan origin. The hog-backs, an unfortunate name since they have nothing whatever to do with the hog, are the solid roofs that covered the graves, which were probably built of stone. As was the case in the actual timber dwellings, the ridge of the grave-roof, which curves slightly downwards towards the gables, was decorated, sometimes with cable-work, a plait or step pattern, the sides of the roof with interlacing or tile-work, the gable ends with animals, the bear being selected in each case at Brompton (Fig. 40). Elsewhere also the bear is the typical animal, probably of totem origin. But at Easington (N.R.) the bear is replaced by that favourite theme, the dragon. On the gable ends are sometimes figures, like the naïve virgin and child at Oswaldkirk, and the less charming group at Bedale. At Dewsbury and Ingleby Arncliffe (N.R.) we find crosses beneath the gable roof. Like the wheel-head cross the hog-backs are most numerous in the North Riding.

Grave monuments other than hog-backs are rare. In the Yorkshire Museum is a unique coped stone, richly ornamented with dragons and beasts, from St. Denis Church, York. In Levisham Church is a broken grave-slab elaborately covered with a bound dragon. In the vestry wall of Spennithorne Church is a grave-slab almost covered by a double-headed cross, nearly penannular. Each side the shaft is knot-work with bifurcated cords, a characteristic Scandinavian device. Above the cross is a panel of strap-work.

In south Yorkshire there appears to have persisted an Anglian style uninfluenced by the Vikings. At Walton Farm, west of Hartshead Church, there is a cross base, nearly 5 feet high, ornamented with birds and beasts more conventionally and less adroitly than in the early Anglian period. The elaborate plaits have a rich effect, but they repeat easy patterns, and contain rings and closed members which indicate the tenth century. A simpler and smaller

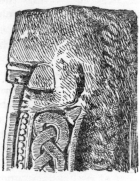

FIG. 40.—VIKING GRAVE COVERS, BROMPTON, N.R.

FIG. 41.—ANGLO-DANISH INSCRIBED SUNDIAL, KIRKDALE, N.R.

example occurs at Rastrick, in the same neighbourhood. The large shaft of a cross from Wakefield consists of an elaborate interlacing pattern, another of the same period at Sheffield bears an archer. Eventually this late Anglian style died out, decadent examples being a crucifix cross at Kirkburton, cross-heads and shaft fragments at Cawthorne (W.R.), Penistone, Ecclesfield and Adel.

About a dozen Yorkshire churches still exhibit architectural features of the Anglo-Danish period. As we already know, the Anglo-Danish folk built their houses of wood, elaborately decorated, as the hog-backs testify. Their stone churches, then, are first essays, wherein the elementary problems involved in stone erections were discovered and tackled. The buildings were small and simple ; the walls of rubble, held together by " through " stones ; and strengthened at the angles by strip or long and short work. The piers were squat cylinders, crowned with rectangular blocks of stone, often unadorned. The windows were small and set high in the walls, a measure taken against thieves. For lighting purposes, when they found glazing too expensive, they depended upon the transparency of linen, or boards pierced with many holes. The belfry windows were of necessity larger, and consisted of two lights, separated by a baluster shaft crowned with an impost from which the two rounded arches sprang. In the lower stages of the tower the windows were but slits. The arches and doorways were simple, and rounded in form. Decoration crept in in the form of horizontal string courses, long and short work, and characteristic carvings on the imposts.

Most of our Yorkshire examples consist of towers, the body of the churches having been enlarged or rebuilt. The oldest building is Bardsey Church tower (W.R.) which dates about 800 to 950. On the west face are traces of what was probably a porch-tower ; that is to say, the tower was erected later upon an already existing porch. The south face has two baluster windows. The west corners of the tower show long and short work. The jambs of the tower arch have no through stones or imposts.

PLATE XI

KIRK HAMMERTON CHURCH, W.R.
Showing Anglo-Danish tower, doorway and South wall

A more complete example of this period is to be seen at Kirk Hammerton (W.R.), where the west tower, nave, and chancel of a church dated 950 to 1066 have become the south aisle of a nineteenth-century church. The remaining wall is built of large blocks. The tower is in two stages, divided by a square string-course. The lower stage is pierced with small rectangular slits, the higher with a two-light opening on each face. The imposts and shafts of the west door are not uniform. There is no true long and short work (Plate XI).

At Ledsham (W.R.) the lower part of the west tower, nave and chancel are pre-Norman. The door on the south side of the tower is not symmetrically placed. The carvings on the imposts and hood are modern restorations of the original knot-work.

At Skipwith (E.R.) the two stages of the west tower are pre-Conquest, with long and short work at the outside angles, and a fine nave arch with roll moulding on each face. A blocked opening above the arch may have led to a gallery. In the east wall of the ringing chamber is a shallow recess lighted by a double splayed window.

Another tower can be seen at Wharram-le-Street (E.R.). Its angles are finished with quoin stones, and there is a single string-course below the belfry stage. The belfry windows are divided by a deeply recessed shaft with a long horizontal stone on top, and a narrow pilaster on each side. The nave arch is horseshoe-shaped. The nave is contemporaneous with the tower. This is post-Conquest work in pre-Conquest style.

The lower stage of the tower, with a blocked doorway, of Middleton near Pickering (N.R.) is late pre-Norman, the angles formed by the dubious long and short work not uncommon in our examples. An Anglian cross-head has been built into the wall above the door.

At Hovingham there is a late pre-Norman tower, into which a large Anglian slab, with eight figures in panels representing the Annunciation, was inserted. This graceful piece of sculpture has now been placed inside the church. It is very weathered, unfortunately. The tower is built in three stages, with a remarkable western door, and two-light belfry windows, with deeply recessed dividing shafts. In the wall are traces of herring-bone masonry.

The pre-Conquest tower (1042–66) of St. Mary's Junior of York is largely built of Roman stone. It contains a typical belfry window, two arched lights, separated by a shaft or baluster, with projecting imposts running through the thickness of the wall.

Appleton-le-Street possesses the best of the pre-Conquest towers. The lowest stage is windowless ; the upper stages have two-light windows, divided by simple shafts. On the highest stage the shafts have zigzag or spiral incisions. All the windows have plain, projecting imposts to shafts and jambs. Those to the shafts are carried right through the thickness of the wall. There is a niche on the north face of the tower above the porch, with the mutilated figures of the Virgin and Child.

At Kirby Hill much of the nave, and perhaps also the chancel, are of Anglo-Danish date, and the south nave door presents a rare instance of a carved impost. Carved imposts can often be seen used over again in walls as building material, and to see a carved impost *in situ* is rare.

At Hornby the three lower stages of the tower are Anglo-Danish. They are built of rough rubble masonry, with small circular-headed slits, and shafts in the upper storey.

The tower at Stonegrave is in three stages, with a round-headed slit in the second. There is no regular long and short work, but something closely approximating to it.

At Terrington the tower shows some fine herring-bone work, and a single, circular-headed slit, thus resembling the tower in the neighbouring church of Bulmer.

At Scarborough, when the Roman fort was excavated, the foundations of an early eleventh-century chapel were discovered within the signal tower. The plan of the chapel revealed that it was without aisles, had an oblong nave and a square-ended chancel. A bronze cross with perforations was all that was left of a book of late Anglian date. In the graveyard was found a skeleton with a jet cross of the same period.

In St. Mary's, Castlegate, York, is a dedication stone, dating after the Danish conquest, impressively lettered, reading as follows :

✠ THIS MYNSTER SET ···
··· RARD & GRIM & AESE : O ···
··· MAN DRIHTNES HAE···
··· CRISTES & SCA MA ···
·· E MARTINI & SCE C ···
·· TI & OMNIVM SCORV ···
··· SECRATA EST AN ···
VISINVITAET
OAERIO THEM F
TER AETSI

The nave and west tower of Weaverthorpe Church are very early Norman, and may be pre-Norman. Above the south doorway is a sundial, 20″ by 12½″, with the following inscription :

✠ IN HONORE SCI ANDREAE
APOSTOLI HEREBERTVS
WINTONIE HOC MONASTERI
VM FECIT IN TEMPORE R

" In honour of Andrew the Apostle Herbert Winton built this monastery in the time of (King ?)." The semicircular frame of the dial has no lettering. The bronze stump of the gnomon still remains fixed to the stone.

Inscribed eleventh-century sundials can be seen at Aldborough Church (E.R.), Great Edston and Old Byland (N.R.). The most famous is that over the south porch of Kirkdale Church, so rich in monuments of Anglo-Danish age (Fig. 41). It is a good example of the English of the period and reads :

Orm Gamalsuna bohte Scš Gregorius minster thonne hit wes ael to-brocan & to-falan, & he hit let macan newan from grunde, Chr(ist)e & Scs Gregorius, in Eadward dagum c(yni)ng, &(i)n Tosti dagum eorl. This is daeges sol-merca aet ilcum tide : & Haward me urohte & Brand pr̃s.

Orm, Gamal's son, bought St. Gregory's minster, when it was all broken and fallen, and he it let made anew from the ground to Christ and St. Gregory, in Edward's days, the King, and in Tosti's days, the earl. This is the day's sun-marker at every time, and Haward wrought me and Brand, priests.

16

The dial therefore dates from 1055-65, when Edward the Confessor was on the throne, and Tosti, son of Earl Godwin and brother of Harald, the last of the Saxon kings, was earl of Northumberland.

Tosti's rule over Northumberland was so brutal that Harald banished him. He thereupon allied himself with Harald Hardradi, King of Norway, doughtiest of all the Vikings. A warrior from the age of fifteen, a captain in the Russian Army before the age of twenty, commander of the Varangian bodyguard of the Emperor at Constantinople, capturer of eighty Arabic strongholds in Asia Minor and Mesopotamia, campaigner in Sicily, Italy and Bulgaria, explorer of Polar seas, Hardradi now descended upon the Yorkshire coast with a fleet of three hundred ships that sailed under his banner, the Landwaster. True to its name, he ravaged Cleveland, burnt Scarborough, pillaged Holderness, and then sailed up the Humber for York. He landed probably at Riccal in order to advance to York along the ridge that rises up between the surrounding marshes. He utterly defeated the English who met him at Fulford, under the leadership of Earls Edwin and Morcar. He entered York in triumph. But a few days later he withdrew his forces to Stamford Bridge.

Now why did Hardradi abandon York so soon after his victory? No satisfactory explanation has yet been given. But by placing his forces at Stamford Bridge Hardradi not only commanded the road to York from the south and east, but also that along the Escrick moraine to the Ouse where his fleet was lying. Advantageous as this position was for battle it does not convincingly explain why he preferred it to York. What vital reason urged him out of that city? It looks as if Hardradi had received news to the effect that Harald was gathering together an army and marching north along the Lincoln-Brough road, which leads into York by way of Stamford Bridge. So here he would intercept Harald, defeat him, and then withdraw again to York, for the second time victorious, and a decisive step nearer to the crown of England. But in Harald the Landwaster met his match. For Harold made a forced march via Tadcaster to York which he entered in the silence of the night ; and before daybreak he secretly pressed on to Stamford Bridge. Taken completely unaware, the Vikings were hurled to confusion ; a fierce battle ensued, and the Landwaster and Tosti were both slain.

Thus ended the epic history of the Viking invasions of Yorkshire. Had Tosti not been a tyrant, had Harald not banished him, had Hardradi not invaded our shores, had Harald's army not become worn and weakened by rapid marching and desperate fighting, Harald would have presented an unconquerable front to William at Hastings, and then his wish for a peaceful reign, as recorded in the single word Pax imprinted on his coins, might have come to pass, and England might have remained English to the core.

For Reference : R. A. Smith, *Anglo-Saxon Remains*, V.C.H., ii, 1912. *B.M. Guide to Anglo-Saxon Antiquities*, 1923. T. Sheppard, *Anglo-Saxon Vases in the Hull Museum*, T.E.R.A.S., xvi ; *Anglo-Saxon Remains in E.Yorkshire*, Trans. Hull Sci. and F. Nat. Club, iv, 1919. W. G. Collingwood, *Anglo-Saxon Sculptured Stone*, V.C.H., ii, 1912 ; *Anglian and Anglo-Danish Sculpture in Yorkshire*, Y.A.J., xix, xx, xxi, xxiii; *Dispersion of the Wheel Cross*, Y.A.J., xxviii, 1925 ; *Angles, Danes, and Norse in the neighbourhood of Huddersfield*, Tolson Museum Publication, 1921 ; *Northumbrian Crosses of Pre-Norman Age*, London, 1927 ; *Pedigree of Anglian Crosses*, Ant., vi, 1932. D. H. Haigh, *Yorkshire Mints under the Danish Kings*, Y.A.J., iv, 1875–6. *B.M. Catalogue of Anglo-Saxon Coins*, i, ii, 1887, 1893. T. D. Kendrick, *History of the Vikings*, London, 1930. George Benson, *Coins, especially those relating to York*, R.Y.P.S., 1913.

CHAPTER XII

THE SCAMRIDGE DIKES AND OTHER EARTHWORKS

YORKSHIRE is rich in earthworks, the purpose and period of which have not been ascertained. In the ancient royal forest of Pickering there is a well-defined system which centres round the famous Scamridge Dikes. The Dikes consist in the main of a central ditch lined on either side by ramparts, running in two lines for more than a mile roughly south and north, converging to the north, though not quite meeting. Beyond this narrow gap one line continues in a northerly direction, until it reaches the southern side of Troutsdale. But this length is much more elaborate, dividing up into six ramparts, with narrow gaps cutting through them, and five ditches, to-day 5 to 10 feet deep; when in use they were considerably deeper. Towards the south, across the broad opening formed by the two main lines of the dike, there appears every indication of a transverse dike, running roughly east and west. It will be seen from the map that the dikes form a more or less horn-shaped enclosure, open at the top, one side of the horn being elaborately extended (Fig. 42).

Now if we survey the whole forest area we find such a system of earthworks repeating itself, with variations. There are the Cockmoor Hall Dikes to the east, comprising as many as eighteen parallel ramparts and seventeen ditches. Although the horn-shape is not so evident, it will be seen that such a shape is approximated to by transverse ditches running westwards to the Scamridge Dikes.

The horn-shape is distinctly visible in the Givendale and Oxmoor Dikes, to the west of Scamridge; indeed, we

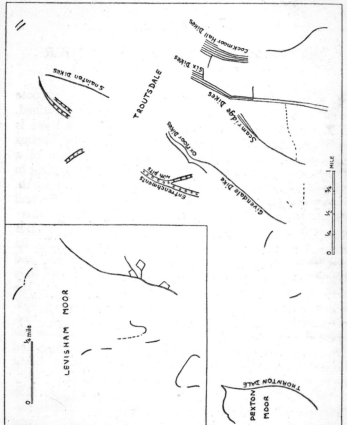

FIG. 42.—SKETCH PLAN OF SCAMRIDGE AND RELATED DIKES, AND EARTHWORKS ON LEVISHAM MOOR (INSET)

get a two-horn system in the case of the Givendale earthworks. The Oxmoor Dikes consist of four broken ramparts and three ditches, whose original depth varied from 10 to 12 feet, 3½ feet wide at the bottom. The Snainton Dikes to the north also form a horn, open at the tip ; and the Pexton Moor Dikes show the same shape even more clearly.

Various opinions have been held with regard to the Scamridge Dikes. Greenwell assumed that they were prehistoric, and that they were erected as tribal barriers, or to prevent the driving off of cattle. Mortimer suggested that they were covered ways of escape for the inhabitants of Troutsdale. Colonel Kitson Clark thinks they are roads, gradually deepened by throwing out on either side the loose stones and earth that impeded the going. General Pitt-Rivers considered them to be the work of invaders, who had landed at Flamborough Head, where they first erected the Danes' Dike.

None of these views appears to us to be tenable. The Dikes are not roads, for hollow ways only develop on hillsides, as they become troughs for descending waters in flood-time. They do not correspond in any way with the Danes' Dike, and so could not have been erected by the same people. Their number and arrangement do not suggest fortifications. The repetition of the horn-shaped enclosure is to us the significant feature, and cannot be regarded as accidental.

A clue to their purpose is found in the ancient Whitby custom observed annually on Ascension eve of ' Planting the Penny Hedge ' on the east fore-shore of the Esk. The Hedge nowadays consists of a row of hazel stakes, but the Abbey records show that the custom was formerly a much more vital function known as the Service of Horngarth, and practised as early at least as the first half of the twelfth century. The word horngarth is of old Norse origin, and as suggested by Major R. B. Turton in his illuminating account of the custom it denoted an angular enclosure bounded by a hedge and dike, the construction and maintenance of which constituted the Horngarth Service. He further suggests that into this enclosure wild animals were driven for slaughter, a method of hunting widely practised in ancient times. He points out that the Penny Hedge ceremony of to-day echoes Anglian observances ; and that therefore the Horngarth originated in Anglian times, when the Whitby district was one of the royal manors in which Oswy, king of Northumbria, loved to hunt.

After discussing in detail the hunting method alluded to, Major Turton states that he does not know of any other existing hedge and dike erected for that purpose. But we venture to suggest that the horn-shaped enclosures, so obvious in the Scamridge dike system, are horngarths. Animals could be driven into them, and slaughtered as they crowded towards the narrow ends. Those that escaped could run along the elaborate system of ditches beyond the angles, where huntsmen stationed at the gaps slew or netted them. Or maybe the animals fell into pits, which can still be seen along the ditches of the Snainton and Givendale Dikes.

Confirmation of this suggestion is afforded by place-names. Near the Snainton Dikes we find the name Hern Head, hern being an old form of horn. A road leading to the Pexton works is called the Haygate. ' Haie ' or ' hay ', which means hedge, is an Anglo-Norman term for enclosures into which deer were driven, as recorded in Domesday. ' Haw ' is another variant, as in Hawdale, near the Givendale Dikes, and near earthworks on Levisham Moor described below.

Now these earthworks cannot belong to the Bronze Age, for they did not interfere with the barrows that lay in their way. Nor have we found as yet any evidence to prove that they were erected in the Early Iron or Roman periods. We know they gave the name to the Wapentake of Dic, mentioned in Domesday, and must therefore have existed prior to 1086. We know, too, that in Anglian times there was surprising activity in hedging and ditching, especially in the erection and maintenance of deer-hunting enclosures. We think, therefore, that these earthworks, concentrated as they are in the royal forest of Pickering (a fact which has never before been emphasized), are mainly of Anglian origin.

There are other earthworks in the forest area, notably those in Blansby Park, west of Pickering, where about eight lines of entrenchment converge towards a centre. These do not make the simple outline of a horngarth, though they may have been constructed for battues.

Another set of works on Levisham Moor undoubtedly takes the form of a horngarth, with the addition of three quadrilateral enclosures on a comparatively small scale. The largest consists of a rampart with an outer ditch on three sides, and a slight embankment on the fourth side. Other earthworks, no longer completely traceable, lie on the moor to the west. None of these works has Bronze Age characteristics, and they are in all probability Anglian or mediaeval.

On the same moor we find two short entrenchments consisting of fosse and ramparts, and running from the steep edge of the Tabular escarpment to the nearest valley head. The Gallows Dike and the Dargate Dikes are similarly situated further east. Their age is uncertain.

On the edge of the forest area are the remains of extensive earthworks on Seamer Moor above Scarborough, and the Thieves' Dikes on Suffield Moor near Scalby Hays. This name suggests a mediaeval origin, and the dikes were mentioned as being on the boundary of the Whitby Strand Liberty in the reign of Henry I.

On the Hambleton plateau the Cleave Dike runs for at least two miles N.W. and S.E., at some distance from the edge of the escarpment, as part rampart, part ditch. Near Hesketh Farm the ditch is repeatedly broken every three yards. Near the Hambleton Hotel it crosses at right angles the Casten Dike, which consists of a rampart with a ditch to the south.

The northern end of the Cleave Dike is obscure. It has not been traced north of the Hesketh Dike which, like the Casten Dike, runs at right angles to it, and consists likewise of a rampart and ditch to the south. The Cleave Dike seems to be later than the Hesketh and Casten Dikes, which certainly resemble the Gallows Dike and the Dargate Dikes.

On Ampleforth Moor we find Studford Ring, consisting of a nearly rectangular bank not more than 11 feet high, with an internal ditch, enclosing a platform 180 feet in diameter, and ¾ acre in area. There is an entrance on the east side. A similar work stands on Great Ayton Moor in Cleveland. Though both works occur in the neighbourhood of Mid-Bronze Age barrows they are certainly not sepulchral, and are probably of much later date.

At Stanwick Park (N.R.) are some of the largest and most extensive earthworks in the county. Known locally as Jack-dike Arches, their high and nearly continuous rampart and outer ditch of 4½ miles form a roughly triangular enclosure of 675 acres. The south-east angle appears to have been destroyed. There are indications of a southern rectangular annexe enclosing 150 acres. Another rampart and ditch extend within the main enclosure from Forcett village towards Stanwick Hall. This line is broken by a small stream flowing eastwards, and likewise dividing the main eastern rampart. Round the church and hall there formerly existed a plexus of banks known as the Tofts (old dwelling enclosures).

It has been suggested that the earthworks were a Brigantian *oppidum*, apparently because the Iron Age antiquities described on p. 110 were said to have been found in them. Actually they were found at Low Langdale, a mile to the south-east. This is the express statement of Maclauchlan,[1] who had every opportunity of knowing the facts, as he worked for the Duke of Northumberland, the owner of the property.

As a matter of fact the enclosure is not likely to be a fortification, for it is commanded by two adjacent hills on the north-east, and by higher ground at the south-west angle. There are no traces of Roman besieging camps in

[1] Roman Roads, Camps and Earthworks between the Swale and the Tees, *Arch. J.*, vi, 339. A bronze spiral armilla and part of a brooch, however, are said to have been found near the church within the works.—*V.C.H.*, ii, 61.

the vicinity, such as we should expect if the Brigantes had been there to offer resistance. Mrs. Armitage, in her account of the Yorkshire earthworks, suggested that these banks formed the enclosure of a deer-park, a view we had independently reached ourselves. The association of embankments with the name park is very frequent in Yorkshire, as Julian Park, Goathland ; Black Park, Cropton ; Oscar Park, Helmsley ; Newburgh Park (N.R.) ; Park Nab, Kildale ; Scale Hill Park, Great Whernside ; Hall Park, near Thorpe Arch (W.R.), and others.

At the northern end of Bilsdale there is a fine example of a contour work associated with the name Park. It follows for the most part the 1,100 to 1,200 feet contour on the eastern side of the dale, and consists of a rampart with a ditch on the western side, $2\frac{1}{2}$ miles in length. At its northern end it turns abruptly westwards across the dale head at Hagg's Gate [1] on the Stokesley road, beyond which point its course has not been fully determined, though it occurs again on the slope of Hasty [2] Bank.

There is a long contour work on the Howardian Hills, stretching for 7 miles just south of the brow of the ridge overlooking Slingsby. This may be another park boundary.

Another earthwork on Commondale Moor consisting of an inner ditch and outer rampart encloses the North Ings valley. In our opinion this was originally stockaded, forming an enclosure for deer-hunting.

It is not possible at the present juncture to form any definite conclusions about the plexus of earthworks in the Wold area. In the first place, since the Wolds have been enclosed and cultivated, the earthworks have been greatly interfered with. Mortimer envisaged them as well as it was possible, and his accounts are full of detailed interest. In the second place, their complexity is the outcome of a long period of occupation by varied peoples from long-barrow times onward, and this in itself makes research work still more difficult. Not only will many of the embankments prove to be village and town enclosures, and

[1] Hagg = haie = hedge.   Gate = road.
[2] Hasty = Haie + sty = hedge + path.

defensive works ; some will be hunting works such as those we have already considered, others will be hollow roads, still others field boundaries.

Here it suffices to say that they enclose areas both large and small, and from them radiate in every direction branches of varying length. Such enclosures have been traced at Fimber, Aldro, Calais Wold and Millington. The ramparts are usually double, separated by a ditch, a favourite form of earthwork. Sometimes they are triple or quadruple. They are not high, rarely exceeding 8 feet. The ditches at the present surface are 10 to 12 feet wide. Such entrenchments also occur along the valley sides, just below their crests, and they can be seen traversing watersheds from dale-head to dale-head. On Huggate Pasture as many as 6 ditches and 5 ramparts running parallel and 200 feet in width can be seen, reminding us of the Cockmoor Hall Dikes. Some entrenchments avoid the roundbarrows, or sometimes cut through them. Anglian interments have been found in others, and this enables us to regard those as post-Bronze Age, but pre-Norman.

The Argam Dike runs for five miles from Reighton to Rudston. It consists of 3 banks and 2 ditches, 35 yards wide in all.

A very different type of earthwork is the Danes' Dike, $2\frac{1}{2}$ miles long, and as much as 18 feet high. It has an extraordinary ditch on the western side 60 feet wide. The counterscarp is well banked up. The Dike runs across the Flamborough Headland, enclosing an area of 5 square miles.

Trenches made by Pitt-Rivers in 1879 revealed more than 60 flints lying on the old surface, and characteristic of Bronze Age manufacture. He thought the dike was thrown up by invaders, but it is hardly likely that a large body of invaders would or could land at Flamborough Head. We have no evidence of foreign objects in this area ; and the dike was probably a work erected by the inhabitants themselves against some enemy. It should be compared with the dikes associated with Mid-Bronze Age settlements in Eskdale (p. 82).

The Scots Dike originally ran from Barforth-on-Tees to Hindwath-on-Swale, and must have been at least ten miles long. It comprises a bank 25 feet high, with a ditch about 12 feet wide on the east side, and a small counterscarp bank. It has no connection whatever with the Stanwick works, to the east of which it lies.[1] Between Barforth and Aldborough it has been destroyed, but it is traceable thence to the neighbourhood of Richmond. Good stretches can be seen at Kirklands, north-east of Gilling, and at Olliver Duckitt, north of the Richmond-Skeeby road. A continuation of the Scots Dike is said to have run along the south bank of the Swale, from Hindwath to Grinton, where in 1821 there was a considerable line of huge stones.

At Grinton, but quite apart from the Scots Dike, there is a roughly circular earthwork consisting of a bank with an outer ditch, and entered by a stone avenue from the east. It is called Maiden Castle. Its age is unknown, but it is associated with cairns and barrows.

A work similar to the Scots Dike is the so-called Roman Rig. It keeps just below the crests of the hills on the west side of the Don Valley between Sheffield and Swinton where it comes to an abrupt end. It runs north-east and then due east and is 11 miles long. It is built of loose stones and earth, 8 feet high where most perfect. The ditch to the east is 30 feet wide, with a small counterscarp bank. It is not connected with the camp at Wincobank, below which it runs. A good length can be seen in Wentworth Park near the Greasbrough entrance. From Wentworth Park to Mexborough runs a parallel embankment. The age and purpose of the Roman Rig and Scots Dike must be decided by future research.

For Reference : Armitage and Montgomery, *Ancient Earthworks*, V.C.H., ii, 1912. Mortimer, *Small Pits near Scamridge Dikes*, Arch. J., Sept. 1895 ; *Forty Years' Researches*, 365–96 (with map). E. Kitson Clark, *Prehistoric Route in Yorkshire*, P.S.A., xxiii, 1911. Wheeler, *History of Scarborough*, 1930. R. B. Turton, *The Service of Horngarth*, Y.A.J., xx, 51–67. E. M. Cole, P.Y.G.S., 1888.

---

[1] *V.C.H.*, ii, 55 ; *Arch. J.*, vi, 223.

ARCHAEOLOGICAL GAZETTEERS

(I.—East Riding.   II.—North Riding.   III—West Riding.
IV.—York.)

These make no claim to be exhaustive.   Only the most important discoveries and sites have been inserted.   Outstanding field antiquities are indicated by an asterisk.

The following contain numerous further records :

V.C.H., I (1907), list of prehistoric antiquities ; II (1912), lists of earthworks and Anglo-Danish sculptured stones.

Hübner's *Corpus Inscriptionum Latinarum*, VII, with Haverfield's *Supplement* down to 1912.

Brit. Ass. Card Catalogue of Bronze Implements deposited with the Society of Antiquaries at Burlington House.

Catalogue of the Bateman Collection, 1899, Sheffield Museum.

Handbook to the Antiquities in the Yorkshire Museum, 8th Ed., 1891 (out of print).

Hull Museum Publications. Yorkshire Archaeological Journal. Transactions of the E.R. Antiquarian Society. Reports of the Yorkshire Philosophical Society ; Proceedings of the Yorkshire Geological Society. The Bradford Antiquary. Halifax Antiquarian Society's Papers. The Naturalist. Tolson M. Publications. Journal of Roman Studies.

I. EAST RIDING

ACKLAM : Bronze Age barrows, Mortimer, 83–94 ; hoard socketed axes (p. 93), *op. cit.*, xlviii [H.M.] ; bronze sword, Whellan, *History of N. Riding*, 1859, II, 209.   Anglian cemetery (p. 182), Mortimer, 94–5 ; *V.C.H.*, II, 92–3.   Stone implements, *A.S.I.*, 140, 415.

ALDBROUGH : Pottery and other Roman remains, T. Sheppard, *Lost Towns of the Yorkshire Coast*, 1912, 124.   Inscribed Anglo-Danish sun-dial, *A.J.*, VIII, 510–12 ; *Y.A.J.*, XXI, 256–7.

ALDRO : Bronze Age barrows, Mortimer, 53–82

ATWICK : Perforated stone axe, *H.M.P.*, No. 122 ; flat bronze axe and bronze spear-head [Hornsea M.] ; Iron Age hut-pits (p. 113).   Ancient British coin, *R.Y.P.S.*, 1913, 9.

BARMSTON : Lake dwelling (p. 103), *Arch.*, LXII, 1911 ; *V.C.H.*, I, 404.   Bronze dagger and spear-head [Hornsea M.] ; socketed axe [Y.M.].   Stone axe, *A.S.I.*, 128.

    Gembling, socketed axe [B.M.].

Gransmoor, flanged axes [H. and Y.M.s.].

Lissett, flat axe [Y.M.], flanged axe [St. Albans M.], socketed axe [Mortimer M.].

BEVERLEY : Iron Age chariot burials and barrow groups at Westwood and Scorborough, Greenwell, *Arch.*, LX, 1906 ; Mortimer, lxxi. Anglian brooch [H.M.], *V.C.H.*, II, 74. Flat, flanged and socketed axes [H.M.]. Palstave [Leeds M.]. Waisted socketed axe (p. 95).

BILTON: Hoard socketed axes, spear-heads, etc. (pp. 92, 98) [S.M.], *J.B.A.A.*, V, 349–50 ; *A.B.I.*, 113, 465.

BINNINGTON : Bronze Age barrow, *B.B.*, No. XXXI. Bronze bell containing twelve silver Roman coins, *Y.M. Handbook*, 245.

BISHOP BURTON : Mid-Bronze Age barrows, Oliver, *History of Beverley*, 1829, 4 ; Greenwell, *Arch.*, LII. Roman tessellated pavements, *H.M.P.*, No. 46.

BRIDLINGTON : Numerous axes and other stone implements (p. 49), T. Sheppard, 'Prehistoric Bridlington', *Nat.*, 1923 ; *A.S.I.*, 91, 96, 125, 128–9, 176 ; *H.M.P.*, No. 74 ; *Proc. Geolog. Assoc.*, I, 273–7. Bronze dagger [Leeds Art Gallery] ; flat bronze axe and halberd, *Nat.*, 1917. Irish jet bead, *B.M. Bronze Age Guide*, 1920, 86.

BROUGH-ON-HUMBER : Roman station (p. 123), T. Sheppard, *Antiquary*, March–April, 1902 ; *H.M.P.*, No. 46 ; Codrington, *Roman Roads*, 127. Beakers and bronze dagger (p. '70), *H.M.P.*, Nos. 43, 45–6, 141 ; *B.M. Bronze Age Guide*, 29. Hoard socketed axes (p. 93), Mortimer, xlviii ; bronze spear-head [Hornsea M.].

BUGTHORPE : Iron Age sword (p. 111), *B.M. Iron Age Guide*, 114–15 ; *V.C.H.*, I. 395. Perforated stone axe, *A.S.I.*, 205 ; *H.M.P.*, No. 122.

BURSTWICK : Large stone battle-axe (p. 62), flanged and socketed bronze axes [H.M.].

BURTON AGNES : Socketed axe [H.M.].

BURTON PIDSEA : Two skeletons with glass ear-rings and plain gold ring [Anglian ?], Poulson, *History of Holderness*, 1840, III, 44.

BUTTERWICK : Bronze Age barrow (p. 65), *B.B.*, No. XXXIX.

CARNABY : Looped spear-head [Y.M.]. Stone axes, *A.S.I.*, 91, 115.

CATWICK : Socketed axe [H.M.].

CHERRY BURTON : Bronze Age barrows, *B.B.*, Nos. LXXII–V.

COTTINGHAM : Four Bronze Age gold armlets (p. 99), *Nat.*, 1927 ; *B.M. Bronze Age Guide*, 51. Flint dagger (p. 57) ; hoard stone axes, *Nat.*, 1926, 262–4 [H.M.].

COWLAM : Iron and Bronze Age barrows, *B.B.*, LI–LIX ; *Y.A.J.*, XX, 491–2 ; XXI, 214–7 ; Mortimer, 336–41. Flanged axe (Y.M.]. Stone battle-axe (p. 70), *H.M.P.*, No. 122, 47.

DRIFFIELD : *Iron Age barrows, the Danes' Graves (p. 107), *R.Y.P.S.*, 1897 ; *P.Y.G.S.*, XIII, 1897 ; *Arch.*, LX, 1906. Anglian cemeteries (p. 182–3), Mortimer, 293–4, 286–93 ; *V.C.H.*, II, 86–7 ; *J.B.A.A.*, II, 55. Kelleythorpe barrow (p. 53), Mortimer, 271–83 ; *V.C.H.*, II, 82–4 ; *Arch.*, XXXIV, 251. Flanged axe [Y.M.] ; socketed axes [Mortimer M.]. Tree-trunk coffin (p. 64), *Y. Museum Handbook*, 12.

DUGGLEBY : *Howe Hill (p. 60), Mortimer, 23–41 ; stone axe, *A.S.I.*, 140.

DUNNINGTON : Plain Roman altars, *York M. Handbook*, 46.
 Scorby, Roman urns and coins (p. 152), Phillips', *Rivers, etc., of Yorkshire*, 1853, 92.

EASINGTON : Pottery and other Roman remains, Sheppard, *Lost Towns*, 120–2 ; *H.M.P.*, No. 46. Bronze Age barrows with urns, skeletons, etc., *op. cit.*, 120 ; *H.M.P.*, Nos. 46, 55.

ETTON : Bronze Age barrows, *B.B.*, LXXVI–LXXXII. Roman hypocaust (p. 169), Mortimer, 342–3.

EVERTHORPE : Hoard socketed axes (p. 94), *Nat.*, 1921, 98 ; 1923, 236–7 ; 1926, 209–10, 242 [H.M.].

FILEY : Roman coastguard fort (p. 173), Cortis, *Trans. Scarborough Phil. and Arch. Soc.*, 1857 ; Haverfield, *J.R.S.*, II, 1912 ; *J.B.A.A.*, XLIV, 353–6. Stone axes [H.M.] ; palstave [Art Gallery, Leeds].

FIMBER : Romano-British cemetery (p. 152), Mortimer, 194–5 ; Anglian remains, *op. cit.* Bronze Age barrows, etc., *op. cit.*, 186–200 ; clay moulds for bronzes (p. 94) ; grooved stone hammer (p. 70), *H.M.P.*, No. 122. Thousands of flint and stone implements [Lady Graves], *V.C.H.*, I, 409.
 Raisthorp, flat axe [H.M.].

FLAMBOROUGH : *The Danes' Dike (p. 235). Three socketed axes [Y.M.]. Perforated hammer and other stone implements, *A.S.I.*, 225. Round barrows, Mortimer, 344–6 ; Greenwell, *Arch.*, LII, 1890.

FLOTMANBY : *Long barrow (p. 41). Round barrows, Greenwell, *Arch.*, LII, p. 16 ; bronze rapier (p. 98).

FOLKTON : Bronze Age barrows, *B.B.*, Nos. LXX–LXXI ; chalk carvings (p. 70), *Arch.*, LII ; *B.M. Bronze Age Guide*, 1920.

FRODINGHAM, NORTH : Wheel-cross (p. 216), *Y.A.J.*, XX, 258–9. Socketed axe, *A.B.I.*, 123.

GANTON : Bronze Age barrows, *B.B.*, XVI–XXX. Numerous flint implements, *A.S.I.*, 73, 89, 94, 241, 267, 335–6, 356, 358.

GARTON : Early Bronze Age barrows (pp. 56–9), Mortimer, 208–70. Anglian cemeteries (p. 182), *op. cit.*, 247–57, 264–9 ; *V.C.H.*, II, 79–82.

GARROWBY : Bronze Age barrows, Mortimer, 134–50.

GIVENDALE : Socketed axe (p. 92), *A.B.I.*, 127.

GOODMANHAM : Bronze Age barrows, *B.B.*, Nos. LXXXIII–CXXI; *Arch.*, XXXIV, 256. Flanged axe [Y.M.]. Anglian burials and brooches (p. 188), *B.B.*, 286; *V.C.H.*, II, 77.

GRIMTHORPE, see MILLINGTON.

HALSHAM : Roman urns, *H.M.P.*, Nos. 46, 60.

HANGING GRIMSTON : Long barrow (p. 44), Mortimer, 102–5. Bronze Age barrows, *op. cit.*, 96–101, 105–12. Hoard socketed axes, *op. cit.*, xlviii.

HARPHAM : Roman villa, *H.M.P.*, No. 23. Socketed axe [Y.M.].

HELPERTHORPE : Long barrow (p. 53), Mortimer, 333–5. Bronze Age barrows, *B.B.*, Nos. XL, XLI, XLIX. Stone axes, etc., *A.S.I.*, 89, 177, 262, 302.

HESLERTON : Long barrow, *B.B.*, 143, 488–9. Bronze Age barrows, *B.B.*, IV–VI. Ground and perforated stone axes, *A.S.I.*, 120, 202, 224.

HESLINGTON : Roman burials, *Y.M. Handbook*, 116–17. Siward's How—round barrow. Looped spear-head [Y.M.].

HESSLE : Anglian cist (p. 181), *H.M.P.*, Nos. 46, 117.

HOLME-ON-SPALDING MOOR : Stone axes (pp. 47–8), *A.S.I.*, 100; stone battle-axe (p. 62) [B.M.]. Flanged bronze axe [Council School]. Roman pottery kilns (p, 169), Corder and Sheppard, *Roman Malton and District Report, No.* 3, Hull, 1930; *H.M.P.*, No. 170.

HORNSEA : Anglian cemetery (p. 187), *H.M.P.*, No. 97. British gold coin (p. 117), Roman coins, *Lost Towns*, 271, 124. Perforated stone axe [H.M.]. Maglemose harpoon (p. 30).

HOTHAM : Hoard palstaves (p. 91), *H.M.P.*, No. 46; *A.B.I.*, 84, 92, 440, 468; *Nat.*, 1921, 97–8, 231; 1923, 141–2. Perforated flint hammer, *H.M.P.*, No. 122.

HOWDEN : Palstave [St. Albans M.].

HUGGATE : Bronze Age barrows, Mortimer, 298–310, 322–32 (p. 70). *Entrenchments (p. 235), *op. cit.*, 370, 376.

HULL : Dug-out canoe, Reid, *Geology of Holderness*, 91. Perforated stone axe, *A.S.I.*, 202. Socketed axe, *A.B.I.*, 118; winged axe (p. 92), *H.M.P.*, Nos. 46, 50. Roman urn [H.M.].

HUNMANBY : Chariot-burial, *Y.A.J.*, XIX, 1908. Stone implements, *A.S.I.*, 184, 455; axes [Bradford M.]; flat bronze axe [H.M.].

HUNTOW : Palaeolithic hand-axe (p. 24), *A.S.I.*, 580, 582. Iron Age barrows, *P.Y.G.S.*, X, 299.

HUTTON CRANSWICK : Bronze Age barrow, *P.Y.P.S.*, 1847–54, 185. Palstave, socketed axes, and spear-head [H.M.]; flanged axe [B.M.]. Flint axe (p. 47), *H.M.P.*, No. 122.

KELFIELD : Carolingian spear-head (p. 183), *V.C.H.*, II, 99.

KILHAM : Long barrow (p. 41), *B.B.*, No. CCXXXIV. Anglian remains (p. 181), Mortimer, 344; *V.C.H.*, II, 87–8. Flint axes (p. 47), *A.S.I.*, 91. Flanged axe, Pockthorpe [Y.M.].

KILNSEA, see EASINGTON.

KIRBY GRINDALYTH : Bronze Age barrow, *B.B.*, No. III.

KIRKBY UNDERDALE : Anglian burials in Uncleby barrow (p. 184), *B.B.*, No. I; Mortimer, 118; *V.C.H.*, II, 89–92 [Y. and B.M.]. Ground flint axe, *A.S.I.*, 91.

KIRK ELLA : Palstave [H.M.].

KNAPTON : Roman kilns (p. 169), *Ant.*, March, 1928, 76. Flat bronze axe [B.M.], *A.B.I.*, 43.

LANGTOFT : Bronze Age barrow, *B.B.*, No. XLVIII. Roman hypocaust, Mortimer, 341–2.

LANGTON : Roman villas (p. 168), Corder and Kirk, *Roman Malton and District, Report No. 4, Y.A.S.*, Leeds, 1932. Bronze Age barrow, *B.B.*, No. II. Flat bronze axe [B.M.]. Hedon Howe (p. 64), Mortimer, 346.

LEPPINGTON : Flat bronze axe and hoard socketed axes [Mortimer M.], Mortimer, xlviii.

LEVEN : Bronze swords [H. and Hornsea Ms.]; looped palstave [Y.M.]; ground flint axe [H.M.].

LOCKINGTON : Flanged axe [B.M.].

LONDESBOROUGH : Bronze Age barrows, *B.B.*, Nos. CXXII–CXXIII. Anglian cemetery, *V.C.H.*, II, 77–8; Mortimer, 353. Roman road (p. 124).

LOWTHORPE : Hoard socketed axes, bronze sword, and socketed spear-head [H. and B.M.], *A.B.I.*, 327; Mortimer, xlviii. Palstave [Beverley M.].

MARKET WEIGHTON : Long barrow (p. 42), *B.B.*, No. CCXXVI. Iron Age barrows at Arras and Hessleskew (p. 109). Looped palstave, *B.A. Catalogue*. Roman pottery, *T.H.S.*, IV, 10.

MIDDLETON-ON-WOLDS : Hoard socketed axes and spear-heads [Cambridge, Pitt-Rivers, and H.Ms.], *A.B.I.*, 118; Mortimer, xlviii. Beaker, jet necklace, and flint dagger (p. 59), *H.M.P.*, No. 55; Mortimer, 353–4. Chariot-burial, Mortimer, 360.

MILLINGTON : Roman villa and burials (p. 169), Mortimer, lxxxiii, 170–1. Iron Age burial (p. 110), Mortimer, 150–2; *B.M.E. Iron Age Guide.*

NAFFERTON : Stone and socketed axes [H.M.], *H.M.P.*, No. 122. Anglian urns (p. 180), Mortimer, 343–4.

NORTH FERRIBY : Bronze spear-head (p. 98), [B.M.]. Roman pottery and Anglian burial, *H.M.P.*, No. 46.

NORTH GRIMSTON : Iron Age burial (p. 111), Mortimer, 354–6.

NORTH NEWBALD : Bronze Age barrows with pygmy-vessels, *B.M. Bronze Age Guide*, 76. Socketed axe [B.M.]. Anglian cemetery, *H.M.P.*, Nos. 3, 11, 117.

NORTON : Roman site (p. 168), *Ant.*, II, 1928, 73–4. Stone axe, *A.S.I.*, 102 ; flanged axe [Y.M.].

NUNBURNHOLME : Viking cross (p. 218), O. Elfrida Saunders, *English Art in the Middle Ages*, 1932, 19 ; *Y.A.J.*, XXI, 265–9.

PAINSTHORPE : Bronze Age barrows, Mortimer, 113–33.

PATRINGTON : Flat and socketed axes [H.M.].

POCKLINGTON : Bronze Age barrows on Calais Wold, Mortimer, 153–170. Roman vases, *H.M.P.*, No. 46.

RISE : Iron Age bridle-bit [B.M.], *B.M.E. Iron Age Guide*, 103, 146.

RISTON, LONG : Socketed axe, *B.A. Catalogue*.

ROLSTON : Iron Age hut-pits (p. 113) ; socketed axe [Hornsea M.].

ROOS : Viking images (p. 202). Anglian bronze pendant, *H.M.P.*, No. 117.

RUDSTON : *Monolith (p. 87). Long barrows (p. 41), *B.B.*, No. CCXXIV. Early Bronze Age barrows (pp. 56, 65), *B.B.*, Nos. LXI–LXIX. Bronze sword fragments, socketed axe [H.M.]. Many stone implements, *A.S.I.*, 34, 176, etc. Anglian barrow burials (p. 183) *B.B.* 261.

SANCTON : Anglian cemetery (p. 179) *H.M.P.*, Nos. 66–7 ; *V.C.H.*, II, 74–6 ; *Arch.*, XLV, 409 ; *T.E.R.A.S.*, V, 115 ; XVI, 50.

SCAMPSTON : Ground stone axe, *A.S.I.*, 126. Flanged axe [B.M.] ; socketed axe [S.M.].

SETTRINGTON : Roman villa, *Ant.*, II, 77. Flanged axe [H.M.].

SHERBURN : Roman coins and pottery, *Ant.*, II, 76. Bronze Age barrows, *B.B.*, Nos. VII–XV. Flat bronze axes and tanged bronze daggers, *A.B.I.*, 43, 223. Stone axe, flint saws, etc., *A.S.I.*, 128, 295, 331, 391.

SKIPSEA : Maglemose harpoon and flints (p. 31). Bone spear-head, *Lost Towns*, 192. Flat axe [Beverley M.], socketed axe [Hornsea M.], bronze spear-head [Y.M.].

SKIPWITH : *Anglo-Danish church tower (p. 223). Barrows and hut-circles on Common, *B.B.*, 70. Coarse woollen garment from barrow [Y.M.]. Flaked flint axe, *Y.A.J.*, XX, 257.

SKIRLAUGH : Hoard socketed axes, spear-heads, sword blades, *H.M.P.*, No. 46.

SOUTH CAVE : Roman pig of lead (p. 135). Roman pottery, *T.H.S.*, IV, 10.

SOUTH DALTON : Socketed axe [H.M.].

SPROATLEY : Hoard socketed axes [Cambridge, H. and Hornsea Ms.] ; perforated stone axe [H.M.], *H.M.P.*, No. 46 ; Wardell, *Notices of Ilkley, etc.*, Leeds, 1881, 54–5.

STAXTON : Flanged axe [Y.M.].

SUTTON-ON-DERWENT : Anglian cross-shaft, *Y.A.J.*, XXIX, 238, 322. Flanged axe [H.M.].

SWINE : Earthwork, Paulson's, *Holderness*, II, 216. Anglian urn, *H.M.P.*, No. 117. Roman coins, *H.M.P.*, No. 46. Socketed axe [Carlisle M.], two socketed spear-heads [H.M].

THIXENDALE : Bronze Age barrows (Riggs group), Mortimer, 172–85 (p. 65). Bronze chisel and ground axe, *A.B.I.*, 168, *A.S.I.*, 128. Socketed axe [Y.M.]. Flat axe [H.M.].

THORPE NEAR RUDSTON : La Tène sword (p. 111) ; Bronze Age urn and food-vessel [Y.M.], *V.C.H.*, I, 394, 413.

THWING : Bronze Age barrow (p. 57), *B.B.*, No. LX. Flat bronze axe [Y.M.].

TOWTHORPE : Bronze Age barrows, Mortimer, 1–43.

ULROME : Lake dwellings (pp. 40, 102). Socketed spear-heads and axe [Y.M.].

WALKINGTON : Triangular bronze dagger and bone hilt [Y.M.].

WARTER : Hoard Roman coins (p. 159), *R.Y.P.S.*, 1913, 9–11. Bronze Age barrows, Mortimer, 311–21.

WATTON : Flanged axe [Y.M.] ; socketed axe [H.M.].

WAWNE : Stone and socketed axes [H.M.].

WEAVERTHORPE : *Pre-conquest church tower and sun-dial (p.225), J. Bilson, *Arch.*, LXXII, 1921–2 ; *Y.A.J.*, XXI, 276. Bronze Age barrows, *B.B.*, Nos. XLII–XLVII.

WELHAM : Early Bronze Age cist burial, *Y.M. Handbook*, 201.

WESTOW : Long barrow, *B.B.*, No. CXXIII. Hoard socketed axes, etc. (p. 92), *Arch. J.*, 1849, 381 ; *A.B.I.*, 85, 462 [some in Y.M.]. Roman coins, *B.R.A.C.*, VI, 1928.

WHARRAM-LE-STREET : Roman glass vessel from barrow, *Y.M. Handbook* 103. *Pre-conquest church tower (p. 223), J. Bilson, *Arch.*, LXXII, 1923 ; *Y.A.J.*, XX, 260.

WHARRAM PERCY : Bronze Age barrows, Mortimer, 44–52 ; flat axe [H.M.].

WILLERBY : Long barrow *B.B.*, No. CCXXII. Bronze Age barrows, *B.B.*, Nos. XXXII–XXXVIII. Four flat axes (p. 57), Greenwell, *Arch.*, LII, 1890.

WINESTEAD : Socketed axe [H.M.].

WITHERNSEA : Roman coins, *Lost Towns*, 124. Pile-dwelling, Sand-le-Mere, *Nat.*, 1898. Dug-out canoe, Owthorne (p. 65), Poulson's *History of Holderness*, II, 407–8. Polished flint axe [H.M.].

WOLD NEWTON : *Willie Howe and other round barrows (p. 61), Greenwell, *Arch.*, LII ; Mortimer, 350–2. Hammer stone, *A.S.I.*, 243.

II. NORTH RIDING

AMPLEFORTH : *Studford Ring (p. 233) and Dikes, *V.C.H.*, II, 59, 64. Bronze Age barrows, *R.Y.P.S.*, I, 1855. Flaked flint axe (p. 47), [Y.M.].

AMOTHERBY : Axe and other stone implements, *A.S.I.*, 105, 391. Socketed axe [H.M.], Swinton. Anglian cist (p. 181), Easthorpe, Whellan's *North Riding*, II, 210.

APPLETON-LE-STREET : Pre-conquest tower (p. 224), *Reliquary*, *N.S.*, VIII, 200. Roman pottery, *Ant.*, II, 74.

ALLERSTON : Perforated axe, *A.S.I.*, 189. Cist and bronze dagger, *O.S. Sheet*, XCII, S.W., 1913. *Bronze Age settlement site, Blakey (pp. 82, 85, 90), *E.M.*, 105, 122, 158. Numerous food-vessels, urns, etc. [S. and Y. Ms.]. *Dargate Dikes (p. 232).

ASKRIGG : *Disc barrows (p. 78), *Y.A.J.*, XXIX, 363. *Earthwork near Mill Gill.

AYSGARTH : Castle Dike earthwork, *V.C.H.*, II, 64.

AYTON, EAST : Long-barrow (p. 43), *E.M.*, 40–1 ; *B.M. Bronze Age Guide*, 104 ; *J.B.A.A.*, IV, 1848. Bronze Age barrows, *J.B.A.A.*, VI, 1850.

AYTON, GREAT : Stone axes, *G.M.*, 1857, 446–7. Hoard socketed axes, Roseberry Topping, *A.B.I.*, 129, 424, 468 ; *P.S.A.*, I, 30 ; *E.M.*, 170–1 ; *Arch. Aeliana*, II, 213. Mid-Bronze Age barrows and earthworks, *E.M.*, 16, 143–4. Roman pottery, Elgee, *Romans in Cleveland*, 11.

BAINBRIDGE : *Roman fort, Brough Hill (p. 131), R. G. Collingwood, *Proc. Liverpool Phil. S.*, VI, 1928. *Prehistoric hut-sites and stone walls (p. 85).

BALDERSBY : Flanged axe [H.M.] ; looped palstave, socketed axe, and bronze ring [Y.M.]. Urns, Wide Howe, *O.S. Sheet* CIII, S.W.

BARNINGHAM : Howe Tallon, cisted Bronze Age barrow, *Yorkshire Post*, Sept. 25, 1897.

BARTON-LE-STREET : Roman pottery, *Ant.*, II, 74. Palstave [B.M.].

BEDALE : Viking sculpture (p. 220), *Y.A.J.*, XIX, 299 ; XX, 259. Viking burial (p. 213), *V.C.H.*, II, 97 ; *Arch. J.*, V, 220.

BOLTBY : *Camp (p. 84), *E.M.*, 157 ; *V.C.H.*, II, 3–4. *Hesketh and Cleave Dikes (p. 232). Silver Hill—beaker barrow, Denny, *P.Y.G.S.*, IV, 1865. Stone axes [Leeds M.].

BOSSALL : Viking ornaments and coins (p. 212), *V.C.H.*, II, 100–1 ; *Y.M. Handbook*, 212 ; *R.Y.P.S.*, 1913, 15.

BOULBY : Bronze Age barrows, W. Hornsby, *Y.A.J.*, XXV, 1918. Cist burials (p. 64), Atkinson, *Handbook to Whitby*, 1882, 11–12 ; *Y.A.J.*, XXV, 51.

BOWES : *Roman fort, Lavatrae (p. 146), *Y.A.J.*, XXII, 400 ; XXIX, 350 ; *J.A.A.*, XLIII, 132 ; *B.R.A.C.*, VIII, 1929 ; *C.I.L.*, VII, 273–5. *Roman camp, Stainmore (p. 133), *V.C.H.*, II, 18. *Rey Cross, Stainmore (p. 218), *Y.A.J.*, XIX, 385, Roman milestones (p. 156), *Proc. Leeds Phil. S.*, I, 138–40. 259–60. Flat axe (p. 67), [Y.M.] ; bronze spear-head [B.M.] ;

gold rings (p. 99), *Y.A.J.*, XXII, 409. Large stone battle-axe (p. 67), [B.M.].

BROMPTON : Perforated stone axe, *A.S.I.*, 202. Flanged axe, *A.B.I.*, 76 ; bronze spear-head and sword, *E.M.*, 170–1.

BROMPTON-IN-ALLERTONSHIRE : *Viking crosses and ' hog-backs ' (p. 219), *Y.A.J.*, XIX, 298–305 ; Greenwell, *Cat. Stones in Durham Cathedral Library*, 1899, 116–26.

BROTTON : Bronze Age barrows (p. 64), W. Hornsby, *Y.A.J.*, XXIV.

BROUGHTON NEAR MALTON : Anglian urns (p. 179), *Y.M. Handbook*, 215.[1] Socketed axe, *A.B.I.*, 122.

BYLAND, OLD : Inscribed pre-Conquest sun-dial, *A.J.*, VIII, 508.

CARPERBY : *Iron Age hut-sites and enclosures ; stone circle, *Y.A.J.*, XXIX, 354–5.

CARTHORPE : Anglian and Viking remains (p. 186, 214), *V.C.H.*, II, 96–7 ; *P.S.A.*, VIII, 407–9 ; *Y.A.J.*, I, 175–81 ; *H.M.P.*, No. 97, 268.

CASTLE HOWARD : Earthwork, *V.C.H.*, II, 12. Round barrow ; Roman pottery kilns (p. 169), Anglian, cist-burials, P. Corder, *Roman Malton and District, Report No. I*, York, 1928.

CASTLETON, see WESTERDALE.

CATTERICK : *Thornbrough, site of Cataractonium (p. 148), *Arch. J.*, VIII, 296 ; *Arch.*, IX, 276–91 ; X, 54–60. Bainesse, Roman site (p. 148), Phillips, *Rivers, Mountains, etc.*, 55 ; *Y.A.J.*, X, 166 ; *B.R.A.C.*, IX, 1929. Anglian brooches, *V.C.H.*, II, 100 ; *Arch. J.*, VI, 215 ; *Mem. Arch. Inst.*, 1846, 34.

CAWTHORN : *Roman camps (p. 137), *Y.A.J.*, XXVIII–IX ; Macdonald, *Roman Britain*, 1914–28. Chariot burial (p. 110), Mortimer, 361. Bronze Age barrows, Bateman, 215, 207–8, 221–2. Tanged bronze knife [S.M.]. Numerous food-vessels and urns [S. and Y. Ms.].

CAYTON : Flanged axe, *B.A. Cat.*; socketed axe, *A.B.I.*, 125 ; spear-head [B.M.] ; dagger [Scarborough M.].

CLIFFE : Roman tombstone, *G.M.*, 1844, 24 ; *C.I.L.*, VII, 421. Flint arrow-heads, *A.S.I.*, 389. Betty Watson's Hill and another round barrow.

CLOUGHTON NEWLANDS : Numerous Bronze Age barrows ; prehistoric settlement site at Hulleys ; stone circle, *E.M.*, 103, 215–17 ; R. Knox, *East Yorkshire*, 1855.

COLD KIRBY : Bronze Age barrows, *B.B.*, CXXVII–CXXVIII ; *P.Y.G.S.*, IV, 1865, 488. Socketed axe, *E.M.*, 170.

COMMONDALE : Mesolithic sites ; *Mid-Bronze Age barrows, earthworks, stone circle (Sleddale, p. 85) ; Celtic fields, *E.M.*, 28–9, 145–8, 217–18.

---

[1] Twenty Roman urns are also recorded (*Ant.*, ii, 74), 9 previous to 1840, 11 previous to 1798. As the Anglian urns were found about 1802, it is probable that all the urns were Anglian.

CROFT : *Anglian sculpture (p. 195), *Y.A.J.*, XIX, 306. Ancient figure (Romano-British ?) in south wall of church.

CROPTON : Long barrows (p. 42), Bateman, 227–8, *E.M.*, 45–6. Urns [Y.M.].

CUNDALL : Anglian sculpture, *Y.A.J.*, XIX, 315. Palstave, *A.B.I.*, 86.

DALTON : Bronze Age barrows (p. 67), *Arch. J.*, VI, 342–3. Flat axe, *Y.A.J.*, XXIX, 359.

DANBY : *Mid-Bronze Age barrows, earthworks, stone circles, etc. (p. 81), *E.M.*, Chap. XV ; J. C. Atkinson, *G.M.*, X, XIV–XVII ; *Forty Years in a Moorland Parish*, 1891. Mesolithic sites, *E.M.*, 27–8.

DUNSLEY : Many urns, probably Anglian, Hinderwell, *History of Scarborough.* *Swart Howe (jet rings and urn) ; *standing stones (p. 86), *P.S.A.*, III, 58 ; Knox, *East Yorkshire*, 1855, 181.

EASBY : Anglian sculpture (p. 195), *Y.A.J.*, XIX, 315.

EASINGTON : Viking sculpture (p. 220), *Y.A.J.*, XIX, 316–17. *Three Howes barrows with urns, etc., *E.M.*, 150–2 ; *G.M.*, XVIII, 16–19.

EBBERSTON : *Scamridge Dikes (p. 228). *Long barrow, *E.M.*, 41–5 ; *B.B.*, No. CCXXI. Bronze Age barrows, *J.B.A.A.*, IV, 101–7 ; Bateman, 225–6 ; *E.M.*, 65. Hallstatt sword and chape (p. 97), *A.B.I.*, 280, 307. Palstave [Scarborough M.], socketed axe [Y.M.], socketed lance head [B.M.]. Numerous axes and other stone implements, *A.S.I.*, 77, 121, 246–7, 335.

EDSTONE : Inscribed Anglian sun-dial, *A.J.*, VIII, 510.

EGTON : Beaker interment (p. 55), *E.M.*, 57. *Mid-Bronze Age barrows and earthworks, *E.M.*, 138–9 ; *B.B.*, Nos. CXXIV–V. Jet necklace, *E.M.*, 112 ; stone axes, *E.M.*, 37 ; urns [Y.M.].

ELLERBURN : Wheel-head cross (p. 219), *Y.A.J.*, XIX, 314 ; XX, 255–6.

ESTON : *Bronze Age barrows and camp (p. 84), *E.M.*, 152–6. Roman coins, *Romans in Cleveland*, 14. Romano-British site, *op. cit.*, 13–14 ; Atkinson, *G.M.*, 1864, XVI, 162–7.

FARNDALE : Obtrush Rook and other Bronze Age barrows, Phillips, *Rivers, Mountains*, etc., 210–12 ; *E.M.*, 70–1. Roman arm-purse (p. 170), *Arch J.*, VIII, 88.

FYLINGDALES : Bronze Age barrows, circles, etc., Peak Moors, Greenwell, *Arch.*, LII, 1890 ; *J.B.A.A.*, VI, 1850 ; *E.M.*, 104 ; *Arch. J.*, XIII, 95. Stone axes [Y.M.], *E.M.*, 34, 37. *Green Dike earthwork, *V.C.H.*, II, 57. Roman coastguard fort (p. 174).

GAYLES : *Castle Steads, camp (p. 119), *V.C.H.*, II, 8–9.

GILLING EAST : Bronze Age barrows, *B.B.*, Nos. CXXXII–CXXXVII. Rectangular mounds with outer trench, Grimston Moor, *op. cit.*, 343–4. Stone axes, *A.S.I.*, 120, 339.

GILLING WEST : Anglian and Viking sculpture (p. 189), *Y.A.J.*, XIX, 322.

GIRRICK : *Herd Howe and other Mid-Bronze Age barrows ; earthworks, etc., *E.M.*, 95–6, 149 ; Atkinson, *G.M.*, XVI, 1864, 705–9.

GLAISDALE : Socketed axe [B.M.]. Mesolithic site (p. 37).

GOATHLAND : *Roman road, Wade's Causeway (p. 138). Anglian relics, Lilla Howe (p. 185), *Trans. Historic Soc. Lancashire and Cheshire*, 1870–71, vol. 23, 200 [Liverpool M.]. *Numerous Bronze Age barrows, *E.M.*, 112, 127. Roman inscribed stone, Young, *Hist. of Whitby*, II, 703.

GOLDSBOROUGH, see LYTHE.

GRETA BRIDGE : *Roman fort (p. 145), *J.A.A.*, XLIII, 127 ; *C.I.L.*, VII, 276–83, a, b ; *B.R.A.C.*, IX, 1929 ; *V.C.H.*, II, 14, 16 ; *J.B.A.A.*, XXII, 182–90. Bronze Age gold armlet (p. 99).

GRINTON : *Maiden Castle (p. 236), *V.C.H.*, II, 65.

GRISTHORPE : Bronze Age barrows (p. 65), W. C. Williamson, *Tumulus opened at Gristhorpe*, Scarborough, 1872 ; Greenwell, *Arch.*, LII, 1890.

GROSMONT : Roman camp (p. 138), Young, *History of Whitby*, 1817, II, 705 ; Phillips, *Rivers, Mountains*, etc., 1853, 246, Plate 34, Fig. 10.

GUISBROUGH : Roman coins and helmet, *B.M. Guide to Roman Britain*, 1922 ; Elgee, *Romans in Cleveland*, 12–13 ; *G.M.*, XVII, 1864, 304–8. Numerous Bronze Age barrows and cinerary urns, *E.M.*, 13 ; Atkinson, *History of Cleveland*, II, 34–40. *Earthworks of uncertain age, J. W. Ord, *Hist. of Cleveland*, 1846.

HACKNESS : *Anglo-Danish sculpture (p. 191), *Y.A.J.*, III, 373 ; XIX, 329–30 ; XXI, 278–80 ; XXVII, 388–407. Baldwin Brown, *Arts in Early England*, VI, Pt. i (1930), 52.

HAMBLETON HILLS, see BOLTBY, COLD KIRBY, KILBURN, OVER SILTON.

HAROME : Bronze sword [H.M.], *E.M.*, 171. Double-bladed axe and other rare stone implements, *A.S.I.*, 89, 133, 177, 262, 302.

HAUXWELL : Anglian cross-shaft (p. 198), *Y.A.J.*, XIX, 330.

HAWES : La Tène sword, Cotterdale (p. 110), *B.M. Iron Age Guide*, 108–9.

HAWNBY : Anglian barrow burials (p. 184), *V.C.H.*, II, 96 ; Denny, *P.Y.G.S.*, IV, 1865. Bronze Age barrows, *E.M.*, 126.

HAWSKER : *Anglo-Viking cross-shaft, *Y.A.J.*, XXI, 281–3.

HELMSLEY : Round barrows, *E.M.*, 121 ; urns [Malton and Y. Ms.] ; socketed axe [St. Albans M.] ; looped spear-head [Y.M.] ; stone hammer, *A.S.I.*, 239.

HEWORTH : Anglian urns (p. 179), *V.C.H.*, II, 103 [Y.M.].

HINDERWELL : Bronze Age barrow (p. 74), W. Hornsby, *Y.A.J.*, XXV, 1920.

HOVINGHAM : Roman villa (p. 168), Gough's *Camden*, III, 85 ; *Ant.*, II, 74. Roman sarcophagus (p. 174). *Pre-Conquest church tower (p. 223), *Y.A.J.*, XIX, 337 ; XX, 255-6. Socketed axes [Y.M.].

HUTTON BUSCEL : Bronze Age barrows, *B.B.*, Nos. CLII–CLX.

HUTTON CONYERS : Bronze Age circles and barrows (p. 78), *V.C.H.*, II, 65-7 ; *Y.A.J.*, I, 116-26 ; XXIX, 364.

INGLEBY ARNCLIFFE : Viking sculpture (p. 220), *Y.A.J.*, XIX, 337-8.

JERVAULX : Perforated stone axe (p. 62), *A.S.I.*, 204 [B.M.].

KELDHOLM : Hoard socketed axes, *A.B.I.*, 452 [B.M.].

KILBURN : Bronze Age barrows, *B.B.*, Nos. CXXIX–CXXXI. Long barrow, Wass Moor, *op. cit.*, No. CCXXV.

KILDALE : Viking burials (p. 213), *P.S.A.* (*Ser.* 2), IV, 52-9 ; *V.C.H.*, II, 96 ; *E.M.*, 220-1, Fig. 67. Bronze Age barrows, *E.M.*, 145-6. *Celtic fields, *op. cit.*, 218.

KIRKBY KNOWLE : Roman gold coins (p. 179), *V.C.H.*, II, 101.

KIRKBY MOORSIDE : Viking cross, etc. (p. 216), *V.C.H.*, II, 125 ; *Y.A.J.*, XIX. Looped palstave [Y.M.].

KIRKBY WHISKE : Flanged axe, *E.M.*, 166.

KIRKDALE : Bone cave (p. 23). *Anglian and Viking sculpture (pp. 198, 225), *Y.A.J.*, XIX, 344 ; XXI, 283-7 ; *A.J.*, VIII, 491. Bronze dagger, *E.M.*, Plate X.

KIRKLEVINGTON : Viking sculpture (p. 217), *Y.A.J.*, XIX, 350-3.

KIRKLINGTON : Large stone battle-axe, *A.S.I.*, 209. Earthwork, *V.C.H.*, II, 57.

LASTINGHAM : Site of Anglian monastery (p. 189). *Anglo-Viking sculpture, *Y.A.J.*, XIX, 352-9. *Black Park earthworks, *V.C.H.*, II, 19. Bronze Age urn of unusual type, *E.M.*, 182.

LEVISHAM : *Viking sculpture (p. 220), *Y.A.J.*, XIX, 360. *Earthworks (p. 232), *E.M.*, 130, 217. Stone battle-axe, *op. cit.*, 96.

LEYBURN : Inhabited cave and terrace (Neolithic ?), W. Horne, *P.Y.G.S.*, IX ; Mortimer, 387. Flanged and socketed axes [St. Albans and Cambridge Ms.], spear-heads, *Y.A.J.*, XXIX.

LYTHE : *Roman coastguard fort, Goldsborough (p. 171). *Viking crosses and hog-backs (p. 216), *Y.A.J.*, XXI, 287-98. Bronze Age barrows, Greenwell, *Arch.*, LII, 1890 ; *E.M.*, 70, 76. *Wade's Stone and other monoliths, *E.M.*, 106.

MALTON : *Roman fortress, *Ant.*, II, 1928 ; P. Corder, *Roman Malton and District, Report No.* 2, 1930. Bronze dagger [Leeds M.] ; socketed axes [Salisbury M.] ; flanged axes [Whitby M.]. Axe and other stone implements, *A.S.I.*, 135. Perforated stone axe [H.M.].

MARTON-LE-MOOR : Dug-out canoe (p. 65), E. Smith, *Reliquiae Isuriane* ; flanged axe [Y.M.].

MASHAM : *Anglian cross-shaft (p. 196), *Y.A.J.*, XIX, 360. Roman sarcophagi (p. 166), *Arch. J.*, VI, 45–8 ; bronze patellae, *op. cit.* Bronze Age gold ornament (p. 100), *Mem. Arch. Inst.*, 1848, Plate I.

MELSONBY : Anglian sculpture, *Y.A.J.*, XIX, 360–1.

MIDDLEHAM : Roman hypocaust (p. 166), *Y.A.J.*, VII, 459. Bronze spear-head and socketed axes, *A.B.I.*, 335 [H. and S. Ms.].

MIDDLESBROUGH : Bronze sword from R. Tees, *E.M.*, 171.

MIDDLETON : *Pre-Conquest tower (p. 223), Baldwin Brown, *Arts in Early England*, II, 340. *Anglian and Viking sculpture, *Y.A.J.*, XIX, 370–2 ; XXI, 298.

NEWBURGH : Bronze Age barrows with cist and food vessels, Gill's *Vallis Eboracensis*, 1852, 153–4.

NEW EARSWICK : Roman site (p. 140), P. Corder, *B.R.A.C.*, VI, 1928 ; IX, 1929.

NORTHALLERTON : Roman site (p. 144), Elgee, *Romans in Cleveland*, 1923, 7–8. Anglian and Viking sculpture, *Y.A.J.*, XIX, 372. Flanged bronze axe [B.M.] and spear-head, *E.M.*, 166–7 ; *Y.A.J.*, XXIV, 106–8.

OULSTON : Roman villa (p. 169), *Y.M. Handbook*, 93. Whellan, *North Riding*, II, 662. Polished stone axe (p. 48), *A.S.I.*, 106.

OVER SILTON : *Long barrow, Kepwick Moor (p. 42), *B.B.*, No. CCXXVIII. *Bronze Age barrows, *B.B.*, No. CXXVI.

PEAK, see FYLINGDALES.

PICKERING : Two British coins, Evans, *Coins of Ancient Britons*, 416 ; *E.M.*, 205. Lake dwelling (p. 103), *J.R.A.I.*, 1899, I, 150–4 ; *Y.A.J.*, XXX, 1930 ; *E.M.*, 183–4. Round barrows, Bateman, *Ten Years' Diggings* ; *Crania Britannica*, 1865, II, 1, Plates 3–4 ; *E.M.*, 68. Beakers, *E.M.*, 56. Bronze dagger, *E.M.*, Plate X ; socketed axes, *op. cit.* ; socketed, flanged and winged axes [St. Albans M.]. Stone axes [Leeds and Y. Ms.]. Viking brooch (p. 213), *A.J.*, IV, 1924, 270.

PILMOOR : Large ground axe and perforated stone adze, *A.S.I.*, 129, 191.

RAINTON-CUM-NEWBY : Bronze flanged axe and spear-head, *Y.A.J.*, XX, 103.

RASKELF : Roman remains, Burrows Hill.[1] Stone axe [Y.M.].

REETH : Flanged axes, *A.B.I.*, 76. Roman bronze horse-harness and other objects, *Y.M. Handbook*, 132. Roman lead mines (p. 135). Polished stone-axe, Marrick [Y.M.].

RICHMOND : Roman coin hoard (p. 175), Whellan, *North Riding*, II, 5. Two prehistoric vessels, German type [B.M.]. Grinding stone from hut-site, Willan's Leap, *Y.M. Handbook*, 196.

ROBIN HOOD'S BAY : Anglian remains (p. 180), *V.C.H.*, II, 93 [Y.M.]. *Bronze Age barrows and entrenchments, John Cross Rigg, *E.M.*, 157–8. *Stone triangle (p. 86). Stone axes [Y.M.].

SALTBURN : Anglian cemetery (p. 180), *Y.A.J.*, XXII, 1913 ; *V.C.H.*, II, 93–6. Roman coastguard fort (p. 172), W. Hornsby, *J.R.S.*, II, 1912.

SCACKLETON : Perforated stone axe, *A.S.I.*, 191 ; flat bronze axe [H.M.].

SCALBY : Gold torc (p. 100), *Arch.*, XXX, 459 ; *E.M.*, 175 ; *P.S.A.*, I, 16. Flanged axe, *E.M.*, 78 ; hoard socketed axes, *Nat.*, 1917–18. Urns [Scarborough and B. Ms.].

SCAMRIDGE, see EBBERSTON.

SCARBOROUGH : Anglian remains (p. 224) ; *Roman coastguard fort (p. 173), R. G. Collingwood in *History of Scarborough*, 1931 (Editor, A. Rowntree). Halstatt remains (p. 104), R. E. M. Wheeler in *op. cit.* ; R. A. Smith, *Arch.*, LX, 1927 ; *E.M.*, 175–6, 179–81. Hallstatt sword [Scar. M.], *Nat.*, 1921. Bronze knife and flat axe [S.M.]. Stone axes [Scar. and Leeds Ms.]. Bronze Age barrows, *J.B.A.A.*, IV, 1848 ; VI, 1850 ; *Arch.*, XXXIV, 1852 ; *Y.A.J.*, XXI, 1912 ; Wheeler, *op. cit.* Long barrows (?), *E.M.*, 40.

SEAMER, NEAR SCARBOROUGH : Anglian cemetery (p. 182), *26th Ann. Rep. Scarborough Phil. and Arch. Soc.*, 1858 ; *V.C.H.*, II, 100. Chariot burial, Mortimer, 358. Bronze Age barrows, *J.B.A.A.*, IV, 101–7. Lead socketed axe [B.M.], *P.S.A.*, XX, 258. Bronze knife and socketed axe, *A.B.I.*, 124, 213. Many stone axes, etc., *A.S.I.*, 91, 96, 105, 126, 290, 371, 379.

SLEIGHTS : *High and Low Bride Stones (p. 86), *E.M.*, 105, 159. *Long barrow, *E.M.*, 47–8. Bronze Age barrows ; flints, etc., from hearths [Middlesbrough M.], (p. 85). Stone axes, etc. [Y.M.].

SLINGSBY : Bronze Age barrows, *B.B.*, Nos. CXXXVIII–CL.

SOWERBY, see THIRSK.

SPAUNTON : Anglian cist burial (p. 181).

SPENNITHORNE : *Viking grave slab (p. 220), *Y.A.J.*, XIX, 393.

STAINMORE, see BOWES.

STAINTONDALE : Anglian urn, *Y.M. Handbook*, 215. *Rudda and Pye Rigg Howes with urns [Scarborough M.], *Arch.*,

XXXIV, 1852. *Three Howes (p. 75). Perforated stone axe, *A.S.I.*, 198.

STANWICK : *Earthworks (p. 233), *Y.A.J.*, XXIII, 402-3; *V.C.H.*, II, 61. La Tène antiquities (p. 110), *V.C.H.*, I, 389; *B.M. Iron Age Guide*, 1925; *P.S.A.*, XXI, 1907, 330. Anglian and Viking sculpture, *Y.A.J.*, XIX, 393-5. Socketed spearheads, *A.B.I.*, 314, 328; socketed axes [B.M.]. Stone axe, *A.B.I.*, 210.

STITTENHAM : Roman bronze patellae, *Y.M. Handbook*, 142; *Arch.*, LXI, 325-32.

STONEGRAVE : *Wheel-head cross and hog-backs (p. 216), *Y.A.J.*, XIX, 398-402; XXVIII, 327. *Pre-Conquest tower (p. 224).

THIRSK : *Pudding Pie Hill, barrow with Anglian interments and Roman pottery (p. 183), Whellan, *op. cit.*, II, 706; *Y.M. Handbook*, 210. Hoard flint implements, *B.A. York Handbook*, 1906, 4.

THORNABY : Dug-out canoe from R. Tees (p. 65).

THORNTON DALE : Iron Age site (p. 113), *Y.A.J.*, XXX, 157. Chariot burial and beaker interment, *R.Y.P.S.*, 1911. Socketed axe, *Nat.*, 1928. *Earthworks on Pexton Moor (p. 230).

THORNTON-LE-STREET : Roman remains and road (p. 134), Whellan, *N. Riding*, II, 337.

THORNTON STEWARD : Viking wheel-cross heads (p. 217), *Y.A.J.*, XIX, 402-3.

TOPCLIFFE : Viking wheel-cross (p. 216), *Y.A.J.*, XIX, 403, 407; XXVIII, 327. Flint dagger and bronze socketed axe [B.M.].

WELBURN : Bronze Age barrow, *B.B.*, No. CLI. Flanged axe, Bulmer [B.M.].

WELBURN (Vale of Pickering) : Four socketed axes, *B.A. Catalogue*.

WELL : *Roman villa (p. 166), *Y.A.J.*, VI, 284-5.

WENSLEY : *Anglian and Viking sculpture (p. 195), *Y.A.J.*, XIX, 407-8. Viking burial (p. 214), *P.S.A.*, XXVIII, 228.

WESTERDALE : *Bronze Age settlement site, Crown End (p. 80); barrows and earthworks, Castleton Rigg, *E.M.*, 139-42; Atkinson, *G.M.*, XV, 1863, 548-52.

WEST TANFIELD : *Thornborough Circles (p. 78), *Y.A.J.*, I, 116-26; *V.C.H.*, II, 65-6; O. G. S. Crawford, *B.A. Excursions Handbook L*, Leeds, 1927. Anglian sculpture, *Y.A.J.*, XXI, 299, 300. Socketed axe [H.M.].

WHITBY : Site of Anglian monastery; Anglian remains (p. 190), *Y.A.J.*, II, 279; XIX, 408; XXI, 302; *V.C.H.*, II, 93; Atkinson, *History of Cleveland*, 1877, and *Memorials of Old Whitby*, 1894. *Burlington Fine Arts Club Cat. Dark Ages Exhibn.*, 1930, p. 29, and Plate LII. Roman potsherds and coins, *Romans in Cleveland*, 1923. Cretan copper (?) axe (p.

70), *E.M.*, 62–3 ; socketed axes, etc. [Whitby M.] *Nat.*, 1918 ; palstave [St. Albans M.]. Numerous stone implements from district, *A.S.I.*, 187, 191, 196, 295, 343, 459.

WHITWELL : Stone axe (p. 49), *A.S.I.*, 122.

WHORLTON : Roman pottery and coins, *Y.A.J.*, XXI, 220 ; *G.M.*, 1811 ; *Romans in Cleveland*, 8–9.

WITTON, EAST : Camp, *V.C.H.*, II, 7.

WYCLIFFE : Cockshot camp, *V.C.H.*, II, 6.

WYKEHAM, see HUTTON BUSCEL.

YARM : Inscribed Anglian shaft (p. 198), *Y.A.J.*, VI, 50 ; VII, 110 ; XIX, 413. Polished axe [S.M.]. *Round Hill barrow.

YEARSLEY : Hoard socketed axes (p. 92), *A.B.I.*, 113 ; *E.M.*, 169. *Long barrow, *B.B.*, No. CCXXXII. Cist-burials (p. 182), *B.B.*, 550–1.

III. WEST RIDING.

ABERFORD : *Becca Banks entrenchments, *V.C.H.*, II, 57. Ethelswith's ring (p. 188). Anglian sculpture, *Y.A.J.*, XXIII, 130.

ACKWORTH : British gold coin (p. 117), *V.C.H.*, I, 406.

ACOMB : Roman villa, *Y.M. Handbook*, 95.

ADEL : Roman station, *Y.A.J.*, XXII, 287 ; XXVII, 320 ; *C.I.L.*, 203–6. Square earthwork, *V.C.H.*, II, 11. Anglian sculpture, *Y.A.J.*, XXIII, 131–2. Flint and stone implements [Leeds M.].

AIRTON : Socketed axe and palstave, *Y.A.J.*, XXIX, 369–70.

ALDBOROUGH : *Isurium Brigantum (p. 163), H. E. Smith, *Reliquiæ Isuriane*, 1852 ; A. D. H. Leadman, *Survey of Isurium*, *Y.A.J.*, XII, 1893 ; F. Haverfield, *Ephemeris Epigraphica*, IX, 561 ; R. G. Collingwood, *B.A. Excursion Handbook Q*, Leeds, 1927 ; *J.R.S.*, XIV ; *C.I.L.*, 260–3. Anglian sculpture (p. 195), *Y.A.J.*, XXIII, 133–4. Stone axes [Aldborough and Edinburgh Ms.].

ALMONDBURY : *Hill fort (p. 118), Petch, *Early Man in Huddersfield District, Tolson M. Publications*, 64–7 ; *V.C.H.*, II, 24 ; Gibson's *Camden*, 1695, 710. Hoard gold British and Roman coins (p. 116), Petch, *op. cit.*, 79 ; Richmond, *Huddersfield in Roman Times, Tolson M. Pub.*, 14–15, 114 ; Evans, *Coins of the Ancient Britons*, 406, 408, 411.

ARNECLIFFE : *Iron Age site (p. 115), Raistrick, *Ant.*, III, 1929. Rock carving (Bryn Celli Ddu type, *Arch.*, LXXX, 179).

BAILDON : Bronze Age barrows, circles, earthworks, cup and ring stones, etc., *V.C.H.*, II, 64–5 ; I, 381 ; *Arch.*, XXXI, 302 ; *Bradford Antiquary*, I, 88–9 ; *A.S.I.*, 388. Palstaves [Bradford M.].

BARDSEY : *Pre-Conquest tower (p. 222).

BARKISLAND : Meg Dike, *V.C.H.*, II, 11 ; Wolf Fold stone circle, Watson, *Hist. of Halifax*, 2nd Ed., 26–7.

BARNOLDSWICK : *Roman road (p. 129). Bronze sword [Skipton M.].

BILTON : Wheel-head cross, etc., *Y.A.J.*, XXIII, 139–41.

BINGLEY : Anglo-Viking Runic font, *Y.A.J.*, XXIII, 141–4. Bronze Age barrows, Harden Moor, *Bradford Ant.*, II, 113. Socketed axes [Bradford and Cambridge Ms.] ; socketed spearhead [Leeds Art Gallery] ; flaked flint axe [Bradford M.] ; stone hammer [Keighley M.].

BISHOPTHORPE : Flanged axe, *B.A. Catalogue*. Plain Roman altar [Y.M.].

BOLTON PERCY : Anglian coin-hoard (p. 201), *V.C.H.*, II, 103. Two looped palstaves [B.M.].

BOLTON-BY-BOLLAND : Flanged axe, *P.Y.G.S.*, IX, 428.

BORDLEY : Two flanged axes ; stone circles, *Y.A.J.*, XXIX, 356, 359.

BOROUGHBRIDGE : *The Devil's Arrows (p. 87), *V.C.H.*, I, 368–9 ; *Arch.*, XLVIII, 426–7 ; *B.A. Excursion Handbook Q*, Leeds, 1927 ; *P.S.A.*, 2nd S., VII, 134–8. Hallstatt brooch (p. 107), *Ant. J.*, X, 54.

BOSTON SPA : Silver coins in vase and other Roman remains, *Y.M. Handbook*, 97–8.

BRADFIELD : Bar Dike, barrows and stone circle, *V.C.H.*, II, 57. Viking hammer-head cross, *Y.A.J.*, XXIII, 146.

BRADFORD : Roman iron workings, Bierley (p. 158). Richmond, *op. cit.*, 115.

BRADLEY : Long-barrow (p. 64) and round barrows, *Y.A.J.*, XXX, 252–3.

BRAMHAM : Anglian gold ring (p. 187). Hoard socketed axes, *P.Y.G.S.*, IX, 427–32.

BROUGHTON-IN-CRAVEN : Mid-Bronze Age barrow with urn, tanged bronze knife, perforated stone axe, etc., *A.S.I.*, 208, 269 ; *A.B.I.*, 217.

BURNSALL : *Anglo-Viking sculpture (p. 218), *Y.A.J.*, XXIII, 146–52.

CASTLEFORD : Roman fort, Legiolium, see Index. Stukeley, *Iter. Boreale*, 76 ; Whitaker's *Loidis*, 201 ; *C.I.L. Addenda*, IV, 1164, 1105 ; Haverfield, *Arch. J.*, XLIX, 191.

CASTLESHAW : *Roman forts (pp. 128, 136), Richmond, *op. cit.*, 48–56 ; *Y.A.J.*, XX, 100–3 ; *Proc. Lanc. and Cheshire, Ant. Soc.*, XL, 1925 ; Bruton, *Roman Forts at Castleshaw*, 1st and 2nd Reps., 1908, 1911, Manchester Univ. Press. Socketed axe, Petch, *op. cit.*, 53–5.

CAWTHORNE : Anglian sculpture, *Y.A.J.*, XXIII, 152–4.

CHURWELL : Flanged and socketed axes [B. and Y. Ms.] ; two spear-heads and hoard palstaves [Leeds and Bradford Ms.].

COLLINGHAM : Roman villa (p. 140), *R.Y.P.S.*, 1854. *Anglian sculpture and inscription, *Y.A.J.*, XXIII, 155–61.

CULLINGWORTH : Camp, *V.C.H.*, II, 7.

DENBY : Castle Hill fort, Petch, *op. cit.* ; *V.C.H.*, II, 7.

DEWSBURY : *Anglian cross and Viking grave-cover (p. 197), *Y.A.J.*, XXIII, 162–71.

DINNINGTON : Anglian (?) barrow (p. 187), Rolleston, *J. Anatomy and Physiol.*, III, 1869, 252–5.

DONCASTER : Roman fort, Danum, Roman pottery and coins. Bronze Age urn and pygmy-vessel ; bronze palstaves and chisel, *Nat.*, 1918 ; flint and stone axes [Doncaster M.].

ELSLACK : Roman fort (p. 129), T. May, *Y.A.J.*, XXI, 113–67. Two small circular earthworks, *V.C.H.*, II, 67.

EMBSAY : La Tène bronze collar, *Arch.*, XXI, 517 ; *Arch. J.*, III, 32 ; *P.S.A.*, I, 265. Socketed axes [Manchester and Skipton Ms.], *A.J.*, VII, 62–3.

FERRY FRYSTON : Round barrow, see Index, *B.B.*, No. CLXI.

FINNINGLEY : Bronze hanging bowls, fourth century, *Y.M. Handbook*, 139 ; T. D. Kendrick, *Ant.*, VI, June, 1932. Bronze spear-head (p. 98).

FLASBY : La Tène sword (p. 110), *V.C.H.*, I, 395.

GARGRAVE : Roman villa (p. 158), Whitaker's, *History of Craven*, 3rd Ed., 1878, 229 ; *Ant. J.*, 1923, 63. Oval camp, Steeling Hill, *op. cit.*, 237. Viking cross-heads, etc., *Y.A.J.*, XXIII, 173–6.

GIGGLESWICK : Dug-out canoe (p. 65) [Leeds M.]. Bronze Age barrows, *Y.A.J.*, XXIX, 361–2. *Celtic Wall (p. 115). Neolithic (?) and Romano-British remains in Kinsey and Little Kelcowe Caves [Settle M.].

GISBURN : Barrows with urns, Whitaker's *Craven*, 53.

GOLDSBOROUGH : Hoard Cufic coins and Viking silver ornaments (p. 212), *V.C.H.*, II, 101–2 ; *Arch. J.*, XVI, 197 ; *Numismatic Chronicle*, N.S., I, 1861, 65. Viking bronze plaque, *Y.A.J.*, XXIII, 179.

GOOLE : Flat bronze axe (p. 68) [H.M.].

GRASSINGTON : Roman pig of lead (p. 135), A. Raistrick, *Trans. Newcomen Soc.*, VIII, 1926–7. *Iron Age settlements (p. 114). Neolithic (?) cave, Elbolton (p. 39), *P.Y.G.S.*, XI, 86, 307 ; XII, 105. Socketed axe, Early and Mid-Bronze Age barrows, disc barrow, *Y.A.J.*, XXIX, 360–1, 364.

GREETLAND : Roman altar (p. 153), *Y.A.J.*, XXIII, XXIV ; Richmond, *op. cit.*, 95–6.

GREWELTHORPE : Romano-British clothing (p. 166), G. Home,

Roman York, 1924, 176. Rectangular earthworks, *V.C.H.*, II, 16.

GRIMSCAR, NEAR HUDDERSFIELD : Roman tile kiln (p. 136), Richmond, *op. cit.*, 57–9.

GUISELEY : Gold torc (p. 99), *Mem. Arch. Inst.*, 1848, 3 ; Whitaker's *Loidis*, I, 212 ; *P.S.A.*, I, 16. Socketed axe, Yeadon, *Y.A.J.*, XXIX, 360. Urn, Wardell's *Ilkley, etc.*, 52. Anglo-Viking sculpture, *Y.A.J.*, XXIII, 17–81.

HALIFAX : Roman coin hoard, *Y.A.J.*, XXIII, 444. Five cinerary urns ; bronze palstave, Watson's *History of Halifax*, 2nd Ed., 54, 58 (Skircoat). Several urns ; greenstone axe (Warley), *op. cit.*, 54, 58–60. Urn in cist (Illingworth) [Halifax M.].

HARROGATE : Viking remains (p. 214), *P.S.A.*, XIX, 55 ; *Y.A.J.*, XXIII, 181–2 ; XXIX, 133.

HARTSHEAD : *Roman camp, Kirklees Park (p. 127), Richmond, *op. cit.*, 24–7. *Walton Cross (p. 220), *Y.A.J.*, XXIII, 250–4.

HATFIELD : Socketed axe and spear-head [Doncaster M.].

HEALAUGH : Inscribed Anglian tombstone, *Y.A.J.*, III, 365, 408 ; V, 223 ; XXIII, 183.

HECKMONDWIKE : Polished stone axe, *Y.A.J.*, XX, 104.

HEPTONSTALL : Roman coins, Richmond, *op. cit.*, 115. Standing stones, Watson, *op. cit.*, 30–1.

HIGH HOYLAND : Anglian and Viking cross-heads, *Y.A.J.*, XXIII, 183–5.

HONLEY : British and Roman silver coins (p. 116), Richmond and Petch, *op. cit.*; *Num. Chronicle, Part IV, 3rd S.*, No. 68, 1897.

HUDDERSFIELD, see ALMONDBURY, HONLEY, MELTHAM, SCAMONDEN.

HUNSLET : Bronze spear-head and hoard socketed axes [Leeds Art Gallery].

ILKLEY : Roman fort, Olicana, see Index, A. M. Woodward, *Y.A.J.*, XXVIII ; A. Raistrick, *Samian Ware from Ilkley*, *Y.A.J.*, XXX, 178. *Anglian crosses (p. 196), *Y.A.J.*, XXIII, 185–97. *Cup and ring-stones and other Bronze Age remains (p. 72), *V.C.H.*, I, 378–80. Swastika carving (p. 112), *op. cit.* See also Wardell, *Historical Notices of Ilkley, Rumble's Moor, etc.*, 2nd Ed., Leeds, 1881.

INGLETON : *Fortified village (p. 119), *V.C.H.*, II, 6–7. *Yarlsber camp, *V.C.H.*, II, 18. Flanged axe, *Y.A.J.*, XXIX, 359.

KEIGHLEY : Roman coins and bronze eagle [Keighley M.]. British coin (p. 117), *V.C.H.*, I, 406. Flat bronze axes (3) ; hoard bronze axes (lost, type not recorded), *B.A. Catalogue*, *Y.A.J.*, XXIX, 359. Stone axes ; grooved stone hammer (p. 70) [Keighley M.]. Flanged axe [S.M.].

KILNSEY : Romano-British remains in Dowkerbottom Cave (p. 159), *B.M. Roman Guide*, 49 ; *P.S.A.*, IV, 111–12. Flint implements [Leeds M.].

KIRK HAMMERTON : *Anglo-Danish church (p. 223).

KIRKBURTON : Anglian sculpture (p. 198), *Y.A.J.*, XXIII, 202–3.

KIRKBY MALZEARD : Hoard bronze socketed axes, *Nat.*, 1910, 340 ; *Y.A.J.*, XX, 254. Viking grave-cover, *Y.A.J.*, XXIII, 204.

KIRKBY WHARFE : Anglo-Viking crosses, *Y.A.J.*, XXIII, 206 ; XXVIII, 328. Roman villa, *O.S. Map Roman Britain, 2nd Ed.*

KIRKLEES, see HARTSHEAD.

KNARESBOROUGH : Hoard Roman bronze bowls, rings, iron hammer, axe-heads, etc., *Y.M. Handbook*, 141–4. Polished axe [H.M.].

KNOTTINGLEY : Bronze Age barrows, G. Roberts, *Topography of Lofthouse*, II, 69–71, 1885.

LEDSHAM : *Pre-Conquest church (p. 223).

LEEDS : *Viking and Anglo-Viking crosses (p. 218), *Y.A.J.*, XXIII, 209–18. Bronze Age urn, Briggate ; socketed axes and flanged axe [Leeds and S. Ms.], *P.Y.G.S.*, IX, 1887. Bronze shield, Thoresby, *Ducatis Leodiensis*, 565. Hoard flanged axes, Roundhay, *P.S.A.*, XX, 261. Socketed axe and palstave, Roundhay, *P.Y.G.S.*, IX, 431. Spear-head, Thwaite Gate, Wardell's *Ilkley*, 91. Bronze dagger, Chapel Allerton [Leeds M.]. Roman altars and lamp, Chapel Allerton and Roundhay, *Wardell, op. cit.*, 81. Roman camp, Hawcaster, Meanwood, *B.R.A.C.*, V, 1928. Perforated stone axes and polished flint axe, *A.S.I.*, 222 ; *V.C.H.*, I, 411.

LIGHTCLIFFE : Gold British and silver Roman coins (p. 127), *Num. Chron.*, I, 79 ; Evans, *Ancient British Coins*, 406, 408, 412.

LONG PRESTON : *Roman forts (p. 130), *Y.A.J.*, XXVII, 410–12.

LUDDENDEN : Two La Tène beads, Watson's, *Halifax*, 60.

MARSDEN : Mesolithic site (p. 32). Bronze Age barrows with food-vessels, etc., Pule Hill, Petch, *op. cit.*, 56–9, *Y.A.J.*, XVI, 1911, 38–42.

MELTHAM : *Roman camp (p. 127), Richmond, *op. cit.*, 21–4 ; *Y.A.J.*, XXVII, 319.

MIDDLESMOOR : *Pre-Conquest cross (p. 219), *Y.A.J.*, XXIII, 219.

MIDHOPE, UPPER : Mid-Bronze Age urns, *Antiquary*, 1897, 147.

MORLEY : Flanged axe, *P.Y.G.S.*, IX, 429 ; palstave found with gold coin (?), Wardell, *op. cit.*, 54.

NESFIELD : *Castleberg camp (p. 84), *V.C.H.*, II, 3, 5.

NEWTON KYME : *Roman fort (p. 126), Codrington, *Roman Roads*, 134 ; Drake, *Eboracum*, 54 ; *G.M.*, 1862, 608.

NORTH STAINLEY : *Castle Dikes, Roman villa (p. 158), *V.C.H.*, II, 17 ; *Y.A.J.*, XXVII ; *Arch. J.*, XXXII, 135 ; T. C. Heslington, *Roman Camps in the Neighbourhood of Ripon*, Ripon, 1867 ; O. G. S. Crawford, *B.A. Excursions Handbook L*, Leeds, 1927 ; *B.R.A.C.*, VIII, 1929.

OTLEY : *Anglian and Viking sculpture (p. 216), *Y.A.J.*, XXIII, 224–30 ; XXVIII, 327.

OTTERBURN : Mid-Bronze barrows with urns, pygmy-vessel and stone battle-axe [Leeds M.], *Y.A.J.*, XXIX, 362 ; XXX, 250–1.

PATELEY BRIDGE : Roman camp, Castle Steads (p. 135), W. Grainge, *Nidderdale*, 1863, 2, 4–5. Roman pigs of lead (p. 135). Bronze Age cairns, Brimham Moor, *Nat.*, 1909, 89.

PONTEFRACT : Anglian iron ladle (p. 182) and stone bead, Mortimer, 95 [H.M.]. Roman coin moulds, Wardell's *Ilkley*, 94.

RASTRICK : Hill fort, Petch, *op. cit.*, 72. Pre-Conquest cross socket (p. 222), *Y.A.J.*, XXIII, 231–3.

RATHMELL : Flanged axe, *Y.A.J.*, XXIX, 359. Lynchets, quern-stones, etc., Swainstead. Barrows, circular banks, etc., Little Bank and Coney Garth, Riley, *The Settle District*, 1923, 51–2.

RIPON : *Anglian crypt ; Anglian and Viking sculpture (p. 193), *Y.A.J.*, XXIII, 233. Anglian coins (p. 201), *Arch. J.*, III, 75 ; *V.C.H.*, II, 103. La Tène sword (p. 111) [Ripon M.]. Bronze Age gold ornaments, Gough's, *Camden*, IV, 231. Bronze sword, socketed axes, and spear-heads [Ripon M.] ; flanged axe [H.M.].

ROTHERHAM : Roman fort (p. 124), T. May, *Roman Forts at Templeborough*, Rotherham, 1922. *Oval (Cæsar's) camp (p. 118), *V.C.H.*, II, 8. Bronze palstave [Manchester M.] ; flat axe, Conklow, Armstrong, *Proc. Sorby Scien. S.*, I, 92.

ROTHWELL : Roman coin moulds and coins, *Y.M. Handbook*, 119 ; *B.M. Roman Guide*, 71.

RYLSTON : Tree-trunk coffin (p. 64), *B.B.*, No. CLXII. Polished stone axes, *Y.A.J.*, XXIX, 361.

SANDAL MAGNA : Flanged axe [Leeds Art Gallery].

SCAMONDEN : Roman fort, Slack (p. 128), *Y.A.J.*, I, 1869–70 ; XXVI, 1918–20 ; Richmond, *Roman Huddersfield*, 30–48, 112–13 ; *C.I.L.*, 199, 201–2. Camp, Lee Hill, *V.C.H.*, I, 8.

SELBY : Tree-trunk coffins (p. 210), *V.C.H.*, II, 107 ; *R.Y.P.S.*, 1876 ; *B.A. Handbook*, 1906, 8–9.

SETTLE : *Victoria Cave, Azilian and Romano-British remains (pp. 22, 159), *B.R.A.*, 1871–2 ; Boyd Dawkins, *Cave Hunting*, 81 *et seq.*; *B.M. Roman Guide*, 49 ; *Arch.*, XXIX, 384–5. Socketed axe, *Y.A.J.*, XXIX, 360 ; urns, Whitaker's *Craven*,

18

1878, 180 ; stone circles opposite Victoria Cave, and at Cleatop Park (destroyed).

SHEFFIELD : *Wincobank camp (p. 118) ; *Roman Rig (p. 236), *V.C.H.*, II, 8, 55, 61. Anglian sculpture (p. 222), *Y.A.J.*, XXIII, 237–9. Roman iron workings, Pitsmoor [objects in S.M.]. Mid-Bronze Age urns, etc., at Crookes, J. W. Baggaley, *Trans. Hunter Arch. S.*, III, Dec., 1928. Stone and socketed axes, Armstrong, *Proc. Sorby Scien. S.*, I, 92.

SHELF : Hoard looped palstaves and two spear-heads, Watson's *Halifax*, 56.

SILSDEN : Palstaves [Y.M.] ; Bronze Age urns, *Y.A.J.*, XXIX, 362.

SLACK, see SCAMONDEN.

SOUTH KIRKBY : *Camp (p. 118), *V.C.H.*, II, 10.

SOWERBY : Roman coin hoard, Richmond, *op. cit.*, 115. Looped palstave, cairns, oval barrow, Watson's *Halifax*, 51, 54–5, 57.

STAINBURN : Bronze Age and La Tène remains (p. 113), *A.J.*, VIII, 526–7.

STANLEY FERRY : Dug-out canoe [Y.M.] (p. 65). Bronze dagger, Woodnook ; flanged axe ; hoard of looped palstaves and socketed axes, Smalley Bight [Leeds M.]. Hoard 7,198 Roman coins, *Y.A.J.*, XXIII, 448.

STANNINGTON : Roman military diploma (p. 146).

STEETON : Flat bronze axes (p. 68), *Y.A.J.*, XXIX, 359.

TADCASTER : Roman site (p. 170), Drake, *Eboracum*, 1736, 20 ; *Y.A.J.*, VI, 112 ; *G.M.*, 1862, I, 610. Socketed axe, *A.B.I.*, 118.

TEMPLEBOROUGH, see ROTHERHAM.

THORNER : Socketed axe, Kiddall [B.M.].

THORNHILL : Anglian inscriptions and sculpture (p. 196), *Y.A.J.*, XXIII, 243–8.

THORNTON : Bronze Age urns, *V.C.H.*, I, 413.

THORPE ARCH : Anglian cross-shaft, *Y.A.J.*, XXIII, 248–9. Bronze Age barrow, *P.Y.G.S.*, X.

TODMORDEN : Mid-Bronze Age burial circle (p. 78), *P.Y.G.S.*, XIII, 447. Pygmy-vessel, Wadsworth [B.M.].

ULLESKELF : Socketed axes and palstave (p. 95).

WAKEFIELD : Pre-Conquest cross [Y.M.], *Y.A.J.*, XX, 185–7. **See also ROTHWELL, STANLEY FERRY, SANDAL MAGNA.**

WENTWORTH : *Stainborough Low earthwork (p. 118) ; Roman Rig (p. 236), *V.C.H.*, II, 10.

WETHERBY : Viking gold bracelet (p. 213), *V.C.H.*, II, 100 ; *P.S.A.*, 2nd S., II, 124. Roman site (p. 166), *B.R.A.C.*, IX, 1929.

YEADON, see GUISELEY.

IV. YORK—EBORACUM

Roman : G. Home, *Roman York*, 1924 ; T. May, *Roman Pottery in Yorkshire Museum, R.Y.P.S.*, 1908–11 ; S. N. Miller, *J.R.S.*, XV, 1925, 176–94 ; XVIII, 1928, 61–99 ; F. Drake, *Eboracum*, 1737 ; C. Wellbeloved, *Eburacum or York under the Romans*, 1842 ; *Reports of the Y.P.S., Handbook to the York Museum*, 1891 ; H. M. Platnauer, *B.A. Handbook*, 1906 ; *Stukeley Letters, Surtees S. Pub.*, III ; *Y.A.J.*, XXII, 127, *C.I.L.*

Anglo-Viking : Sculpture, *Y.A.J.*, XX, 149–214, XXIII, 260–1, XXVIII, 328 ; urns and glass, *V.C.H.*, II, 102, *Arch.*, XLII, 433 ; coin hoards, *V.C.H.*, II, 102 ; Viking remains, *V.C.H.*, II, 104–8, *Museum Handbook*, 216–18 ; *R.Y.P.S.*, 1905 ; Lamel Hill barrow (p. 186), Thurnam, *Arch. J.*, VI, 27–39, 123–36 ; Latin gospels (950 c.) [Dean and Chapter Library].

Prehistoric : Beakers [B. and Y. Ms.] ; bronze implements of all periods including hoard socketed axes [Liverpool, Y., and S. Ms.]. Flint and stone implements (p. 47), *Y.A.J.*, I, 47–51 ; *B.A. Handbook*, 1906, 3–4 ; *Nat.*, 1905, 226 ; *R.Y.P.S.*, 1904.

Early Iron Age bronze situla, two Italian Hallstatt brooches (said to have been found at or near York), C. F. C. Hawkes, *A.J.*, XII, 1932, 453–5.

LIST OF MUSEUMS EXHIBITING YORKSHIRE ANTIQUITIES

Aldborough (W.R.). Museum Isurianum. Roman antiquities from Isurium.

Alnwick Castle Museum. Yorkshire bronze sword and Viking brooch, Bedale.

Beverley (E.R.). Public Museum. Stone and bronze implements from East Yorkshire.

Bradford (W.R.). Cartwright Memorial Hall. Prehistoric antiquities from Elbolton Cave. Stone and flint implements from East and West Ridings. Bronze Age pottery and cup-and-ring stone from Baildon Moor. Local bronze implements. Roman urn from York.

Bridlington (E.R.). Bayle Gate Museum. Local stone, flint and bronze implements. Roman coins.

Bristol. Public Museum. Stone implements from Skipton, Scarborough and East Riding (Pease Collection).

Cambridge. Museum of Archaeology and Ethnography. Skulls from Dowkerbottom Cave, from barrows at Cawthorn, Acklam and Arras. Socketed axes from Bingley, Leyburn and Sproatley, spear-head from Beverley.

Trinity College. Roman inscriptions from Bowes and Greetland.

Doncaster (W.R.). Local stone and flint axes; Bronze Age implements and pottery; Roman pottery, Samian ware, coins.

Durham. Cathedral Library. Anglo-Viking inscribed and sculptured stones and crosses from N.R. Roman inscription from Northallerton.

Edinburgh. Museum of National Antiquities. Flint implements from the Wolds, greenstone axe from Aldborough, bronze dagger from Kirkdale, N.R., bronze sword from Brompton, N.R., Roman knitted fabric found in York, and a Viking brooch, Bedale.

Giggleswick (W.R.). School Museum. Antiquities from Victoria Cave, Settle.

Halifax (W.R.). Bankfield Museum. Mesolithic flints from Rishworth Moor, local stone axes, eight stone axes from York, flint and local bronze implements, cinerary urns and food vessels.

Harrogate (W.R.). Public Library and Art Gallery. Runic stone and other Viking relics from Pippin Castle.

Hornsea (E.R.). Morfitt Museum. Stone, flint and bronze implements, British gold coin, pottery from Iron Age hut pits, Roman pottery and coins, Anglian beads, pins, brooches and pottery from Holderness.

Huddersfield (W.R.). Tolson Memorial Museum. Tardenoisian industries of the Southern Pennines ; local stone, flint and bronze implements ; food-vessels from Pule Hill ; Roman antiquities from Slack.

Note beautiful coloured models of Pre-Conquest crosses (W.R.).

Hull (E.R.). Mortimer Museum of Prehistoric Archaeology. Contains the pottery and implements from more than three hundred Bronze Age barrows, described in Mortimer's *Forty Years' Researches.* Large collections of stone and bronze implements from all parts of East Yorkshire. Large series of Neolithic, Bronze, Iron and Roman Age skulls. Large collections of Anglo-Saxon antiquities from cemeteries and barrows in East Yorkshire. Roman antiquities from Brough, Malton, Harpham, Throlam, etc.

Ilkley (W.R.). Public Library and Museum. Roman antiquities from Olicana. Anglian sculptured stones.

Keighley (W.R.). Corporation Museum, Victoria Park. Human bones from Elbolton Cave ; numerous stone and flint implements ; bronze axes and palstave. Cup-and-ring stone. Roman bronze eagle from Keighley, and various Roman antiquities from Slack and Gargrave (villa site). Anglian beads from Saltburn.

Leeds (W.R.). City Art Gallery. Bronze dagger from Bridlington ; spear-heads from Morley, Churwell ; palstaves from Churwell ; flanged axe from Sandal Castle ; hoard of socketed axes from Carr Moor Side between Beeston and Hunslet.

City Museum. Relics from Victoria Cave. Numerous stone axes and perforated hammers. Casts of cup-and-ring stones from Ilkley Moor. Giggleswick dug-out canoe. Many bronze implements. Beakers, pygmy and food vessels. Roman milestone from Castleford ; Roman remains from

York, Ilkley, Slack, Aldborough and Dowkerbottom Cave. Viking sculptured stones.

Liverpool. Free Public Museum. Cinerary urns, food and pygmy vessels, beakers from Whitby district ; Anglian silver ornaments and gold-ornamented filigree work from Lilla Howe on Goathland Moor (Mayer Collection). Socketed axes from York.

London. British Museum. The Atkinson and Greenwell collections of prehistoric antiquities from Cleveland and East Yorkshire. Maglemose harpoons from Holderness. Numerous stone and bronze implements from all parts of the county. Ulrome lake-dwelling relics. Early Iron Age remains from Stanwick, the Danes' Graves, Grimthorpe, etc. The Arras chariot burial. Roman remains. Anglian crosses from Dewsbury and Sheffield. Anglian urns from York and Ganton Wold, and bronze bowl from Hawnby ; needle-and-thread boxes from Kirby Underdale. Viking coin hoard from Goldsborough, W.R. Ethelswith's gold ring, W.R. Gold carbuncle pendant, Acklam, E.R., brooches from Rudston ; lion's head on bronze plate, Malton ; girdle end, Cowick, W.R. ; square-headed brooch, seventh century, Fridaythorpe ; silver gilt tabs with pearls and garnets, long bronze brooch, late sixth century, Goodmanham ; long brooches, Bulmer ; bone combs and case, Viking Age, York ; pewter brooch with iron pin, late Saxon and Viking, York.

Royal College of Surgeons of England. Skulls from Yorkshire, also skeletons, of Bronze, Iron, Roman and Anglian Ages.

Malton (N.R.). Museum of Malton Field Naturalists' Society. Stone implements and Roman vessels.

Museum of Roman Antiquities, Manor House. Local finds ; Roman pottery and cists from Castle Howard.

Manchester Museum. Socketed axe from Embsay, palstave from Templeborough.

Middlesbrough (N.R.). Dorman Memorial Museum. Local Tardenoisian, Bronze Age, Roman and Anglian antiquities from the Cleveland coast, including Huntcliff coastguard fort. Dug-out canoe from the Tees at Thornaby.

Oxford. Ashmolean Museum. Neolithic, Bronze, Iron Age and Romano-British skulls (Greenwell Collection). Stone and bronze implements (Evans Collection). Anglian urns and antiquities from Sancton and Londesborough.

Ripon (W.R.). Cathedral Library. Anglian relics (p. 193).

City Museum, Thorpe Prebend House. Local stone, bronze, Iron Age and Roman antiquities [Castle Dikes villa].

Rotherham (W.R.). Clifton Park Museum. Roman remains from Templeborough. Local flint implements.

St. Albans. Hertford County Museum. Loan exhibit of Yorkshire bronze implements (Ball Collection).

Scarborough (N.R.). Museum of Philosophical and Archaeological Society. Stone, flint, jet, Bronze Age, Hallstatt and Roman local antiquities. Gristhorpe burial.

Settle. Local prehistoric and Romano-British remains, chiefly from caves.

Sheffield (W.R.). Weston Park Museum. Bateman collection of prehistoric antiquities from Pickering and Whitby area, including beakers, food vessels, cinerary urns, flint implements, stone axes ; note skeleton and associated pottery and flints from cist ; bronze implements including the Roseberry hoard, Hallstatt sword and chape from Ebberston, the Bilton hoard.

Skipton (W.R.). Craven Museum. Mammalian remains from Elbolton Cave. Stone and flint implements (local). Cinerary urns from Baildon Moor. Bronze swords and spears. Iron Age remains from Grassington. Local Roman antiquities, including sword, lamps, vase, bronze stamps, seals ; Samian bowl, platters and finger bowl (Ilkley). Roman antiquities from Elslack.

Whitby (N.R.). Museum of Literary and Philosophical Society, Pannett Park. Flint implements, stone axes, urns, pygmy and food vessels, Bronze and Early Iron Age implements ; Roman inscription from Peak, antiquities from Goldsborough and Whitby ; Anglian relics from Abbey site and kitchen midden.

York. The Yorkshire Museum. Boynton and Harland collections of Yorkshire stone and bronze implements. Kendall collection of urns, food vessels, flint, stone and bronze implements from the Pickering district. Dug-out canoe from Stanley Ferry. Beakers from York and Thorntondale. Early Iron Age remains (including chariot burials) from East Yorks. Roman inscriptions, altars, tombs from York. Tessellated pavements from York, Oulston, Dalton Parlours near Collingham. Roman pottery, coins, glass, ornaments, statuettes, jet work. Anglian urns from Heworth. Anglian bronze bowls. Contents of the Uncleby barrow. Anglian wood coffins and cist. Anglo-Viking sculptured stones from York,

Ripon, etc. Collection of Viking bone combs from York. Large collections of Anglian and Viking coins minted at York.

The Mount School. Roman urns, stone coffin and VI Legion inscription.

INDEX

913.4274
572369

Printed in Great Britain by Butler & Tanner Ltd., Frome and London